WEST SCRÆFTUN

A UNIQUE COVERDALE VILLAGE

Foreword
by Sir Richard Branson

It is many a long year since I walked in the Dales and, frankly, I had only a lingering memory of those times and the sense of tranquillity and stability that part of the country seemed to exude.

In between times, of course, life has had its fill of very different sensations, most arising at a frantic and exciting pace in an atmosphere of constant change - a roller-coaster ride on an ever changing track; so it is good on occasion to be reminded of that other world where one year is very much like the rest and variations are just sufficient to be interesting; where change is barely perceptible and many families have occupied the same land and houses for generations.

So, when I learned of this book from an old Yorkshireman I know, I was intrigued. The old memories of the Dales flickered into life again, maybe tinged with a little nostalgia, and, what is more, there was something familiar in a venture carried to success by a small group of people without any previous experience and no outside help.

I'm looking forward to my next visit to that part of the world, either in person or via the pages of this book. I hope you will too.

Richard Branson
Necker Island
August 2001

WEST SCRÆFTUN

Printed by Marford Lithographic, Darlington
Published by the Villagers of West Scrafton

ISBN 0-9541336-0-9

WEST SCRÆFTUN

A UNIQUE COVERDALE VILLAGE

The Small Village Green

This book was written and produced by the inhabitants of the village as a celebration of over one thousand years of its existence.

It is a collection of narratives centred around a remote dales community of some 30 old houses and 60 people, recalling tragic accidents, idyllic childhoods, some characters from another age and a brave railway venture. It also contains sad coal mine and slate quarry chronicles and glimpses of a long history. All this is set against a record of the daily lives of farmers and residents today.

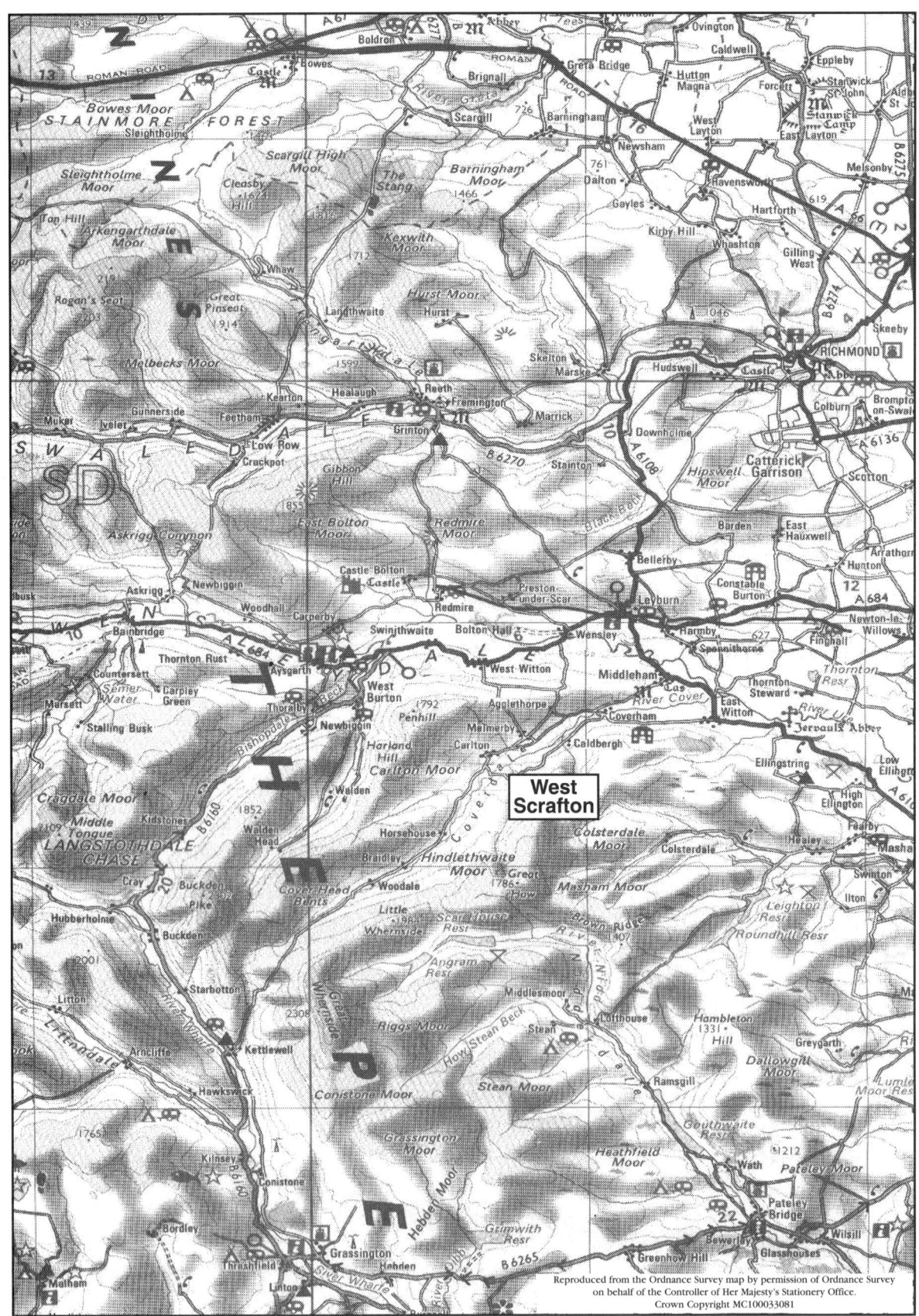

Fig 1 Map showing Location of West Scrafton

PREFACE

We knew when we started that the local inhabitants of many, perhaps several hundred, communities in the United Kingdom would also have decided to write a book about the place in which they lived as a way of commemorating the second millennium. Undeterred by this absence of originality, we, that is, the villagers of West Scrafton, decided to press ahead and not only produce a book about the village itself and its history (which goes back to the first millennium - hence the spelling in the title), but also attempt to create for posterity a record of a very varied way of life that is slowly becoming extinct and therefore increasingly unique.

It should perhaps be said that we had very little recourse to outside help or advice apart from final printing and binding. This is therefore our book, produced in a way that we conceived, and which reflects, for better or worse, the multiform contributions and styles of the contributors, themselves a diverse group as is shown in various chapters. We hope that it will be of interest, not only to the mere thirty six households in the village, but to our own offspring and far-flung families; and perhaps to other Dalesfolk and those who might know West Scrafton from their travels or want to know it in the future. For this reason, it is being put on the market in the hope that many more people might find some pleasure in reading it.

In this book there are numerous pieces of information and extracts handed to various members of our village community by family and friends who thought they might be of interest. Because of this, it was not feasible to trace the origins of much of this material and therefore few specific acknowledgements are possible. However, we are most grateful to Jim Wight for permission to reproduce a few paragraphs from "James Herriot's Yorkshire", to David Webster for the happy outcome of an accidental meeting which resulted in his jewel of a contribution "A War-time Evacuee" and to Marion Moverly for pointing us in the right direction towards much historical material. Thanks are also due to John Rendall for his good publishing advice which we seem to have ignored to our cost. Otherwise our apologies and grateful thanks are due to those who might recognise possible examples of plagiarism. We hope that we are excused!

That being said, we hope that you enjoy what you read.

The Villagers of West Scrafton

CONTENTS

Preface — Page 3

Introduction — Page 9

History
The First Beginnings — Page 15
Bringing us Up to Date — Page 27
A Welcoming Verse — Page 33

Past Inhabitants
Population Records — Page 37
Some Stories from the Past — Page 45
The Foster Trust — Page 51
The Gold Find — Page 53
A War-time Evacuee — Page 56
The Most Famous Vet in the World — Page 61

Present Population
House and Home — Page 69
The Women's Institute — Page 157
Schooling — Page 159
Some Children's Stories — Page 161

Farming
Farming in West Scrafton — Page 167
A Farming Diary of 1971 — Page 175
The Farming Calendar Today — Page 179
Tommy Handley's Charolais Bulls — Page 193

Gamekeeping
  The Gamekeeper's Story   Page 199
  A Gamekeeper's Year   Page 203

Village Records
  The Civil Parish Meeting   Page 211
  Chapel Records   Page 217
  Weather Records of 1999   Page 223
  Three Winter's Tales   Page 236

Local Amenities Past and Present
  The Village Shop   Page 243
  A History of the Water Supply   Page 245
  The Installation of the Water Sterilisation Plant   Page 251
  The Postal Services   Page 258
  A Brief Look at Road Transport   Page 260
  The Yorkshire Dales Railway Proposals   Page 265

Local Items of Interest
  The Pot-holes   Page 275
  The Coal Mine   Page 280
  The Quarries   Page 288
  Wild Flowers   Page 290
  Birds   Page 295
  Some Walks around the Area   Page 299

A Monthly Diary compiled by a Few Residents   Page 303

List of Figures

Fig 1	Map showing Location of West Scrafton	Page 2
Fig 2	Map of Hang West Wapentake	Page 21
Fig 3	Some Pictures from the Past	Page 36
Fig 4	Map of 1849 showing Old Field Names	Page 41
Fig 5	The Ancient Terraces of "Granny Banks"	Page 63
Fig 6	The ". . . Smallest Village Green . . ."	Page 63
Fig 7	Plan of Village showing Present House Names	Page 68
Fig 8	A few of the Village Cottages	Page 111
Fig 9	Some more of the Cottages	Page 147
Fig 10	Some Farming Scenes from the Past	Page 166
Fig 11	Map of Farmers' Holdings	Page 171
Fig 12	A couple of Farming Activities	Page 189
Fig 13	Tommy Handley's Charolais Bull	Page 195
Fig 14	Map showing the Civil Parish Boundary	Page 210
Fig 15	The Installation of the Water Sterilisation Plant	Page 255
Fig 16	Cyclist's Map of 1881	Page 263
Fig 17	Route of the proposed Yorkshire Dales Railway	Page 267
Fig 18	The Yorkshire Dales Railway Proposal - Gradients	Page 269
Fig 19	The Yorkshire Dales Railway Proposal - South	Page 270
Fig 20	The Yorkshire Dales Railway Proposal - North	Page 271
Fig 21	Map of Village showing position of Pot-hole	Page 274
Fig 22	West Scrafton Colliery as surveyed in 1908	Page 286
Fig 23	Map showing position of Last Working Colliery	Page 287
Fig 24	A few local Items of Interest	Page 298
Fig 25	A couple of Rural Activities	Page 334
Fig 26	The Millennium Party	Page 357
West Scrafton from Roova Moor		Front Cover
Roova Crag from Poverty Street		Rear Cover

INTRODUCTION

At a point roughly half way between the Irish Sea and the North Sea and some 1670 feet above them, where the moor and its heather stretch out in all directions and the dales are small green gulleys cut into it, a spring of cold clear water seeps out below the crest of Carle Fell. This spring becomes Lead Up Ghyll and then Great Ghyll as it is joined by innumerable streams and runnels on its way down into Coverdale and its confluence with the River Cover. The enormous sky which stood over its start is diminished after about three miles as the stream reaches lower levels; riverine copses, farms, lanes and buildings close in, gradually contracting and then obscuring the horizon.

A few hundred yards from the River Cover, which gives its name to the dale, the much smaller Great Ghyll disappears underground beneath Bow Bridge into a channel through a number of vast chambers to emerge later at the bottom of the ravine, which, over endless millennia, has been cut through the rock by the ghyll in flood when the mouth of the chamber is able to take only part of the torrent.

It is at this point that the village of West Scrafton originated, being built on the small ridge covering these underground chambers. The fortunes of the village have fluctuated, sometimes dramatically, over the last thousand years or so, but the number of people (rarely more than a hundred souls) and the number of buildings (less than forty) have surprisingly not changed in any great measure. Moreover, it still remains unchanged as a place on the edge of the mainstream (somewhat like its ghyll), not quite remote and certainly not a backwater, for its people still participate fully in the life of the dale and the county and throughout its history more than one has risen to national status; but it is still off the beaten track and easily missed by the hasty traveller.

From the earliest settlement, well before records began, it has been essentially a farming community and, despite a current downturn in its economy, remains such. At one stage, mining on a small scale changed the balance of activity in the village for a brief period, as no doubt did Scandinavian invaders a thousand years earlier in a more dramatic way. The current, and certainly gentler, invasion of non-farming "incomers" over the last few decades has not changed the basic nature of the village but only, as mining did, changed the mix.

This influx has to a large extent been responsible for the rescue of many buildings which were in severe decline and have now been renovated to make relatively substantial homes with the concomitant effect of raising the value of property dramatically. It has not, however, increased the actual number of buildings. All this seems to have been done without disturbing the community or creating schisms between old established families and the newcomers, perhaps in part due to many of the later arrivals having had holidays or even having had family in the village over many years prior to their becoming resident. Of course, no small community is without its frictions but anecdotal evidence suggests that there was more open hostility over water and grazing rights at the beginning of the last century (when an Utley and a Bell came to blows over bracken cutting rights, for instance) than there is today over any current issue; indeed it is difficult now to find even a minor question which divides old from new.

However, a more profound change is taking place, one that is not at first visible to the casual eye, but disguised by the discreet prosperity of the village and its inhabitants. Hill farming is possibly in long term decline. The reasons for this are much debated, but inescapably the market for its products (sheep, wool, mutton, cattle, milk and beef) has changed. Despite a standard of efficiency and productivity that would dazzle present farmers' grandparents, the market (and possibly government support) continues to be less accommodating. Talk now is of declining involvement in traditional farming and increasing attention and government support to conservation of the countryside.

We stand too close to this steady shift of direction to have any view on its outcome but its impact may be more substantial and deeper than the finding of coal on Roova Moor or the influx of newcomers to the village.

Arguably, in its thousand years of existence, West Scrafton has never known such a golden age as it has now, thanks mainly to a thriving world economy and its advanced technology. But change is inevitable and no doubt the 21st century will bring its share along with differing fortunes for the inhabitants.

But one thing is certain. For as far into the future as anyone can imagine, there will be a small spring rising at a point half way between the Irish Sea and the North Sea and running down the vast body of the fell to a place once called Scræftun.

This book is an attempt to show in a rough mosaic form what we, the inhabitants, thought it looked like at the beginning of the 21st century. It is perhaps a scrapbook, a compilation of contributions provided by the villagers themselves, and covers all manner of subjects from a brief historical background, through descriptions of local buildings and inhabitants, to a résumé of modern living by means of a monthly diary, and it also includes accounts of local farming and other gainful occupations.

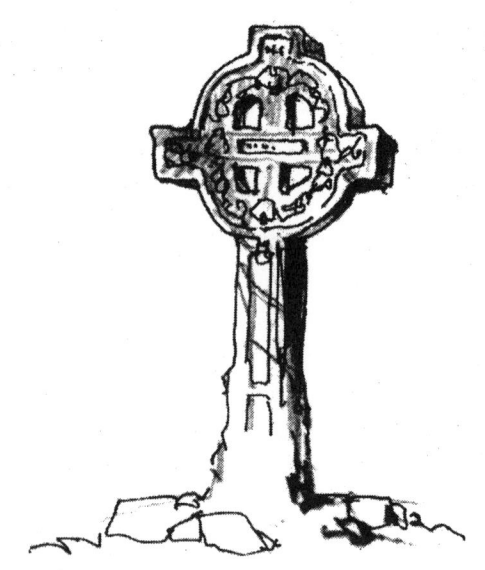

HISTORY

The First Beginnings

West Scrafton is built on a small promontory on the south-east side of the River Cover from which the dale gets its name. The word "Cover" is derived from the Norse word "cofa" which means "ravine" and it should be pronounced to rhyme with "hover". The village of Carlton on the opposite  side of the river contains evidence of what is generally believed to be tumuli from the bronze age. The largest of these is on the left-hand side of the village as one progresses up the hill and has the remains of an elm tree on the top (see page 24). It is thought by many that this could be the site at which an ancient parliament was held.

Many millennia ago, in the ice age, the dale was a glacial lake which was held in at its lower end by the ice of Yoredale. There were no glaciers scouring its sides to fill it with what would have become earth and consequently it has no flat bottom, a feature which has made it rather unsuitable for arable cultivation; but it is generally wetter and therefore greener than other dales in the vicinity, with an abundance of ghylls feeding into the main river. Because of this, the area was once well covered with forest and was a favourite hunting ground during the first part of the millennium.

At the beginning of the first millennium this part of the country was known as Brigantia and was inhabited by the celtic Brigantes tribes who had their main settlement at Aldborough. When the Romans arrived in the first century AD they were kept out of Coverdale at its north-eastern end by the high ground of what is now Middleham Moor and at its head by the enormous earthworks of Tor Dyke which had ramparts that had been built by the Brigantes people helped by using the natural terrain. The only place name in the area believed to be surviving from the Brigantes era is Penhill.

Looking across the valley from Carlton, the terracing of the ancient arable fields of West Scrafton can be seen between the river and the village on the land known locally as "Penny Banks" or "Granny Banks" (see fig 5).

It is well known that, following the departure of the Romans around the fifth century, there was a succession of invading tribes from over the North Sea, each of which came for the purpose of colonising the whole area. The first of these to arrive were the Anglo-Saxons and these were later followed by the Danes and then the Norsemen from Scandinavia. Place names can give a good indication of how far the various invading tribes managed to penetrate into the dale. The Saxons covered the dale towards the end of the sixth century but the Danes who followed some time later did not advance very far into dales territory.

The first recorded settlement of these Scandinavians in England was in 876 when a chieftain by the name of Healfdene meted out the land that had previously been inhabited by the Northumbrians; this infiltration had been effected by a Danish army. Names of various places in Yorkshire indicate that the Danish settlement was confined to the most fertile parts of the county, including the central and southern parts of what is now the North Riding. The term "riding" is of Scandinavian origin and is a corruption of the word "thrithing" which meant one-third. The division of Yorkshire into three ridings must therefore have been carried out later than this Danish settlement of 876.

Early in the next century, a new Scandinavian invasion began, this time by Norsemen who came in from the west side of the country by way of Ireland. They arrived in greater numbers than the Danes and this infiltration culminated in the capture of York in 915. These Norsemen managed to over-run Coverdale to quite a large extent, such that it was inhabited from then on by both the remaining Anglo-Saxons and the newly arrived Norsemen; they subsequently came to share the land between them. It is believed that Carlton (originally meaning Karl's farm) was the dividing point in the dale between the two clans, with the upper half, known even then as the High Dale, being the territory of the Norsemen. Place names once again can be used, this time to provide evidence that the Norsemen would have entered Yorkshire from the north-west. In Richmondshire, Nordic influence was very strong and the large proportion of Scandinavian names must be due almost entirely to the Norwegians.

The meaning of some of the place names in Coverdale gives an indication of what the landscape would have been like in those days. A few of the present day names from around this area are shown below together with their original meanings; these are followed by some words and suffixes that will help to show how the meaning of some other names may be derived.

Agglethorpe - Aculf's village	Arkleside - Arkil sætr (Arkel's pasture)
Braidley - broad clearing	Braithwaite - broad clearing
Caldbergh - cold hill	Carlton - Karl's farmstead
Dove Scar - dove cliff	Elliker - Helaghker (marsh by forest clearing)
Fleensop - Fleemis ghyll	Gammersgill - Gammall & skali (Gamel's hut)
Hindlethwaite - forest clearing for hinds	Ings - meadow
Melmerby - Maclmuire's dwelling	Nathwaite - clearing (with a ford?)
Swineside - Sven's pasture	Woodale - wulf dæl (wolves valley)
Roova - rook	

·akr - field	·beck - stream
·berg - hill (Caldbergh)	·by - dwelling (Melmerby)
·eller - alder	·gil - stream
·thorp - farm, village	·toft - homestead
·tun, ·ton - farm, village	·thwaite - clearing
dæl - valley (dale)	sætr - pasture
scræf - hollow, cave	·sop - ghyll

It can be seen that Scrafton (Scræf-tun) probably meant "village in a hollow" or perhaps "village near the caves". The suffixes "-ton" and "-thorp" can be found all over the country, the meaning of "-ton" changing, as building development took place, from "farmstead" to "village" and then eventually becoming the word "town".

The names of East Scrafton and West Scrafton most likely relate to their position, "east of the caves" and "west of the caves", the caves in question being Otter's Hole near the remains of St Simon's Chapel by the River Cover and a cave near Caygill footbridge more recently known as Tom Hunter's Parlour, so called because a highwayman of that name is reputed to have been captured there. The story goes that he apparently hid his loot in this cave and operated from there as he preyed on travellers using what was then a much used route from London to Richmond. The terms "East" and "West" do not appear in any early documentation but were in use by the middle of the 13th century, although the two villages have over the years been known variously as Scrafton Parva or Little Scrafton (for East) and just Scræftun (as in Domesday Book) or sometimes Scrofton or Scalftun (for West).

There are a few rather insignificant sites of antiquities around West Scrafton, all of them being near to the road approaching from East Scrafton. The first (NGR SE 0770 8382) is visible only as a slight rise in a ploughed field and could possibly be the remains of a small pond or dam; the second (NGR SE 0783 8392) shows slight traces of a diamond shaped enclosure, also in a cultivated field, about 17 metres across, the purpose of which remains unknown; a third (NGR SE 0809 8413), again in a cultivated field, consists of the remains of a rectangular turf covered platform measuring 21 metres by 17 metres and overlaid by a mediæval field bank; the purpose of this is also unknown. There are also records of two other sites (NGRs SE 0775 8376 and SE 0836 8398), but these have apparently been ploughed out and there are no visible remains.

In 1089, a few years after the famous Norman invasion of 1066, King William led his followers north and organised the "harrying of the North", the term given to the plundering, destruction and ravaging the countryside and properties in the north of England from Durham to York by these Norman invaders. The dales country did not escape, but life not only survived under its new Norman masters, but eventually it tended to prosper.

West Scrafton was one of five granges in Coverdale that are mentioned in Domesday Book and the entry for West Scrafton in an 1896[1] transcription of the Yorkshire Section reads as follows:

> In Scræftun, for geld, three carucates, and two ploughs may be [there]. Ghilepatric had a manor there; now, Ribald has, and it is waste. Underwood, and plain, four leugæ in length and half [a leuga] in breadth. T.R.E., it was worth ten shillings.

A "carucate" was the term given to the amount of land that could be cultivated and ploughed by an eight-oxen plough team over the period of one year and this, of course, varied considerably in size

---

[1] "Domesday Book for Yorkshire" · Transcribed by Robert H Scarfe · 1896.

depending upon the quality of the soil. A later word for it was a "hide". In terms of modern measurements it would have been somewhere between 70 and 170 acres.

Ghilepatric was a Saxon thane from Spennithorne, the village in which he was living at the time of the Norman conquest. The parish of Middleham was given to Ribald by Count Alan Rufus whom William had installed at Richmond as the governor of the whole area. Ghilepatric, however, continued to hold Scrafton on behalf of Ribald. In 1086, the year the Domesday Book was compiled, Scrafton seems to have been the only place in the parish of Coverham in the hands of Ribald.

The monks of Jervaulx Abbey, which was founded in 1156 by the Cistercian order from France, had several thousand sheep in the area and are said to have bred the famous Swaledale flocks. During the 13th century, these helped to support a very flourishing export trade to the Venetians in Italy, who operated very tight agreements on the amount of wool to be received each year. From Jervaulx, this amounted to 50 sacks, which might not sound very much until it is realised that a sack was equal to 172 fleeces, a quantity which, due to the vagaries of sheep health, was very difficult to maintain.

Coverham Priory was founded by Ralph, son of Robert Lord of Middleham and a descendant of Ribald, in about the year 1215. A further descendant of Ribald by the name of Waleran granted the priory small tenements in what is now West Scrafton, and, after the priory had been upgraded to become an abbey, the abbot was given a grant of free warren (the right to preserve and hunt small game and birds, but not large game such as boar or deer) in the West Scrafton area in 1271.

By 1286 the township of Scrafton had been divided into East and West Scrafton, West Scrafton being composed of one carucate of land held by the abbot of Coverham on behalf of the then lord of Middleham, who was a yet further descendant of Ribald. The parish of Coverham comprised the six townships of Agglethorpe, Caldbergh (with East Scratfon), West Scrafton, Melmerby, Carlton and Carlton Highdale (comprising Gammersgill, Horsehouse, Swineside, Arkleside, Black-rake, Braidley and Woodale). These same six townships have since become the present civil parishes in the dale and the original extensive Coverham parish is nowadays part of Agglethorpe.

St Simon's Chapel, a hermitage or "chapel-at-ease", was built on the bank of the River Cover near East Scrafton for the convenience of people from outlying villages. There was a monk's cell at the west end of the chapel which was manned by a monk from Coverham Abbey. The abbey was ravaged in 1314 during a raid by invading Scots, but it managed to recover from this attack and, by the payment of 3d a year to the mesne (intermediate) lord, it continued to hold the village until the "dissolution of the monasteries" in 1538. The dissolution allowed large monastic holdings to be split up and sold off to smaller proprietors, allowing greater prosperity in the dales and the consequent building of many of the stone houses and barns.

Throughout the centuries considerable lead and coal mining was carried out on the sides of the dale and there is evidence that as early as 1301 there was a "ledebeter" working in Coverham. Collieries and other mineral-seeking earthworks came into being at several of the villages in Coverdale, including West Scrafton, although rudimentary mining activities had undoubtedly been carried out since pre-Roman times. Coal from the West Scrafton mine was transported via a purpose-built route over the moors and down to Jervaulx for use by the abbey.

In 1538 a Sir Arthur d'Arcy, who owned the manor of Green's Norton in Northamptonshire, exchanged this property for ownership of all lands in Scrafton, Caldbergh, Carlton, Arundel (near Horsehouse) and Slape Gill (Coverhead), together with the five respective granges. However, a year later it seems that he gave these back as "manors" to the Crown. These same five properties and their associated lands were, only a short time afterwards, awarded to Matthew, the Earl of Lennox, and also "in tail" (restricted rights of inheritance) to Margaret, his wife. Later they again returned to the Crown by virtue of the accession of their grandson, who became James I in 1603. During the early part of this period, in 1545, legend has it that Lord Darnley, the future husband of Mary Queen of Scots, was born in the Manor House at West Scrafton. This is quite probable as he was the son of the Earl of Lennox.

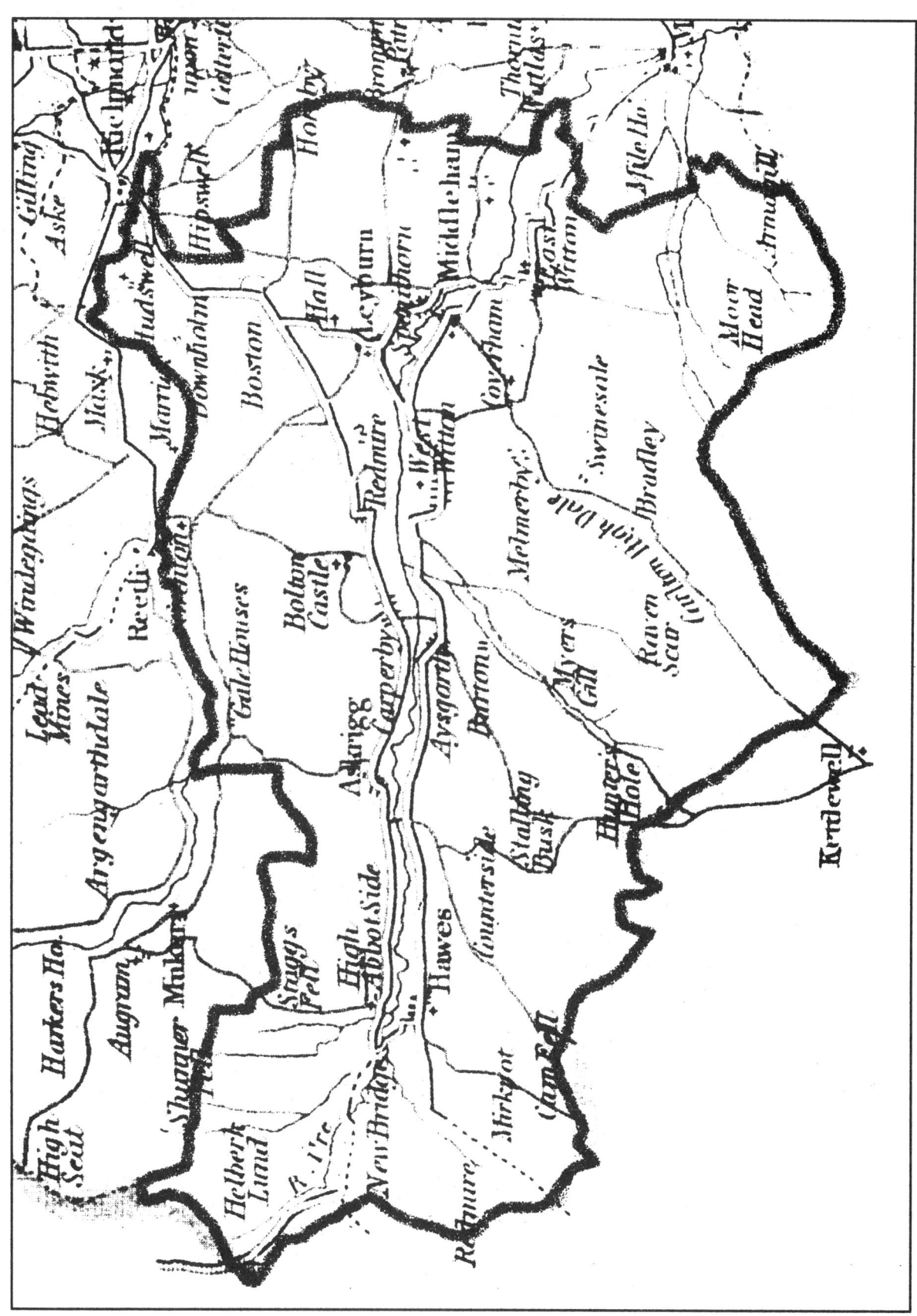

Fig 2   Map of Hang West Wapentake

In a document dated 1605[2] there is an account of the number of people living in what was then known as the Coverdale Chace and it also mentions the quantity of land and other property in the possession of each village. Carlton was the largest of the villages and contained thirty-four inhabitants; it commanded 459 acres and 3 roods of land and possessed 115 beast gaits (see page 26). It also had one brewing house, for which the yearly rent stood at five shillings, and an overshot mill with an annual rental of £1·6·8d. Gammersgill had thirteen tenants and 214 acres of meadowland with 84 pasture gaits, while Horsehouse apparently had eight tenants, 98 acres of meadow and 53 pasture gaits. Further up the dale, Braidley had nine tenants and 172 acres of meadowland as well as 132 pasture gaits, and Woodall (Woodale) had eight tenants (half of them related), 142 acres of meadowland and 157 pasture gaits. Flernshope (Fleensop) had only four tenants but possessed 54 acres of meadowland and 12 pasture gaits. There is, however, no mention of any of the villages or people on the south-east side of the River Cover such as East and West Scrafton and Caldbergh, although it is known from the Domesday Book references already mentioned that they existed long before that time.

In this document it is written of Coverham parish, which at that time was in the wapentake of Hang West, that:

Mr Loftus holdeth certeyne lands at the rent of £4-12-2d. Medow - twenty eight acres one rood. Pasture - 48a 2r - worth yearly both of them £10-10-0d.

The Generall of Coverdale Chace being the Second division of Middleham.
Number of tennants in this division -		77
Quantity of Medow	-	1216a 2r
Pasture gates	-	553
Fines paid in 20 years	-	£216-4-3d
Yearly rent	-	£71-12-1½d
Yearly Value	-	£300-19-4½d
Cleare yearly improvement	-	£299-7-3d

A "wapentake" was an administrative division consisting of a number of parishes. In some parts of the country this was known as a "hundred". Hang West was a division which roughly covered Coverdale and Upper Wensleydale (see fig 2). The "Mr Loftus" mentioned in the above extract was undoubtedly the Adam Loftus from Swineside who became the archbishop of Armagh and Dublin in 1570 and who ultimately rose to become lord chancellor. He

---
[2] "A Survey of the Lordships of Middleham and Richmond" 1605.

had a nephew, also an *Adam*, who was inaugurated as the first viscount of Ely. The Loftus family was the last family to take up residence in Middleham Castle.

In 1625 the same five granges of Scrafton, Caldbergh, Carlton, Arundel and Slape Gill were leased to the trustees of the City of London and were subsequently granted to a John Rushworth and a William Claxton in trust for a John Lambert of Calton Hall in the nearby parish of Kirkby in Malham Dale. In 1628 Charles I sold the neighbouring manor of Middleham to the City of London to pay off some debts, the estate having previously come to the throne through Richard III. The City of London, however, did not keep the land, but sold it off to the various tenants.

At that time deer were plentiful in Coverdale where they enjoyed a comparatively secure existence in the wide forest tracts which then prevailed in the area. Large numbers of pheasants, partridges, hares and other small game were kept in warrens in both Scrafton and nearby Melmerby. These warrens belonged to the successors of a Geoffrey Pygot who had been given the right of pasture in Coverdale Forest by Mary de Neville of Middleham by a deed signed in 1286.

In 1660 fifty-four tenants of the five granges asked for a continuation of their leases as they were on the point of being evicted by John Lambert who had by then risen to the rank of an army colonel. The granges were leased in 1661 but conveyances in 1662 transferred their ownership to John Lord Belasyse in trust for Dame Frances Lambert and her children. John Lambert, who was now a celebrated parliamentary major-general, was attained (inheritance rights removed) at the Restoration and subsequently died a prisoner in 1683. His son, also a John Lambert, together with his wife Barbara and another member of the Lambert family by the name of Thomas, made a settlement for the properties and lands in 1690. This John was then the sheriff of Yorkshire and, when he died in 1701, he left two daughters. One of these was Frances, wife of Sir John Middleton of Belsay castle in Northumberland, and she inherited the Lambert properties. She died in 1712 and Sir John then inherited the five granges and the associated lands from her. He died five years later leaving a son, William. William kept the granges until 1727 when he decided to sell them to the reverend Oliver Marton, vicar of Lancaster, together with his other acquisition, the Malham Dale estate.

One of the main sources of income for the dales in the 17th century was from the textile trade. Many a family in the dale spun yarn and made up cloths for which at that time there was not only a demand for the rag rugs for which the dale was well known, but also a considerable demand for cloth in the towns of Lancashire. This local industry later went into decline as Lancashire's own textile establishments grew and matured. In the dales it was gradually replaced by the growth of the local coal mines and stone quarries which had already been in existence for a number of centuries. Mining and quarrying were in those days what could be called a family concern and offspring as young as seven and eight were frequently sent down the mines. The Butterfield family in West Scrafton was largely responsible for getting the expansion of this industry going and it was around the 1770s that it reached a peak.

As has been mentioned, the route through Coverdale out over Hunter's Sleets to Upper Wharfedale was once a haunt of highwaymen and robbers and it is likely that the protection of this route was the reason for the lords of Middleham building a tower at West Scrafton. The remains of the tower now form part of the cottage known as Hilltop Cottage. In places the walls are five feet thick and there is still one ancient window remaining. The original guard post was possibly on the other side of the dale at Carlton where there is a medium-sized "motte" still standing (one school of thought suggests that this is the mound generally believed to be a bronze age tumulus as mentioned on page 15) but the tower at West Scrafton had a more commanding position and was quite close to Caygill Scar where the robber's caves were situated.

In 1777 there was a man living in West Scrafton by the name of James Geldart who was probably the descendant of the Geldarts recorded in the population record of 1673. In that year he decided to expand his horizons and he journeyed to Nova Scotia in search of fame and fortune. He apparently did very well as he managed to acquire a considerable amount of land out there. However, he succumbed to the call of the dales as he returned to West Scrafton three times and was eventually buried at Coverham. But, to this day, there is a valley in Nova Scotia called Coverdale which is the name that he nostalgically gave to the land that he purchased there.

The 1840 records show that a James Dearden was then the major single land owner and consequently known as the lord of the manor of West Scrafton, although the greater part of the land was owned by individual proprietors. Around that time many of the small rural localities in England became rather run down as the rapidly developing industrial towns provided much more remunerative work than the local village industries. In Coverdale, West Scrafton in particular went into decline. This was considered sufficiently serious for the village to be specifically mentioned in the Parliamentary Report of 1851 as an example of a place that was gradually becoming depopulated. It will be seen from the population records that many people were recorded as having more than one occupation. The reason for this is that the income derived from a single source would not have been sufficient to support a family in the rather weak rural economy.

By 1889, a Christopher Other had become the principal landowner in West Scrafton and the so-called lord of the manor. On his death the ownership went to his daughter, a Mrs Annie Agnes Wright, together with some farms in West Scrafton, Arkleside, Arundel Grange and Hindlethwaite Hall. When she died in 1921, her trustees became the moor owners and remained so until 1937.

During the first part of the millennium, West Scrafton Moor, along with East Scrafton Moor and Swineside Moor, consisted of wide open unobstructed moorland. There were no walls or gates to separate the livestock which could therefore graze within the village and on the wastes and verges. Some form of enclosure had taken place in the late 16th century and the land rents were raised to pay for the cost of this exercise. This imposition resulted in local riots and the subsequent legal battles were fought not only in the West Scrafton Manor Court but were taken as high as the Star Chamber in London. No record exists of when the present gates, walls and fences were erected on West Scrafton Moor, but it can be assumed that these probably appeared following the Enclosure Acts of the 1750s. Nowadays, however, the moor has no unhindered access. Until recently, it seemed that the responsibility of ownership of West Scrafton Moor had been exercised by the inhabitants of the village for a very considerable period of time with the gait-holders renewing and maintaining the walls, gates and fences themselves as and when required. The word "gait" is derived from the same period as the word "stint", which was an allotted amount of work particularly pertaining to the coal mining industry (hence the modern phrase "to do one's stint"). Gaits represent the right to graze a certain amount of livestock on the moor, the definition of a gait seeming to be decided by local agreement. A document of 1843 (an extract of which is shown on page 168) records a village meeting in which gaits were defined and awarded to bye-law men for their services. Nowadays, for example, a sheep gait represents the grazing needs of one ewe and its immediate offspring. Gaits can be bought and sold and they used to change hands when the associated property was sold, but they can be, and these days often are, sold separately.

West Scrafton, along with many other places in the dale, has its own legends, such as the ghost reputed to appear at St Simon's and the strange lights that have been seen in the windows of The Chantry. Many of these legends have been handed down by word of mouth but, in these modern times of mass media and electronic communication, such stories are unfortunately becoming lost.

Bringing us Up to Date

During the first part of this century, until the outbreak of the second World War, West Scrafton, and indeed the whole of Coverdale, had remained practically unchanged. It was a community dependent almost entirely upon farming and contact with the outside world was largely confined to the weekly visits to the livestock markets in Leyburn and Hawes; so far as the younger ones were concerned, this outside contact involved cycle rides to Leyburn for an evening at the Elite Cinema followed by fish and chips.

Redundant houses were recycled into byres and shelter for livestock, and the square that now contains the village green was in those days used as a parking dump for horse-drawn and tractor trailers, in winter a very muddy one. There was a quoits pitch and a bench mainly patronised by the old men of the village where they would sit on warm days to reminisce and discuss their neighbours, not always very kindly.

The children all went to the village school in Carlton where most of them completed their education and left at the age of 14. Some of them did go on to secondary education at Wensleydale Grammar School in Askrigg but, because this involved a weekly train journey from Leyburn and lodgings in Bainbridge for the week, for financial reasons it was not an option that was open to all. The lives of the women of the village were ruled in the main by domestic and family responsibilities, but several of the farmers' wives in particular made farmhouse Wensleydale cheese which could be sold to provide an additional income.

There is a story that, in the memorably bad winter of 1940 when the snow was rather deep, Mr Pickersgill, the butcher at Middleham, could not get his meat deliveries through to West Scrafton. This was reported in the local paper and was taken up on the radio in the national news as an example of how the bad weather conditions were affecting people in the countryside. Phrases such as "West Scrafton in North Yorkshire is one village that could not get its food supplies through" were used. The Germans picked this up and the propagandist William Joyce ("Lord Haw-Haw") reported that the people in West Scrafton (at that time known locally as the "Holy City" since the closure of the Moorhen Inn) were on the point of starvation. Apparently, when Adolf Hitler heard this, he said that, when the war had been won and he was in England, he would make a point of visiting this "Holy City" of West Scrafton to see the poor people and terrible conditions in the village for himself!

The early 1950s saw, not only the arrival of electricity in the village, but also the first signs of intrusion by the outside world. At this stage, the intrusion was not so much the arrival of new residents as the purchase and restoration of old properties as holiday bolt-holes at bargain prices. This did, however, have the positive effect of stemming the decay of empty and abandoned buildings as well as giving the village an enhanced appearance and a new life.

Among those who came was a Harry Watson, a draper and ex-mayor of Wakefield, who bought Manor House in the centre of the hamlet. He brought with him John and Tom Dunford, both plasterers also from Wakefield, to help him with his modernisation plans. John Dunford subsequently bought Moor Ghyll, while Tom purchased a cottage in Melmerby and their sister Vy Dunford acquired Chapman's Cottage. A few years later a Mr Brown, a timber merchant from Darlington, bought and restored two cottages and combined them into what is now Bridge Cottage; and Derek and Brenda Thiede, both doctors from Thirsk, did the same with Great Ghyll Cottage.

Of all these early incomers, Harry Watson was probably the most influential in stamping his personality on the village. He very quickly became clerk to the Civil Parish Meeting and in that capacity he submitted the village's claim to the rights of ownership of all the common land within the village under the Commons Registration Act of 1965, rights which were confirmed at a Hearing in Richmond before the Chief Commons Commissioner in the early 1980s.

Harry Watson was also actively involved with the installation of the 10,000 gallon water supply tank in 1976, but many years before that he was personally responsible for the creation of the present village green (see picture). In 1961 West Scrafton won the "Best

Kept Village" award for which the prize of a flowering crab-apple tree for the green was gratefully received. A year later Harry Watson decided that a further improvement would be beneficial and to this end he donated a second tree to tone in with the first. Unfortunately both these trees are now in decline and will at some stage have to be replaced, but for almost four decades their spring-time blossom and autumn fruit have enhanced the village scene (see inside rear cover). Of course Harry Watson's activities may not have been entirely without self-interest, for when he first arrived the area outside his house where he created the village green was the muddy parking lot for old tractors and trailers, but without doubt what he did was of great benefit to the village and its people.

The 1970s saw the arrival of more incomers, many of them as residents rather than occasional visitors. Some of these were retired but many of them like John and Liz Watson were still engaged in full-time occupations and very quickly became absorbed into the local community.

But, in spite of the growing number of incomers, the main purpose and core of the village continued to be farming and, even when two of the village farming stalwarts retired in the 1970s and sold up (Thomas Hogg and Tommy Handley), their land was bought by one or other of their neighbours or kept in the family and retained as farming land.

With regard to the moor, unbeknownst to the village, the trustees of Mrs Annie Agnes Wright transferred the ownership to a consortium from Harrogate in 1937, but, as has been said, the gait-holders continued to look after it. Under the 1965 Common Land Registration Act all common land had to be registered for ownership, grazing and shooting rights. The village had registered grazing rights but, as no-one had registered ownership, in 1978 a document was drafted to register ownership by the village (see page 268). However, a Mr Vallance then appeared and claimed ownership as he had apparently acquired it from the consortium. Shooting rights were then advertised on all the enclosed land right down to the River Cover, including the farmland owned by West Scrafton farmers, but the farmers, of course, won that legal battle, although they couldn't do anything about the moor.

As we enter the new millennium, West Scrafton is, as it has been throughout the 20th century, still a living, thriving farming community and not, as so many other villages are becoming, a holiday village or a residential area for commuters, empty by day and alien by night. Nor is it a retirement lot for the aging, for, although many incomers are retired, out of a population of 68 only

17 are retired or semi-retired, while, at the other end of the age scale, there are 14 (soon to be 17) children between infancy and higher education, and this has to be a hopeful mix for the future.

Looking back at the immediate past serves to remind us of how much has in fact changed within living memory. Although progress has in several ways been slower here than in many comparable settlements, this perhaps enables us to look forward into the new millennium from a more stable base and therefore with more confidence. However, it would be very foolish to believe that we can remain as we are, because, not for the first time in the 20th century, farming is again in crisis.

But West Scrafton has been in this position before and has survived as the following pages will show, as they describe the village, its people and their lives at the door of the 21st century.

A Welcoming Verse

We people of Scrafton looked on in despair
To see all the cottages in sad repair;
Moulding, derelict, a haven for rats;
A Pied Piper we needed; no use were our cats.

Alderman Watson was first on the scene;
He rebuilt his house and fenced off the green.
Tidy and neat, we hear people say;
But the kids of the village have nowhere to play.

Dr Ralph Dubberley was next to appear;
From him and his building we had nothing to fear.
Tall, dark and handsome, athletic and lean;
A dashing young bird, his wife, our Jean.

Derek and Brenda, Freddie and Mike;
They came to relax, to garden or hike.
Philip Brown and his family we see now and again,
But they, we are told, have a villa in Spain.

All you good people who come to our dale,
We bid you all welcome and hope you'll not fail.
On the life of the village you'll all leave your mark
And give thanks for your house in the Dales National Park.

(From a collection of poems by Betty Hogg written around 1980).

PAST INHABITANTS

The Hay Raker

Collecting Wool

A local Cattle Show

A Shooting Party around 1930

Milk Churns outside the Old Chapel

Hilltop Farm and the Old Barns

Fig 3   Some Pictures from the Past

Population Records

The following table of the population of West Scrafton was compiled from the available tax lists, census records and local directories. The latter were mostly produced for commercial purposes and they vary in their accuracy.

1673	1840	1851	1881	1921	1931	1954	1999
25	145	139	106	69	73	55	58

The table gives an indication of the rise and fall of the village population over the years. The 1673 figure taken from the tax records is not a record of the population and should be increased to take account of the families of the taxpayers who would also have been resident at the time. The population was probably at its highest during the time when the mines and quarries were working at their peak in the 1700s, causing the houses to be filled to the brim with the miners and quarry workers. In those days the number of houses did not change very much to accommodate the population increases; the houses just got fuller! But, in more recent years, with the various conversions to houses that have taken place from a few barns, a shop, two inns and a chapel, the dwelling count has increased; it was 21 in 1954 and 38 in 1999. Six of the present-day houses are now either holiday lets or part-time accommodation for their more-or-less absentee owners, but the figure in the table for 1999 includes only the permanent residents.

It is interesting to look at the names and occupations of some of the inhabitants taken from various old records and directories; these very roughly coincide with the above census dates. The tables shown below are extracted from a mixture of both the "Post Office

Directory" and "Kelly's Directory", and the entries in both of these publications include only the main or "business" residents; they therefore cannot be correlated with the population count. The 1673 tax list does not include the occupation.

1673

J Geldart
W Walker
W Horne
A Geldart
C Forster
R Lobley
C Lobley
G Cagill
F Spanton
L Loftus
T Butterfield
R Hammond
R Place
T Kipling
J Harrison
F Foster
F Thompson
J Spanton
J Egling
C Barwicke
B Geldart
E Copland
C Donkin

1840

W Chapman (joiner)
J Hanby (blacksmith)
J Horner
M Minethorpe (land agent)
J Morrell (shopkeeper)
J Spence (stone mason)
S Fairey (farmer)
J Horner (farmer & shoemaker)
R Horner (farmer)
T Horner (farmer)
G Paley (farmer)
J Spence (farmer & slater)
J Swales (farmer)

1857

Ann Bell (shopkeeper)
J Blackbird (butcher)
W Chapman (wheelwright, joiner & farmer)
J Cradock (shopkeeper)
J Falshaw (farmer)
J Calvert (agent & quarry manager)
J Harrison (farmer)
J Hogg (seior farmer)
J Horner (innkeeper))
R Horner (farmer & slater)
J Morrell (farmer & slater)
M Pearson (farmer & shoemaker)
John Spence (farmer)
James Spence (mason)
A Swales (butter factor & farmer)
W Utley (farmer)
H Walker (quarrymaster & farmer)
T Walker (quarrymaster & farmer)
H Horne (coal mine manager)
John Whitfield (farmer)
James Whitfield (farmer)
Mary Whitfield (schoolmistress)

1890

J Butterfield (farmer & quarryman)
T Chapman (farmer)
W Chapman (wheelwright & farmer)
T Hogg (yeoman sheep farmer)
J Hogg (cattle dealer)
J Horner (farmer)
R W Horner (farmer)
T Horner (yeoman farmer & cattle dealer)
W Matthew (cowkeeper)
S Metcalfe (farmer)
Anne Morrell (shopkeeper)
G Paley (shopkeeper)
J Paley (shoemaker)
J Paley (yeoman farmer)
R Paley (farmer & quarryman)
F Raynor (innkeeper)
J Spence (yeoman farmer)
M Ball (farmer)
J Stubbs (farmer)
J Swales (yeoman farmer)
E Utley (yeoman farmer)

1929

J Handley (farmer)
T Harrison (junior farmer)
T Harrison (senior farmer)
T Hogg (farmer)
J Horner (smallholder)
R Metcalfe (farmer)
J Robinson (gamekeeper)
G Spence (farmer)
O Utley (farmer)

1937

J Handley (farmer)
T Harrison (farmer)
T Hogg (farmer)
R Metcalfe (farmer)
G. Robinson (farmer)
J Robinson (gamekeeper)
G Spence (farmer)
O Utley (farmer)

1999

J Bainbridge (farmer & draughtsman)
R Baxter (retired)
I Brotherton (lecturer)
G Burgess (retired)
M Deare (insurance broker)
A Dent (farmer)
W Dobson (retired)
G Forrest (builder)
P Gower (mineralogist)
R Hall (retired)
T Handley (retired)
A Harrison (retired)
B Harrison (farmer)
P Harrison (farmer)
R Hogg (farmer)
P Hudson (social worker)
E Hullah (airline consultant)
F Johnstone (landscape builder)
N Oddy (retired)
K Suttill (farmer & welder)
Brenda Thiede (retired)
D Thomas (retired)
C Utley (farmer)
K Utley (farmer)
W Utley (farmer)
J Watkins (landscape gardener)
J Watson (builder & electrician)
R Wilson (botanist)

The number of people who are quoted as having two jobs indicates that the local economy was rather poor and that often a single occupation did not bring in sufficient income to maintain a family.

The census records of 1841 noted that the population of West Scrafton included six persons living in tents! The census was taken on the 6th of June so this may have been a temporary measure during the summer weather.

The following list has been compiled from the records mentioned above and shows the current house name, the present owner and the owner and occupier in 1851.

House Name	1999 Owner	1851 Owner	1851 Occupier
Appletree House	Baxter	John Spence	Owner
Bridge Cottage (part)	Burgess	Edward Bell	Owner
Bridge End & Roova Barn	Utley & Forrest	Eliza Hill	Thomas Whitfield
Burnside	Hudson	Ralph Wilson	Mark Pearson
Chantry	Deere	Thomas Chapman	John Hogg
Chapman's Cottage	Wight	William Chapman	Owner
Crag View	Elsby	Isabella Dobey	Owner
Culverham Farmhouse	Hullah	William Thompson	James Swales
Dem. (now Culverham House)	Handley	John Dawson	John Horner
Cullen House	Utley	William Utley	Owner
Dem. (now Curlew Cottage)	Harrison	Eliza Hall	John Horner
Fell View	Watson	Thomas Simpson	Joseph Horner
Forester's Cottage	Dobson	?	Joseph Horner
Garth House	Bainbridge	Ann Atkinson	Richard Whitfield
Great Ghyll Cottage (part)	Thiede	John Glue	James Swales
Great Ghyll Cottage (part)	Thiede	John Glue	Robert Morrell
Hilltop Cottage	Utley	John Lofthouse	John Blackbird
Hilltop Farm	Harrison	Rev. E Wyvill	Tristram Walker
Inverburn House	Oddy	William A ?	Owner
Lane End Cottage	Watkins	John Morrell	Owner
Manor House	Elliot	Paul Stubbs	George Blades
Moor Ghyll	Brotherton	John Falshaw	Owner
Old Inn	Neale	James Deardon	John Horner
Dem. (rear of Old Inn)	Neale	James Deardon	William Whitfield
Town Head	Dent	Eliza Hall	Richard Horner

The records of 1851 include against each person's name the reference numbers of both his dwelling house and the plots of land and fields owned by him; in addition the names of the fields are given in these records. These field names can therefore be identified on a contemporary map (dated 1849) of the village environment which also shows these reference numbers; moreover, the 1851 home owner can be established and compared to a village map showing the present-day houses. The 1849 map with the old field names added is reproduced in fig 4 and a map showing the present-day house names is at fig 7.

In addition to the total count, the census of 1851 provides a breakdown of population into age groups and also gives the place of birth. The following two tables show these details and, out of 139 residents comprising 28 households, there was a surprising number of children under the age of 20, 69 in fact, 48 of whom were under 10 years old.

Place of Birth		Age Distribution	
West Scrafton	76	0 - 10 years	48
Other Coverdale	30	11 - 20 years	21
106 from Coverdale		69 children	
Nidderdale	9	21 - 30 years	14
Wensleydale	5	31 - 40 years	17
Colsterdale	3	41 - 50 years	13
Wharfedale	2	51 - 60 years	15
Swaledale	1	61 - 70 years	7
126 from Dales		66 adults	
Other Yorkshire	11	Over 70 years	4
Non-Yorkshire	2		

Total 139

The most detailed information about past members of the village community comes from the census taken in 1881 of which the following is an extract.

West Scrafton Village

	Name	Relationship	Trade	Marital status	Age	Where born
1	William Pearson	Head	Boot and shoe maker	Unmarried	43	Fewston
	Ann E Pearson	Niece	Scholar		13	West Scrafton
2	Tristram Hogg	Head	Farmer (25 acres)	Married	43	West Scrafton
	Elizabeth Hogg	Wife		Married	40	West Scrafton
	Mary J Hogg	Daughter	Scholar		8	West Scrafton
	Thomas Hogg	Son	Scholar		6	West Scrafton
	Ellen Hogg	Daughter			2	West Scrafton
	Mary A Nicholson		Farm servant	Unmarried	18	Ilton Cum Pott. Yorks.
3	Joseph Butterfield	Head	Slate miner	Married	43	West Scrafton
	Ann Butterfield	Wife		Married	34	West Scrafton
	Dinah Paley	Step-daughter	Scholar		9	Carlton Highdale
	Elizabeth Butterfield	Daughter			3	West Scrafton
	John Butterfield	Son			1	West Scrafton
4	Fanny Walker	Head	Farmer's widow	Widowed	75	Carlton
	Isabell Walker	Daughter		Unmarried	35	West Scrafton
5	John Paley	Head	Slate miner	Widowed	43	Carlton Highdale
	John Paley	Son	General labourer	Unmarried	20	Carlton Highdale
	Thomas Paley	Son	General labourer	Unmarried	16	Carlton Highdale
	Isabella Paley	Daughter	Scholar		10	West Scrafton

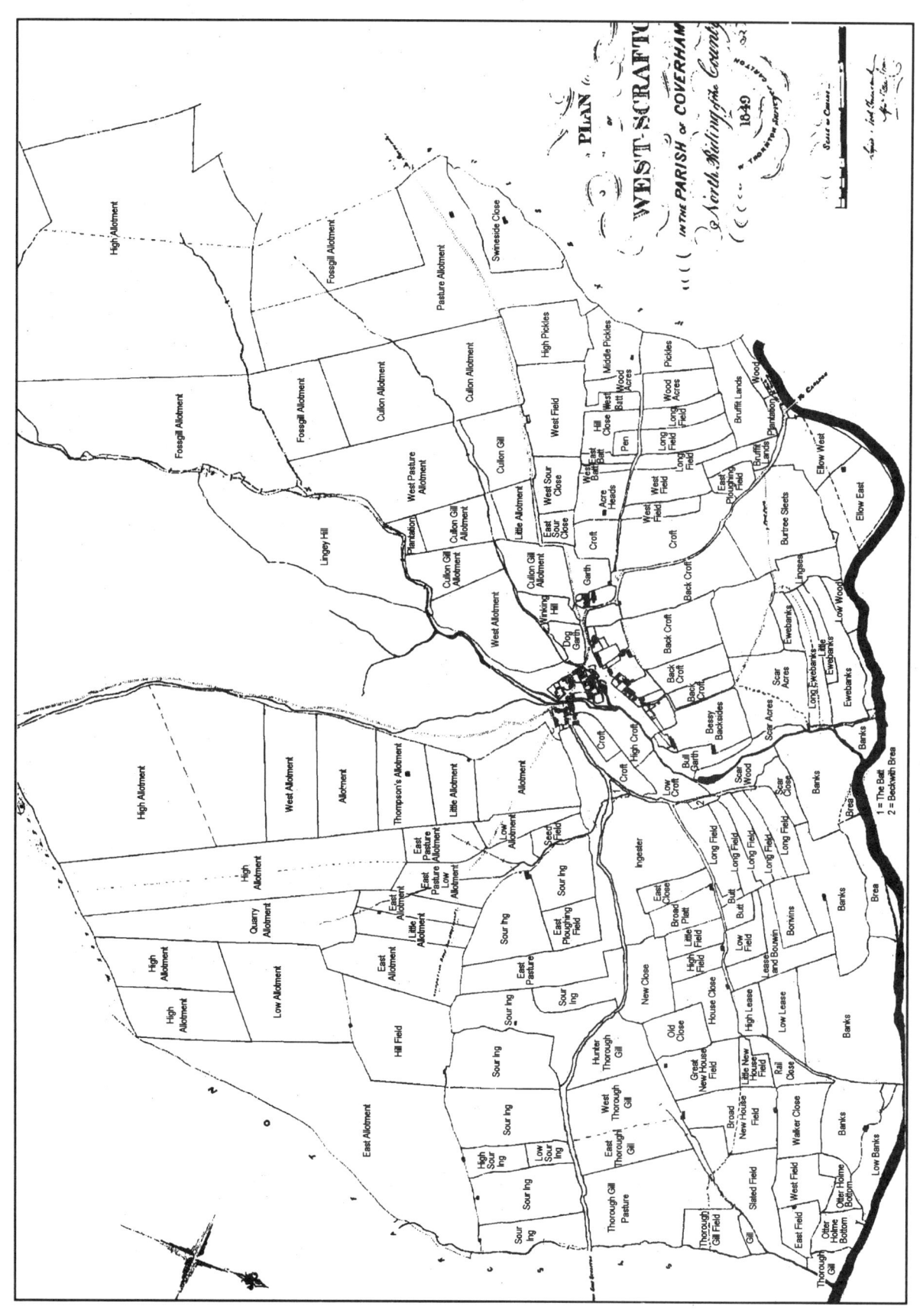

Fig 4   Map of 1849 showing Old Field Names

6	Thomas Falshaw	Head	Farmer (30 acres)	Married	44	West Scrafton
	Ann Falshaw	Wife		Married	39	Melmerby
	Thomas L Falshaw	Son	Scholar		10	Melmerby
	Mary G Falshaw	Daughter	Scholar		7	Melmerby
7	John Hogg	Head	Farmer (14 acres)	Married	59	West Scrafton
	Sarah Hogg	Wife		Married	50	Caldbergh
	Sarah M Hogg	Daughter		Unmarried	21	Cauldbergh
	Elizabeth Hogg	Daughter		Unmarried	14	Cauldbergh
	Annie Hogg	Granddaughter.			2	Tadcaster
8	Edward Utley	Head	Farmer (51 acres)	Married	59	West Scrafton
	Elizabeth Utley	Wife		Married	54	Barrow. Westmoreland
	William Utley	Son		Unmarried	27	West Scrafton
	Thomas Utley	Son		Unmarried	21	West Scrafton
	Joseph Utley	Son			15	West Scrafton
	Dawson Utley	Son	Scholar		12	West Scrafton
	Elizabeth Utley	Daughter	Scholar		9	West Scrafton
9	Uninhabited					
10	Paul Stubbs	Head	Farm labourer	Married	43	Carlton Highdale
	Hannah Stubbs	Wife		Married	40	Keithley
	John Stubbs	Son	Farm servant	Unmarried	22	Carlton Highdale
	James Stubbs	Son	Farm servant	Unmarried	18	West Scrafton
	William Stubbs	Son	Scholar		15	West Scrafton
	Anne Stubbs	Daughter	Scholar		12	West Scrafton
	Joseph Stubbs	Son	Scholar		10	West Scrafton
	Elizabeth Stubbs	Daughter	Scholar		7	West Scrafton
11	Robert Morrell	Head	Grocer / Farmer (15 acres)	Married	66	West Scrafton
	Ann Morrell	Wife	Grocer	Married	67	Carlton
	George Morrell	Grandson	Scholar		10	Ravensworth
12	John Harrison	Head	Farmer (retired)	Married	69	Lofthouse
	Ann Harrison	Wife		Married	69	West Scrafton
13	Moorhen Inn					
	Thomas Horner	Head	Farmer / Inn keeper	Married	34	West Scrafton
	Alice Horner	Wife		Married	35	Caldbergh
	Leonard Horner	Son			2	West Scrafton
	Elizabeth Swanbank		Domestic servant	Unmarried	21	Dent
14	Moses Stubbs	Head	Farm servant	Married	47	Carlton
	Margaret Stubbs	Wife		Married	41	West Scrafton
	Richard Stubbs	Son	Scholar		13	West Scrafton
	Thomas Stubbs	Son	Scholar		10	West Scrafton
	Elizabeth Stubbs	Daughter	Scholar		8	West Scrafton
	Ellen Stubbs	Daughter	Scholar		6	West Scrafton
	Alice Stubbs	Daughter	Scholar		6	West Scrafton
	Anne Stubbs	Daughter			4	West Scrafton
15	Jonas Swales	Head	Farmer (70 acres)	Married	59	Carlton
	Elizabeth A Swales	Wife		Married	48	Preston. Yorkshire
	Jonas Swales	Son			16	West Scrafton
	Christopher J Swales	Son	Scholar		14	West Scrafton
	John T Swales	Son	Scholar		12	West Scrafton
	Elizabeth A Swales	Daughter	Scholar		9	West Scrafton
	William Swales	Son	Scholar		6	West Scrafton
16	Uninhabited					
17	John Spence	Head	Farmer (20 acres)	Married	61	West Scrafton
	Elizabeth Spence	Wife		Married	61	Carlton
	Eleanor Spence	Daughter		Married	21	Carlton
18	Daniel Cradock	Head	Miner (gypsum)	Married	30	Carlton Highdale
	Elizabeth Cradock	Wife	Dress maker	Married	35	West Witton
	Francis H Cradock	Son	Scholar		9	Darlington
	Elizabeth Cradock	Daughter	Scholar		7	Darlington
	Joseph W Cradock	Son			1	West Scrafton
19	William Chapman	Head	Farmer (32 acres)	Married	66	West Scrafton
	Esther Chapman	Wife		Married	60	Masham Moorheads
20	John Brown	Head		Married	23	West Witton
	Elizabeth Brown	Wife		Married	38	Fewston
	Frederick Pearson	Step-son			7	West Scrafton

21	Uninhabited					
22	Joseph Horner	Head	Farmer (32 acres)	Married	48	Caldbergh
	Elizabeth Horner	Wife		Married	31	Caldbergh
	Joseph Horner	Son	Scholar		7	Caldbergh
	Jane Horner	Daughter			3	Caldbergh
	Mary Horner	Daughter			1	West Scrafton
	William Horner	Brother-in-law			10	Caldbergh
23	John Walker	Head	Farmer (21 acres)	Married	48	Carlton
	Fanny Walker	Wife		Married	48	Thirsk
24	Richard W Horner	Head	Farmer (100 acres)	Married	49	Caldbergh
	Jane Horner	Wife		Married	44	Melmerby
	Elizabeth Horner	Daughter		Unmarried	19	West Scrafton
	Janie Horner	Daughter	Scholar		9	West Scrafton
	Alice Horner	Daughter	Scholar		5	West Scrafton
	John Horner	Brother	Farmer	Unmarried	47	Caldbergh
25	Benjamin Whitfield	Head	Farmer (80 acres)	Married	52	Coverham
	Isabell Whitfield	Wife		Married	51	Caldbergh
	Ellen Whitfield	Daughter	Dress maker	Unmarried	20	West Scrafton
	Jane A Whitfield	Daughter	Scholar		10	West Scrafton
26	West Close House					
	John Paley	Head	Farmer (30 acres)	Married	66	Carlton Highdale
	Hannah Paley	Wife		Married	46	Garsdale
	George Paley	Son	Scholar		13	West Scrafton
	Elizabeth A Paley	Daughter	Scholar		10	West Scrafton
	Isabell Paley	Daughter	Scholar		6	West Scrafton
	Thomas R Paley	Son			4	West Scrafton
	Atkinson Parker	Step-son	Farmer	Unmarried	18	Ingleton Westmoreland

Caldbergh with East Scrafton

Lane House

Thomas Stubbs	Head	Farmer (80 acres)	Married	33	Highdale, Yorkshire
Margaret Stubbs	Wife		Married	35	Castle Bolton
Margaret Stubbs	Daughter			5	Caldbergh
Joseph Stubbs	Son			2	Caldbergh
Bartholemew Stubbs	Son			1	Caldbergh
Mary A Robinson		Farm Servant	Unmarried	21	Ilton Cum, Yorkshire

Lane House was undoubtedly what is now Lane Farm House as the present Lane House was only a cow-byre at that time.

In West Scrafton there were 25 households and 111 occupants of which a breakdown is as follows:

Place of Birth		Age Distribution	
West Scrafton	54	0 - 10 years	38
Other Coverdale	37	11 - 20 years	18
91 from Coverdale		57 children	
Nidderdale	1	21 - 30 years	9
Wensleydale	4	31 - 40 years	12
Colsterdale	1	41 - 50 years	17
Wharfedale	2	51 - 60 years	7
Swaledale 1		61 - 70 years	8
100 from Dales		53 adults	
Other Yorkshire	7	Over 70 years	1
Non-Yorkshire	4		

Total 111

Unlike the 1851 records, this 1881 census has no map available on which the household reference numbers are recorded and therefore it is not possible to link them to particular properties. However, there are various clues in the form of old deeds of some of the houses and, together with other known facts, the reference numbers may be attributed to the present houses as in the following list. The "guesswork" is shown by the use of query marks and it must be remembered that Great Ghyll Cottage and Bridge Cottage each used to be two separate cottages and also that there were two cottages along the frontage of Curlew Cottage which itself was then a barn. A rough indication may be seen of the way the man collecting the information worked his way through the village.

1	Forester's Cottage	14	Manor House
2	East Leigh	15	Culverham Farm House
3	Bridge Cottage ?	16	Fell View
4	Bridge Cottage ?	17	Appletree House
5	Bridge End Farmhouse	18	Lane End Cottage
6	Moor Ghyll	19	Chapman's Cottage
7	The Chantry	20	Curlew Cottage (dem.) ?
8	Cullen House	21	Curlew Cottage (dem.) ?
9	?	22	Burnside ?
10	Inverburn House ?	23	Hilltop Farm
11	Great Ghyll Cottage	24	Town Head Farm
12	Great Ghyll Cottage ?	25	Garth House
13	The Old Inn	26	Allaker

Some Stories from the Past

It may be that some people are remembered more for the trials and tribulations of their lives than for anything else; the former certainly make a bigger imprint on the memories of their surviving contemporaries.

The first two members of the community mentioned below, who survived until the first half of the 20th century, are recollected as being significant largely because of their misfortunes or handicaps and that at a time when life was considerably harder than it is nowadays.

Joe Bell

Joe Bell, who lived in what is now Crag View on the edge of the minute green then known (doubtless without any irony) rather grandly as "The Square", was a devout "chapel man". He was remarkable for his ability to sing with a quite beautiful (to some) falsetto voice, perhaps not as rare a quality then as now as fashion has changed, but certainly it distinguished him in the chapel and elsewhere.

A bachelor, he made a living painting, decorating and even spring-cleaning for households over an area that stretched as far as Bedale; but alas, during Christmas of 1954 at the age of 63, for reasons known only to God and himself, he hanged himself and now he lies buried in Coverham Dale cemetery.

* * * * *

James Utley, who was not related in any way to the Utley family farming in West Scrafton, was one of the last of the dying breed of "length-men". Living first as a child in what is now the garage of

Manor House and later in Lane End Cottage, his task was to maintain the length of road between East Scrafton and Field Heads, the latter being the T-junction on to the Carlton to Kettlewell road. Every day except Saturday and Sunday he would be engaged in repairing the surface of the road and gutters, cutting the grass verge with his scythe in summer and generally ensuring that the road was kept in a usable condition. It was not a five-day week for him, of course; the long weekend was not established in this part of the world during his lifetime. Saturday morning was devoted to keeping the village itself tidy, sweeping the road, cutting the grass and removing any litter, while Sunday was, naturally in those days, a sacrosanct day of rest and chapel.

His misfortune was to be an epileptic. On a number of occasions he was found lying in the road in the throes of a fit or perhaps even unconscious. The affliction is no respecter of weather or location and he was fortunate not to have died of exposure or to have severely injured himself; his scythe would have been a hazard in itself and passers-by would never have been very frequent.

It was a hard life and, no doubt partly as a result of his affliction, it was a short one. He died at the age of 48 in 1969.

* * * * *

In the very early part of this century there was a man living around the West Scrafton area who rejoiced in the name of John Wilkinson. At that time, life was very hard and work was very difficult to come by and so a number of people had to invent some kind of work for themselves in order to scrape a living.

John Wilkinson was apparently such a person. The story has it that he seemed to have made a living by searching Roova Crags for pieces of soft sandstone which was used in those days for scouring stone steps. He used to hawk these pieces of stone around the dales, selling them for a penny each. For this reason he acquired the nickname of "Scouring Stone Johnny". He

Scouring Stone Johnny

died in the 1920s, but at least he deserved the local honour of having had his photograph taken, which was not a very common thing in those days.

*   *   *   *   *

Ann Robinson, who for fifty years ran the village shop (see page 243), was known affectionately as "Old Ma Rob". She was born in Halifax in 1873, grew up in Stockton and then went into service as a laundress. This work took her all over Britain with various employers; it even took her to the Vice Regal Lodge in Ireland with the Zetland family.

She came to West Scrafton in 1897 when she married the local gamekeeper, John Robinson. They had three children, George, Peggy and Frank, who all grew up in the village. Her husband died in 1947, but she kept the shop open until 1954 when she left West Scrafton to live in North Cowton.

The two Robinson sons lived and farmed in the village, but Peggy went to live in Swaledale. Frank lived in The Old Inn, and George, his wife Mary and daughter Eva lived in The Chantry. Mary grew up in Melmerby where her father was the publican. She knew George from school in Carlton, and they moved to West Scrafton after their wedding at Coverham. She recalls life at the Chantry as a

George, Frank & Peggy

newly-wed, especially the memento that remains there yet; shortly after moving in, she was throwing some garden waste over the wall into the ghyll when her wedding ring flew off her finger after it; over and down it went, never to be seen again!

After the 1939 - 1945 war, the two brothers and their families moved to Kettlewell over a period of years, Frank being landlord of the King's Head. Eva went over to work for his family and then married into a Wharfedale farming family, the Listers. Her parents, George and Mary, moved to Kettlewell four years later.

At the end of the millennium, Mary is still living in Kettlewell and has recently celebrated her 99th birthday. It was Mary who kindly provided the information here.

* * * * *

At the end of the summer of 1948, a massive hunt for a marauding Alsatian took place. Sheep had been found on the moor seriously mauled; killed for pleasure, not food. The number of carcasses had passed twenty and was increasing, and the culprit had been identified as a feral dog, believed to be an abandoned pet animal from Catterick Camp. Groups of armed men, making some eighty guns in all, assembled at points in Wharfedale, Bishopdale, Nidderdale, Arkleside and Coverdale with the intention of sweeping the vast area of moorland and field between them.

The West Scrafton contingent had assembled at the gate to Culverham Farm under the watchful eye of the local policeman, PC Potter, who claimed to be turning a blind eye to the ratio of guns to licenses in the interest of the chase, but nevertheless kept a record of who was in the party. They had got as far as Arkleside when the photograph was taken with Bobby Hogg and Tommy Handley in the rear.

Not shown are the groups of spectators who inevitably turned out to see what this unusual circus would produce, but they themselves played a bigger part than intended. The story has it that the dog appeared and loped unawares towards a couple of the guns crouched silently in a hollow. They believed that they had got him in their sights when the spectators caught sight of the animal as well and, waving their arms, shouted "There he is, there he is!". The guns comments are not on record.

In the end the whole hunt was unsuccessful, the area too large and the number of hunters too small. The alsatian slipped through the cordon but the poor dog was eventually shot by a policeman at Askrigg some considerable time later.

* * * * *

Tommy Dent came to West Scrafton from Lunds in 1939, the same year in which he married Mary, a Garsdale girl. They acquired the tenancy of Town Head Farm. Fifteen years later, while still in the prime of life, he was struck down with poliomyelitis and he was destined to spend the rest of his life without the full use of his legs.

Before his illness he had been noted for his energy and stamina and it is said that his clogs often made sparks when he walked on stony ground. On many occasions he would milk his cows before setting off to walk the six miles over the moor track to West

Tommy and Mary Dent

Burton where he would catch a bus to Hawes in order spend a few hours at the cattle market before taking the same route back. The cows would need to be milked again on his return. Moreover, in

Page 49

the early days, there was no milk parlour or shed on their land and the cows were milked in the field down by the river. He was, however, known as the fastest milker in town (if not the west) and was suspected of being able to pull two teats in each hand. This would have been a useful ability after a visit to Hawes.

But he was a man of enormous determination and spirited independence who spurned any kind of assistance, especially if related to his affliction. Not only did he manage to work his farm virtually single-handed, except at the peak times of lambing and hay making when he had a hired hand, but he was successful enough to buy the farm in 1958 and later win the "Milk Maid Award" for the quality of both milk and milking. It was accepted that he would refuse the smallest offer of help, even if it was merely with the opening of the chapel door on a Sunday. When the leg irons, which he had had fitted in the early days, malfunctioned, he threw them away and insisted on dispensing with them entirely. From then on he used two stout walking sticks to get about and stuck them beside him after swinging himself up on to his tractor. Relatively simple tasks, such as baling hay or opening a gate, presented daily challenges which he had to solve with a mix of ingenuity and head-on attack.

But he had to abandon his beloved motor bikes and instead bought a car which he taught himself to drive, although his getting it into the garage was an experience the memory of which delights his family even now. He carried on working well past the age when many have stopped and died at the age of 82, mourned with typical directness as "the best of neighbours, but stubborn".

The Foster Trust

Quarry Lodge is a very old farmstead situated near the River Cover at Nathwaite. It has a history going back at least until the 17th century, at the end of which it was in the ownership of a man by the name of Thomas Foster. In 1698 he left this building and the associated farmlands in trust on the understanding that the rent realised from all subsequent leasing arrangements should be used to help the poor and needy folk of the dale. The local vicar, who happened to be resident at the time, was to get 25% of the monies received.

Quarry Lodge

The appointed board of trustees comprised one person from each of the parishes in Coverdale with each trustee having responsibility for the people within his own parish. This arrangement remained throughout the intervening centuries, but in recent times, although the trustees still remain as one from each parish, the Charity Commission has assumed the responsibility for the administration of the fund. In 1969, the trustees recommended to the Commission that the farm should be sold, a proposition to which they agreed. The subsequent sale realised the sum of £2,400 and this money was invested by the Charity Commission on the stock market. This proved to be a wise move, as the proceeds from the investment brought in more income than had been obtained from the previous rental arrangement.

Times have changed considerably over the last few decades, and nowadays the money is distributed in a way that is rather different from that at the end of the 17th century when the charity was started. The people from the dale now benefit in a way that is more appropriate for present day life styles.

The second millennium is entered with donations being given to organisations such as Friarage Hospital, the local Retirement Homes in Leyburn, the Leyburn Medical Surgery and the local Ambulance Service. Young people in the dale also benefit from the trust, as donations are given to the playgroup and to the local school, and, in addition, individuals still receive consideration as, for example, students going on for further education each receive a sum of £100.

This is a far cry from the original concept of the trust as set up by Thomas Foster, but he would perhaps be greatly surprised and gratified to know that his generosity would still be of benefit to the local community three hundred years after his death.

The Gold Find

One of the many responsibilities falling upon a farmer is the repair and replacement of dry stone walls which, in this part of the country, account for by far the greater part of the field boundaries.

A number of years ago, there was a farm-hand by the name of Simon Horner (possibly a descendant of the Horner family living in West Scrafton during the 19th century), who unfortunately had the affliction of being both deaf and dumb.

He had a brother who lived in Fell View at the time, and who reportedly was afraid of him. One day, they apparently had a violent argument which caused Simon to leave home and he subsequently spent the greater part of his life sleeping rough. Much of the time he chose to sleep in the barn on Ewe Bank, but often he spent the night in any rough spot that took his fancy. With the customary innocent cruelty of children, he was called Dummy by them and was often taunted, but with caution, as they were careful not to be within reach of receiving a clipped ear.

Simon Horner

However, in common with many an afflicted person, he was an excellent craftsman and he remained a good hand at dry stone walling. He was also a first-rate joiner so, along with being good at a number of other odd jobs, he was generally well occupied and derived a small income for his labour. In fact, it seems that he would never leave a household until he had been both paid and fed. Moreover, it was his rather unnerving habit to appear at meal times in village houses, unconnected with any job that he might be engaged upon at the time, and mutely wait until he had been fed, before silently disappearing again.

Against all expectations, he appeared to have earlier notice than any one else of deaths and funerals in the dale. But, even more noteworthy, was the fact that he attended them all wearing a very respectable suit, and, to this day, no one can work out where he could have kept it stored between internments.

One day in the autumn of 1972, Tommy Handley set about repairing part of a dry stone wall that had collapsed. He had just started the operation by clearing away some of the fallen stones, when he noticed a coin on the ground. On bending down to pick it up, he saw that there were quite a few more spread around. One can imagine his surprise when he started turning up some gold sovereigns. Sheep and farmers must have been passing backwards and forwards over this area for many years, totally unaware that they were spreading gold around in doing so!

That stretch of the wall ended up by being taken right down to the ground. In order to ensure that as many of the coins as possible were found and retrieved, a metal detector was brought in and used to good effect.

In all, there was a total of forty-two coins dating from between 1815 and 1913, and the find consisted of a mixture of denominations including sovereigns (£1), half-sovereigns (50p), crowns (25p), double-florins (20p), half-crowns (12½p), florins (10p), shillings (5p), sixpences (2½p) and silver threepenny-bits (1¼p). The present-day equivalents have been inserted to remind younger readers that what was once a considerable amount of money is nowadays worth very little.

It has never been discovered how the coins had come to be there, as they had been hidden in a corner of a field where they would not have been noticed by anyone until the wall collapsed.

As for poor Simon Horner, his income may have been meagre, but it undoubtedly well exceeded his expenses, and there is still speculation about where he put the money that he must have acquired over many years. Could it have been Simon's "bank" that had been uncovered? He is reputed to have died penniless, but at least the West Scrafton gold find ensures that his name is not forgotten.

Reproduced below is the reply from the coroner to Tommy's letter reporting the find.

H. M. CORONER
WESTERN DISTRICT N. R. YORKS.

PETER HATCH
(ALSO AT THIRSK.)

TEL. NORTHALLERTON 2643.
THIRSK 3156.
THIRSK (HOME) 2358.

124 High Street,
Northallerton,
Yorkshire.

PH/DEA   5th February 1973

Dear Mr. Handley,

I confirm that you have reported to me the finding of four sovereigns, four half sovereigns and various coins in silver and that this find, made in re-building of a wall indicates that there was a deliberate concealment at some time past. You have produced the coins to my Officer P. C. Lagan at Middleham and in the circumstances that these are substantially current coin of the realm it is not necessary for me to hold an Inquest.

I confirm therefore that the Crown makes no claim upon this Treasure Trove.

Given by virtue of the Royal Perogative,

Mr. T. Handley,
West Scrafton,
Middleham,
LEYBURN.

Peter Hatch
H. M. Coroner.

A War-time Evacuee

In the autumn of 1940, my younger brother Geoffrey, my mother and I were evacuated from Hartlepool to West Scrafton. I was just eight years old and a "townie". We moved into the house called Burnside, rather a strange name in West Scrafton, where "Beckside" would have been more natural as the beck ran just below the garden. The house stood on its own, fifty or sixty yards from the rest of the village. It had been lived in by an old lady with German connections of some kind. Her name was Seifert and she had left the house to go to live with relatives. We arrived by taxi from Middleham where we had spent a couple of months billeted on not very willing hosts.

"Burnside"

We explored the house, a kitchen and a living room on the ground floor and, between them, a flight of stairs to two bedrooms. The kitchen had a fire range with a hot water boiler to the right and an oven to the left. There was one small window out to the west with a view of Penhill. There was also a stone-benched larder with a cold water tap. In the winter the supply pipe froze solid and water had to be carried from the tap at the end of the lane which is now marked "Not for Drinking". We drank from it! There was a flight of external steps up into a loft which, when we explored, yielded envelopes with German stamps on - a great addition to my collection. There were also outbuildings in which we eventually housed a pig and two goats. During the day the goats were tethered to graze on the beck side.

The most unwelcome discovery was that the lavatory was a two holed seat of wooden planks over an ash pit which had to be emptied from time to time. It was out of the kitchen door and round the corner and in winter time no place to sit and read the "Beano". The dirty water from washing up drained into a cesspit in the garden. There was no electricity in the village at all, so cooking was on the fire or in the oven, bathing was in a tin bath in front of the kitchen fire, and lighting was by oil lamp and candle. The nearest telephone was at the Post Office in Carlton.

Our wireless was powered by two batteries. One was a dry battery which lasted about three months, the other an accumulator. A van drove to the village once a week to swap the exhausted accumulator for one newly recharged. The wireless was essential for news of the war, as there were papers only if someone had been into town. Old Ma Robinson kept the village shop in a room of her house just where the beck entered the village and the track began up on to the moor by Roova Crag. All we could buy there were our rations for the week. There was no public transport to the village but there was a taxi which was run by Charlie Utley's dad. Every day during the term it picked up children who attended the school at Carlton from a distance of more than two miles, which meant that it collected children from East Scrafton and Caldbergh but not from West Scrafton because the track through the fields was less than two miles. Charlie, however, got a lift because his dad was the driver.

One of the other lads going to school, a little older than me, was Les Brown, whose dad drove a lorry that, with sides up, was a cattle truck and, with no sides up, collected the full milk churns along the roadside and returned them empty. Mr Brown sometimes took me, perhaps for company, on some of his journeys if I was not at school, so I got to know the district. Eva Utley was nearly old enough to leave school but when I first started she looked after me. Robbie from Swinniside (as we called it) also walked to school with us. He had difficulty in reading, a problem which was made much worse by the attitude and actions of the teacher, which would never be tolerated today.

My town shoes were no use at all in the lane which led from the village because I was over the tops in mud and cow pat. So we had to have boots, which I had never worn before. There was a bootmaker in Carlton who also made clogs. I had thought that clogs were a picturesque feature of Dutch life and had not known that they were part of life in the dales and I was fascinated to see them being made.

The people in the village that I remember were: Mr Handley, the farmer, Tommy's dad (I do not know if it was in one of his fields that, at hay making time, I found myself turning the hay as it dried with a big hay rake half as tall again as myself; it was a dusty and exhausting job); Mr Robinson, whom I used to watch milking and who would ladle a pint or a quart out of the bucket into my metal milk can; Mrs Hogg, who played the piano and came to play duets with Mother (I lay in bed and listened to them romping through "Marche Militare" and the "War March of the Priests"); and Mr Bell, who would do wall papering on the very uneven walls of the cottages. He also played the harmonium in the chapel. We were "church" but for the sake of solidarity I was required to take part in the "chapel" anniversary. I was allotted what I thought was a soppy poem to learn and recite. It was about daffodils, but not those of Mr Wordsworth beside the lake, beneath the trees. Under protest, I half learnt the poem but events in the chapel that afternoon nearly drove it from my head. Mr Bell pedalled his harmonium and sang at the same time with a horrendous vibrato. I had never heard anything like it and it quite frightened me. Somehow or other I got through the poem but I refused point blank to return for the evening's performance.

The winters of 1940 and 1941 were savage. One night a Whitley bomber crash-landed on the moor tops. When we heard about it, we went up to see. Soon a recovery team from the air force arrived. We had two lads billeted on us, Robert and Bob. They both played, or perhaps one might say, vamped, the popular tunes of the day on the piano which annoyed Mother, who was a better pianist but could not vamp, being dependent on having the music in front of her. The flight sergeant, with a flourishing ginger RAF moustache, was billeted on the Browns. As the squad dismantled the plane to take it away, the lads bet "flight" that he would not use a section of the fuselage to sledge naked down the hillside. So he did, at the bottom going head over heels into a deep drift from which he had to be dug out half frozen. Mrs Brown told Mother she wished she had had binoculars which, as a very proper eight-year-old, I thought was very naughty. Bob and Robert also used to hang Geoffrey by the belt of his trousers from the hooks in the ceiling beams.

It had seemed that the winter would never end and Mother bewailed its length to me. That very night the wind changed, we woke to hear the beck running again and, though the two feet of snow had not altogether melted, there were flowering snowdrops to be seen.

In the summer of 1941 there was a tragic event. We had a family of mother, father and two lads and another boy, Billy, all from West Hartlepool, staying with us for the summer holidays. Billy was three years older than me and had been my great friend both at school, where he protected me, and out on the road, where he taught me how to ride my bicycle. One morning the two lads and I were shelling peas grown in the garden ready for lunch when Billy appeared at the little gate that opened on to a field alongside which ran the beck. The beck had carved itself a deep ravine through the soft stone. Billy was soaking wet, without his shoes, and clearly had had a very serious accident. The adults took charge and a doctor was sent for. Eventually he arrived, bundled Billy into his car, mother cradling him in her arms. Billy died on the way to hospital and mother had to continue her journey to tell Billy's parents of the disaster. It was discovered that Billy had been walking along the top of the ravine, perhaps collecting kindling wood, had slipped in the wet leaves and fallen over the edge. His shoes were found in the stream and the X-rays revealed a fractured skull in spite of which he had made his way back to the house.

Mother was very keen on the war effort and started a War Savings group in the village. She would collect the sixpences and shillings every week and sell the saving stamps in return. In the summer of 1942, she organised a fancy dress and sports day to raise war savings. The event was in Mr Handley's field. I was told very clearly that I would not be allowed to win the fancy dress, but I still had to dress up as a pierrot, which I hated. Part of the sporting events was a slow bicycle race. Mother could not understand why I objected to her ruling that if you put your foot to the ground you had to go back to the start.

One day in great distress she met me on the way home from

school. The great battleships the Prince of Wales and the Repulse had just been reported to have been sunk. All those boys lost! She had a fierce disagreement with the vicar Reverend Chadwick; when Hitler invaded Russia, he thought that we should not be allied to a godless communist regime. Mother insisted that anyone who would fight Hitler was our ally, as the first thing was to win the war.

By the spring of 1943, the luftwaffe had almost ceased bombing our home town, so all our furniture and one goat and one pig were loaded on to Mr Brown's lorry and our days of evacuation to West Scrafton were over. There will always live with me the outline of Penhill seen from our window; the Roova Crag outcrop of millstone grit crowning the moor at the other side; the call of the curlew up on the moors; the brown water running below the footpath bridge on the way to school, and the smell of wild garlic just across the bridge as we made our way through the wood; picking the field mushrooms in the meadows; the, to me, unpleasant smell of the cooking of sheep's head broth and the wonderful smell of the dough, covered with a tea towel, rising before the fire; the black buds on the ash tree in the garden, always the last to open; the narrow path cut through drifts of snow higher than a man when the village was cut off for weeks at a time.

The Most Famous Vet in the World

As has already been noted in previous chapters, after the war, in the 1950s and 1960s, there was a gradual increase in the number of people who bought cottages in the village and made them habitable for use as second homes and for letting for short periods to holiday makers. Ralph Dubberley and his wife Jean were one such couple and they bought the cottage on the edge of the village green called "The Chantry" or, as it was sometimes known, "Grange Cottage" (see above illustration). On many occasions they let it out to other holiday-making families and one family in particular who used to come on quite a regular basis for exploring the local countryside was an Alf and Joan Wight from Thirsk and their children Jimmy and Rosie. As readers will know, Alf Wight became the "most famous vet in the world" writing under the name of James Herriot. He wrote many books about his early days as a vet in Yorkshire and not only the books, but also the films and the many television adaptations shown under the title of "All Creatures Great and Small", will be fondly remembered by a vast audience throughout the world. Some of the early television episodes were, in fact, shot in and around West Scrafton, even using Tommy Handley's dog at Culverham Farm House in one of the scenes, for which he got paid (see page 65).

The family spent many a holiday in The Chantry and enjoyed every minute of them; but we can let "James Herriot" speak for himself as the following paragraphs are extracted from his book "James Herriot's Yorkshire".

"I have said a lot about my deep feelings for Swaledale and Wensleydale and yet it is in Coverdale that I have spent my holidays.

"To be exact, in the tiny village of West Scrafton. The word Scrafton means "town by a hollow" and the village is a closely packed group of ancient houses around the smallest green I have ever seen (see fig 6).

"We stayed in Grange Cottage, rented from the then owner Dr Ralph Dubberley. It is a characterful old house with the green on one side and a deep gill and beck on the other. It was originally one of the granges of the monks of Coverhan Abbey and has a magnificent fifteenth-century window stretching from the kitchen into the main bedrooms, giving an unusually ecclesiastical look to both rooms. It also means that every word spoken in the kitchen can be heard upstairs.

"When we first went there, we had never seen the place and since it was October we were prepared to rough it in a no-frills rural dwelling with its full share of dampness and draughts. We were understandably enthralled when we found a gracious country home, with the central heating going full blast and a pile of logs roaring and spluttering in an enormous fireplace and throwing its warmth into a sitting-room with comfortable furniture.

"It was a cold day with frost in the air and it all seemed too good to be true. We thawed out by the fine dog grate, then explored the well-equipped kitchen, the dining-room and the three bedrooms and bathroom upstairs. It was perfect.

"And what did we do in October in West Scrafton? Well, you only have to walk out of the door and look up at the long rocky comb on the crest of Roova Crag to feel you have found somewhere exciting. The Crag overhangs the village from a height of over fifteen hundred feet and it is the pleasantest of strolls to follow the track to the summit, then along to the old mine workings and come back to the village via the beck with its hidden pools and falls which are seen only by the farmers and shepherds. It was fine that October, but foggy on the low country and I spent many afternoons up on the Crag with my dogs, either wandering over the mounds and tussocks or stretched out on the crisp grass looking at the grey blanket rolling over the plain.

"Down there it would be dank and dark but on the Crag it was a glittering world of sun and blue skies with the peace and silence wrapping me round as I lay.

Fig 5   The Ancient Terraces of "Granny Banks"

Fig 6   The ". . . Smallest Village Green . . ."

"Or there was another, even gentler walk, very suitable when my daughter visited us with our grandchild, Emma. The road up and over the hill to Swineside was ideal for pushing the little girl in her buggy and though it was a short way the feeling of Pennine beauty was deeply satisfying.

"On one side, above the stone walls, rose the Crag, leading in a noble ridge over Great Haw, Carle Fell and Little Whernside and on the other the land dipped to the floor of the dale with the steep slopes rising to Penhill and Carlton Moor. The long village of Carlton was like a grey thread against the green. . . .

". . . .And what else, you may think, did we do on a holiday in West Scrafton? Well, Helen and Rosie did a lot of shopping. Shopping? In those remote parts? Of course. Since we were catering for ourselves, we had to buy provisions regularly and the food shops were abundant and excellent. Even in lonely Carlton there was an excellent store and when I saw their selection I thought of the days when I was in my twenties and felt lucky to be able to buy a digestive biscuit and a slice of Wensleydale cheese to sustain me on my rounds. . . .

". . . .Of course I spent most of the time roaming among the fells with an Ordnance Survey map tucked in my anorak. It may not sound very exciting to follow those lines of dots which cross the contours of the hillsides but in Coverdale I found it a continual thrill. Especially when my peregrinations took me to the wild country at the dale head. . . .

". . . .All around, the sweet smell of the miles of moorland grass and the silence, complete except for the distant bleating of a sheep. And the sensation, which is comforting at times, of being quite alone; there was no living creature in sight - just me and my dogs. . . .

". . . .When I reached West Scrafton, it was late dusk and banks of dark cloud were crowding over the rim of Roova's crest into the last pale light of the sky. But the yellow gleam in the window of Grange Cottage gave promise of an evening of warmth and cheer around that wonderful log fire."

The Wight family enjoyed their many holidays while staying in The Chantry so much so that, in 1978, they bought Chapman's Cottage as their own rural retreat. One day, not long after that, Alf was walking his dog up the Swineside road when he met Tommy Dent who asked him why he had chosen to come and spend so much time here amongst all the mud and muck of the village and surroundings when he could afford to holiday anywhere in the world. The reply was that Alf loved the countryside around these parts so much that he felt part of it and could spend hours just being in it, contemplating all the unending changes in the weather, the skies and the landscape. Alf Wight died in 1995 and his wife, Joan (Helen in the books and in the above extracts), died a few years later leaving his son Jimmy as the present owner of Chapman's Cottage.

Brenda Thiede, who lives in Great Ghyll Cottage, and her late husband Derek, were rural GPs in Thirsk. They shared the same area as Alf Wight and not only did they have him as a patient from long before he started writing, but they also looked after many of the real characters who feature in his "James Herriot" vet books; and so Brenda, too, is firmly rooted in "Herriot Country".

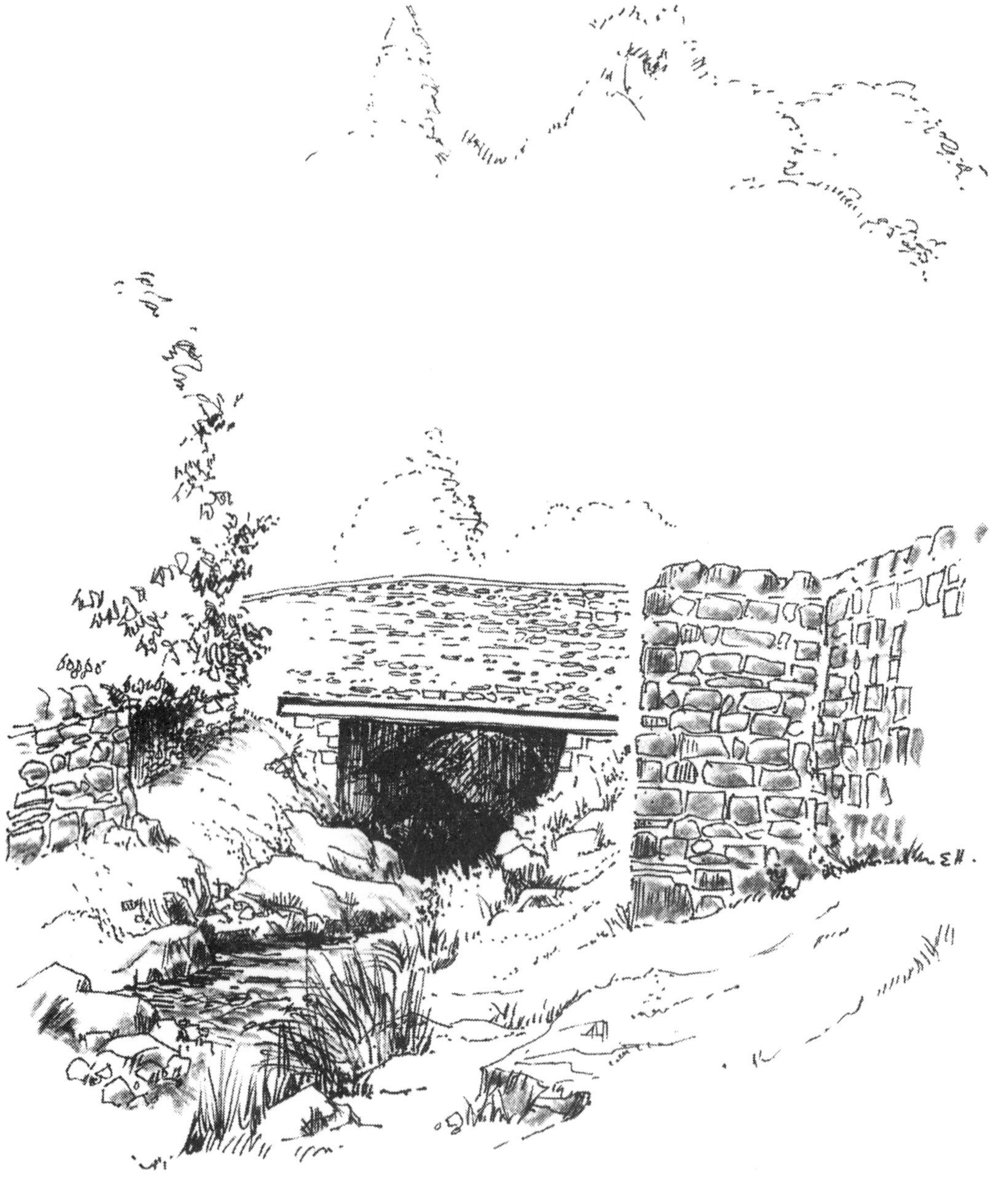

PRESENT POPULATION

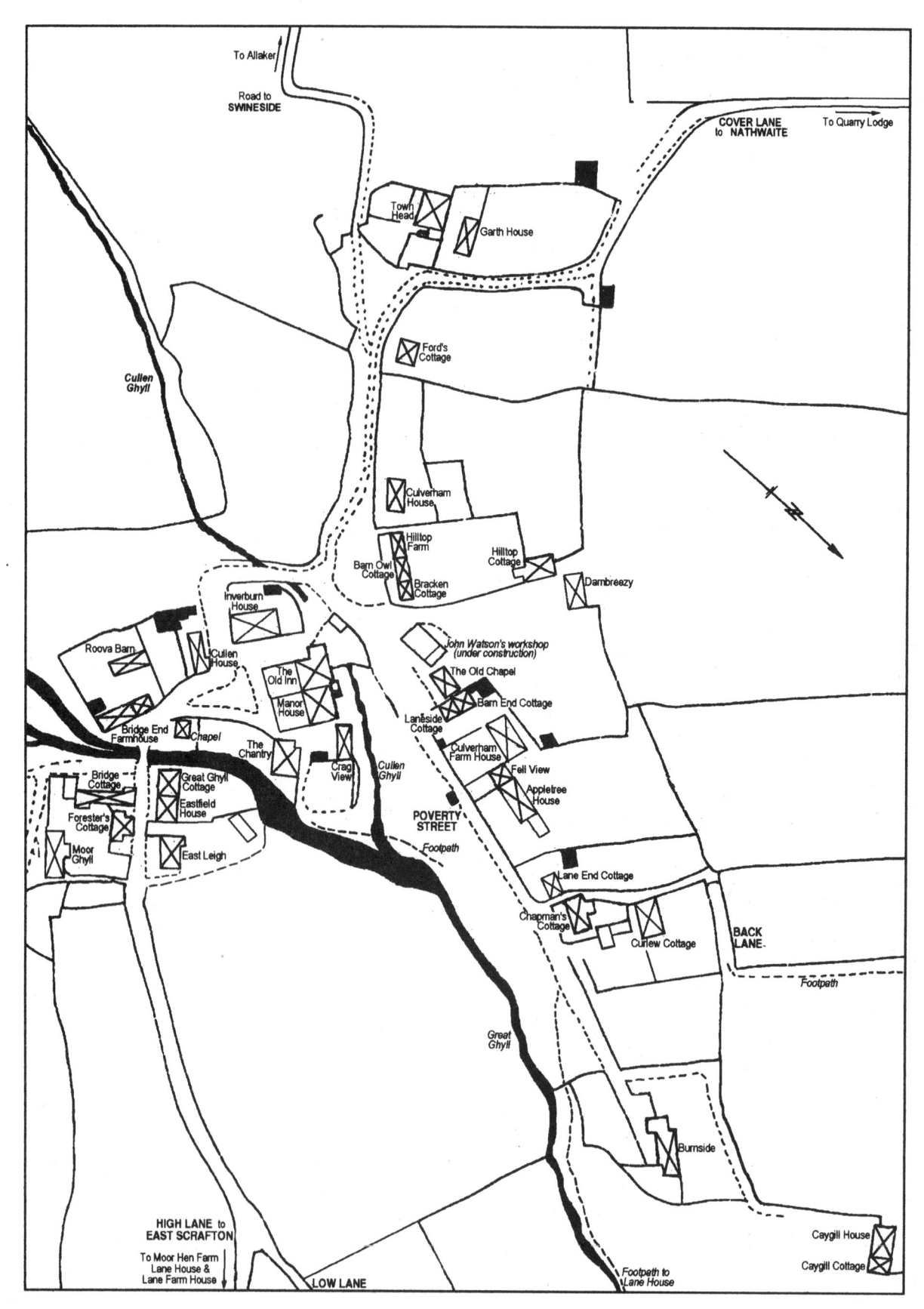

Fig 7 Plan of Village showing Present House Names

House and Home

The following list shows all the householders in the village as at 1 January 2000 including those outwith the parish boundaries who have been included for the purposes of this book. Non-residents who own holiday cottages within the village are shown in square parentheses.

	Name	House	Occupation
1	Bainbridge	Garth House	Audrey · farmer / John · structural draughtsman
2	Baxter	Appletree House	Accountant (retired)
3	Brotherton	Moor Ghyll	University lecturer
4	Burgess	Bridge Cottage	Headmaster (retired)
5	[Cave]	Allaker	Architect
6	Deare	The Chantry	Insurance broker
7	Dent	Town Head	Farmer
8	Dobson	Forester's Cottage	Headmistress (retired)
9	[Elliot]	Manor House	Farmer's wife
10	[Elsby]	Crag View	
11	Fobbester	Quarry Lodge	Micro-electronics engineer (retired)
12	Forrest	Roova Barn	Julie · Town Clerk / Geoff · builder
13	French	Lane Farm House	General maintenance
14	Gower	East Leigh	Mineralogist
15	Hall	Bridge End Farm (cottage)	Ch. Supt. of police (retired)
16	Handley T	Culverham House	Farmer (retired)
17	Harrison A	Curlew Cottage	Telecommunications consultant (retired)
18	Harrison B	Hilltop Farm	Farmer
19	Harrison P	Bracken Cottage	Farmer
20	Hogg	Moorhen Farm	Farmer
21	[Howarth]	Old Chapel	
22	Hudson	Burnside	Social workers
23	Hullah	Culverham Farm House	Airline consultant (retired)
24	Johnson	Caygill House	Landscape builder
25	Neale	The Old Inn	
26	Oddy	Inverburn	Merchant navy captain (retired)
27	Southgate	Lane House	Gamekeeper
28	Suttill	Ford's Cottage	Farmer & welder
29	Thiede	Great Ghyll Cottage	Doctor (GP) (retired)
30	Thomas	Eastfield House	Felicity · secretary / David · army officer (retired)
31	Utley C	Cullen House	Farmer
32	[Utley G]	Hilltop Cottage	Mechanical engineer
33	Utley K	Dambreezy	Farmer
34	Utley W	Bridge End Farmhouse	Farmer
35	Watkins	Lane End Cottage	Landscape gardener
36	Watson	Fell View	Liz · social work leader / John · building services
37	[Wight]	Chapman's Cottage	Veterinary surgeon
38	Wilson	Caygill Cottage	Botanist

The year 2000, however, saw two or three changes to the above list. The Hullahs sold Barn End Cottage to the Hannabuss family and Laneside Cottage to the Schofields, the latter now having been renamed Gillside Cottage. In addition, another holiday cottage was taken over by permanent residents, as Leone Neale, after more than twenty years as owner, sold The Old Inn to John Sheehan, a silversmith, and his wife Liz.

Eleven of the buildings are Grade 2 Listed and brief notes about each of the houses and their occupants follow, some of which reveal interesting secrets and historical facts about the village and its past inhabitants.

Allaker

The following is what Adrian Cave says is his best hypothesis for the history of Allaker, based on information obtained from a wide variety of sources including looking at the building in detail, studying maps and place names, and reading local and regional histories.

Inspection of the stonework of the walls, including the quality of workmanship, corner stones, blocked windows, etc. shows clearly that the oldest part of the existing building is the end of the barn which is next to the house. This may well have been built around 1680 to 1700 when many local walls and buildings were being constructed. The barn was then extended towards the south-west, probably in three phases, of which the last coincided with the construction of the first phase of the cottage.

1800 is the possible date of construction of the cottage, which was certainly completed before 1849, as it is shown on the six-inch ordnance map of that date. The cottage was built as an extension of the barn, forming a traditional dales laithehouse, with the cottage and the barn under one long continuous roof. The cottage would have consisted of the main kitchen/living room, with a traditional range (dating from about 1875) with one bedroom above. There would also have been a washroom (now the bathroom) supplied by water from the roof, with a stone slab with a drainage hole for washing clothes; this stone slab is still in place. The present kitchen would have been a pantry and the existing stone slab was probably used for salting meat, as it took years of redecoration before we were able to clear the salts out of the wall. The kitchen also has a curious wooden hook nailed to a ceiling joist and, although we did not know what it was for, we kept it carefully as we kept most features when we started converting the cottage. The answer came after a thunderstorm in 1977 when the milk curdled and we looked for somewhere to hang a cloth to strain the milk and make cheese: the wooden hook was in exactly the right place over the stone slab.

The whole cottage had a stone ground floor, which is still in place, and the marks of a dog-leg staircase were found on the walls of the present kitchen in 1975. The original door to the kitchen is still in use, but it provides very low headroom. It is made of wide boards shaped by an adze, the adze marks being clearly visible. The cottage, which at that time had no door to the barn, was possibly a hind-house, used for a farm labourer.

Our estimate for the approximate date for the construction of the north-east part of the house is 1875. This part has two rooms with higher ceilings than the original cottage, a new staircase and improved timber doors, window panels and shutters. We think that the posh name of Westclose House was probably introduced at that time and that the building may have belonged to someone involved in local mining or quarrying, as it seems unlikely that the house had sufficient land or buildings to be the home of a prosperous farmer.

We have no information about Allaker in the early part of the 20th Century, but it does not seem to have been changed at all during this time. I once met an elderly man who had lived at Allaker from about 1945 to 1950 and who said that he had met someone who had been born there in the early 1900s. The building was unoccupied and used as a barn (including the house) from about 1950 until we found it in 1974.

We found Allaker by chance because of bad weather. During a family walk in July 1974, we sheltered in the barn during heavy rain and immediately realised from the character of the building and the superb views over Coverdale that Allaker was special. Several people had been interested in buying it, but no one had done so because, although Allaker had never had electricity and the only toilet was an earth closet (which still exists) in an outbuilding, the real problem was that Allaker had never had a water supply other than rainwater from the roof. Standing at an altitude of about 925 feet (280 metres), Allaker was too high to be served by the village water supply. When we bought Allaker from Mr and Mrs S Harrison in 1975, we arranged with them that we could pump water from their cow shed in the village. This we continued to do until the new water tank was built higher above the village in the 1980s, enabling water to flow up to Allaker by natural pressure for the first time.

The electricity supply was connected in 1975 and, since then, internal alterations and improvements have continued almost every year. We have tried always to enhance and conserve the original character of the building, without showing how much work had actually been carried out, and this has been a challenging undertaking for me as an architect. The building works are funded partly by renting out the building as a holiday cottage, and several families, including our own, try to have a holiday at Allaker every year. Allaker was used several times by the BBC in the 1980s for filming the TV series "All Creatures Great and Small" and more recently as a remote location for training highly specialist security guards.

As we are witnessing the end of the sustainable farming traditions of the Yorkshire Dales, it is worth noting the features that applied at Allaker. The balance between sheep and dairy farming included the cattle being kept in the barn in the winter and fed with hay from the surrounding fields. In the springtime, the manure was distributed in the same fields, minimising the distances for transport. There was so much manure on the ground floor of the cottage that we did not know that there was a stone floor until the sale had been agreed!

The oldest part of the barn has the newest timber roof structure, probably because this part of the roof needed renewing at about the time of the construction of the house extension. The beams used at this time in both the barn and the house are rectangular sections cut by machinery, presumably in about 1875, using Victorian technology and means of transport. All the other main roof timbers in both the barn and the cottage are made of rough cut circular tree trunks that were probably cut locally. The building stone is from local quarries, the roofing slabs are from the old Nathwaite mines on the slopes below Allaker, and the lintels and stone door frames are millstone grit, probably from Roova Crags. The lime mortar for the stonework would have come from the many lime kilns in the fields below Allaker (see fig 24).

A local feature is the tradition of rag rugs, made from remnants of old cloth. All the rag rugs at Allaker were made in the 1990s by a lady who lived at Horsehouse.

When we found Allaker there were no trees or shrubs, apart from the white roses (of Yorkshire) in front of the house. Since I planted the trees, the variety of birds around the house has increased considerably. Birds which have nested on or in the building now include swallows, pied wagtails, blue tits, stock doves, jackdaws and kestrels.

Perhaps the most interesting thing about Allaker is the name. Although shown on maps as Westclose House, the building has always been known locally as Allaker. We preferred this name and asked several people in the village how to spell it. No one knew, as they had never seen the name written. We adopted the phonetic spelling, knowing that Aller or Eller is an ancient word for Alder tree, that there are Alders on the banks of the Cover and that there is a local field called Ellers. Years later, having walked almost everywhere in Coverdale and after studying maps, books about place names, and the history of Norse settlements in the Dales, we came to the following conclusions. Allaker is on the line of the best drained route from West Scrafton to Swineside and may mean either Aller-akr (Alder field), Elliker or Helaghker (marsh near the high forest clearing). One thousand years ago the stream in Cullen Gill, close to Allaker, would have been very marshy and there could well have been a clearing in the high forest beside the track to Swineside. A Norse farmstead called Allaker, in this high clearing in the forest, would have been built of timber and no traces could be expected to have survived. But what is extraordinary is that, although the name Allaker is undoubtedly of Norse origin, it does not appear on any maps and had apparently not been written down until we did so in 1975. Therefore, the only way in which the name could have survived is by continuous verbal tradition for more than 1000 years.

This Norse or Scandinavian connection gives cause for thought as we doze at Allaker on modern IKEA chairs in front of a Danish wood-burning stove. We also remember that, when Caroline Harrison, who looks Swedish, told us that her dog was loppy, only our Danish friend knew that this meant that the dog had fleas!

Appletree House

The date stone over the kitchen door says "1688". This may or may not be the true date of the building, but, if true, then the front elevation was rebuilt some time later as its style is more like 1788. The house was internally re-organised at some time, probably around 1930 at which time the property was owned by one James Hammond of Hornby Castle. Until it was removed by the present owners in 1991, the main fireplace was formed by a sort of breastsummer beam of oak, which was 14ft long and reputed to have come from Hornby Castle; the castle was indeed "reduced in size" at about that date.

In 1851 the house was owned and occupied by John Spence, together with just over twelve acres of land in the parish. He was born in West Scrafton while his wife, Elizabeth, had been born in

East Scrafton. They had a daughter, Ann, a dressmaker, and two sons who were both masons. The records show that on the night of the 1851 census they entertained visitors, John Coblet, a butcher, also born in West Scrafton, and his two children.

The house probably remained with the Spence family until 1904 when it was sold to Thomas Horner, passing to James Hammond in 1929. He held it for only four years selling it to Joseph Bell of Crag View in 1933. Soon after, and certainly prior to 1940, the house was leased to William Brown who continued to occupy the house (as owner, following the death of Joseph Bell in 1954) until his own death in 1961. William's sister Edna had come to live in the House in 1941 to care for the family after the death of William's wife. Edna inherited the house and continued to live there until 1987. Two short-term owners followed before the house was purchased by the present inhabitants, Roger and Sandra Baxter, towards the end of 1990.

Over the following two years a comprehensive restoration was undertaken by John Watson (who had never worked so close to home) starting with rebuilding the roof and working downwards. All plaster and internal rendering was removed and most of the beams and joists were replaced. New floors were fitted throughout the ground floor.

After these modifications had been carried out, Roger and Sandra moved into the house as residents in April 1992.

Bridge Cottage

Like most of the properties in West Scrafton, Bridge Cottage, which is situated delightfully by the bridge overlooking Great Ghyll, has been knocked about a bit in the best Cromwellian tradition. Not that Bridge Cottage was actually around in the Protector's day so far as we can ascertain. Though its origins are indeed obscured in the mists of antiquity, that fog descends in mid-Victorian times prior to which no trace of its existence can be found.

For all we can tell "BC", so far from having been built when these initials might suggest, actually started life as a coal miner's "two-up two-down" sometime during West Scrafton's heyday as the Pittsburgh of Coverdale. With the abandonment of the coal mines around the turn of the last century, due to too much water (both below and above ground), faulty geology and even faultier economics, BC "fell into desuetude" as they say; ie it became an uninhabited and uninhabitable farm outbuilding and hay store. At some time thereabouts a separate shippen appeared between the original cottage and the road and thenceforth the property remained deserted and increasingly derelict throughout the two world wars. It was only as recently as 1970 that BC's fortunes took a turn for the better. At that time one Philip Brown acquired first the house and, eighteen months later, the barn, joined the two buildings together (resulting in an impressive 3ft thick interior wall) and set about making BC a magical holiday home. Alas, unable to cope with this sudden upturn in its affairs, most of the cottage walls promptly fell down. As it subsequently turned out, however, even this debacle had its bright side in that, when the new BC rose phoenix-like from the rubble of the old, it was (a) larger and (b) blessed with some foundations, the lack of which had caused its downfall in the first place. To be truthful, not all of the walls succumbed and the original (and unusual) banded stone facade luckily survived, as did the robustly built shippen or "barn room" as it was now christened. The Browns then gutted the entire interior including the whole of the first floor. Pine beams and "mod. cons." of modest pretensions were installed and the whole edifice re-roofed. This latter restoration, however, proved to be an unmitigated disaster. Due to some feeble excuse about running out of the original roofing slates (but in truth, more due to the owners partying in Spain at the crucial time and thus losing track of what was going on) the new extension, which, very unusually for Dale's cottages, is at right angles to the line of the main building, was finished off with a <u>flat</u> roof instead of the planned and approved gable end. This was a calamity, both aesthetically and practically; flat roofs and Coverdale weather being antipathetical. However, what was done was done and retrospective planning permission was obtained!

History moves on to 1983 and so do the Browns (move on, that is). Consequently Bridge Cottage comes once more to the market and, by a devious set of machinations too complicated to explain, is next acquired by an impecunious schoolmaster and his wife with the aid of a 90% mortgage and the loan of the remaining 10% deposit from the same source!

In the event, BC had to continue its rough and ready existence as a letting holiday cottage, since the new owners, encumbered as they were by having to live in at their school, could only manage infrequent sojourns in Coverdale; but it was always their intention to retire to West Scrafton and in due season (1993) they did just that, despite the very basic accommodation and facilities which they had inherited from the holiday makers.

There ensued, consequently, two major development phases. The first involved a complete reconstitution of the interior (once again). Lounges became kitchens; kitchens became dining rooms; bedrooms became bathrooms and vice-versa! Staircases were repositioned and fireplaces summarily moved from room to room and/or reconstructed; even the dramatically expensive underfloor electric heating was abolished.

When they had recovered, phase two was initiated. This resulted in the addition of a built-on garage; a porch to prevent the soufflé from being blown off the dining room table, and the construction of Hadrian's Wall (otherwise known as a car-park to overlook Great Ghyll); but above all it resulted in the demise of that disfiguring flat roof and its replacement by a properly pitched gable adorned by proper Yorkshire slates!

That all took place seven years ago, since when the present owners, Graham and Ruth Burgess, have continued to enjoy their "Little Grey Home in the West", its ever-changing weather and its everlasting scenery. As one of their erstwhile happy holiday hirers once wrote in the guest book, "Who needs a garden when blessed with ten thousand of God's Own Acres on the doorstep?"

According to Graham, "not, apparently, two of our early visitors. During the 1993 excavations, when we were knee-deep in mud and JCBs, endeavouring to turn the morass that lay feet deep outside our front door into a passable tarmac driveway, two Barbour-jacketted and green-wellied gentlemen came picking their way gingerly through the quagmire. 'What's going on here?' one of them politely inquired. Somewhat facetiously, in dread fear lest they proved to be planning officers, I replied 'Not a lot! Just an amateurish attempt to redesign the Yorkshire Dales National Park!' With slightly forced smiles, William Hague and Sir Leon Britton strode on to rejoice in what was left of God's Own Acres and I was left wondering where I had seen those faces before."

Bridge End Farmhouse

Bridge End Farmhouse has had a varied history over several centuries. It was the home of a good many coal miners during the time when work in the mine on Roova Moor was at its peak. Possibly around the same time, when the village community was large enough to sustain a second public house in addition to the Moorhen, it was an inn, although by what name it was known seems to have been lost in the mists of antiquity.

The building, which is grade 2 listed, has a 17th century square stone arched door surround at the front and 17th century mullioned windows at the rear which set its date of origin pretty firmly. Cannibalisation of old buildings over the years has been commonplace and the lintels of a couple of the upstairs sash windows at the front have been re-cycled from the 18th century stone architraves. There is also an interesting small blocked-in window with a gothic surround on the right of the facade.

One of its more intriguing features is the white painted front door which is in two halves, hinged in the centre and on the right jamb in order to make access possible to the minute entrance lobby behind and to either of the two internal doors leading off it. In place of locks, security is ensured when the door is closed, by drawing the substantial beam from its recess in the wall until it can be fitted into a similar recess in the opposite wall.

The house came into the Utley family in the '50s and when Charles Utley married June Sutill in 1964 it became their first home and where their children were born. They all moved out to Cullen House in 1976 and Bridge End was rented out for fourteen years until Will started a major renovation in 1990 and in 1992 family history repeated itself. Will married Kath and they in turn moved into it as their first home, where likewise their children were born. They have three, two of whom are twins; Bret William and Liam John are both eight, and Kim Ruth is nearly four. Will of course is part of the family farming partnership and Kath like many farmers' wives participates on the farm as well as being a housewife and mother.

At the moment the house is divided into two, with the right hand portion consisting of a self-contained cottage currently occupied by Dick Hall, who moved across from the Manor House a few years ago.

Burnside

Burnside is an attractive house but has no claim to fame over and above any other house in West Scrafton, each of which has its own history to tell.

The house was probably built in the 1700s and was two separate "one up one down" adjoining cottages which have, over the years, been extended to give the kitchen and stone-shelved pantry with a bathroom upstairs. The original outbuildings were bought and attached to the house in two stages and converted first into a garage and store room with a "state of the art" hen house and by the present owners into a garage and extra living accommodation.

It has the attributes of being a dales "long house" in only being one room in depth from front to back with each downstairs room opening off each other.

The deeds to the house go back to 1883 where it is described as a dwelling-house, "formerly two dwellings but now in one with the garden and paddock". It was sold at that time by a brewer from Coverbridge to a spinster lady in West Scrafton for £70. Apparently some time between 1883 and 1915, when the house was sold again, its spinster owner had married and moved to Newbiggin in Bishopdale and the house had been occupied by tenants. When it was sold in 1915, the price was only half that which had been asked for it in 1883. Was this drop in value a result of the economic conditions during the First World War - a prelude to the Great Depression or had the tenants allowed the property to deteriorate? Strangely, on this occasion it was once again purchased by another spinster, this time one who was living in Maunby near Thirsk, and who continued to live there after the purchase.

By 1918 it seems that this lady had moved from Maunby and was living in Bradford when she sold the house in that year to the widow of a German gentleman, a Mrs Seifert, who was also living in Bradford at the time. It is thought that this unfortunate widow had suffered some harassment in Bradford as a result of her "unpatriotic" marriage and took the opportunity to buy this house and retreat to West Scrafton. She owned the house right up until 1942 but went to live with relatives when the war started. It stood empty for a couple of months until it was occupied by a family of evacuees from Hartlepool (see page 56). After her death, the house was sold to a gentleman described as "a director" from Knaresborough for a price that was only just over double that originally agreed for it in 1883. However, this new ownership does not seem to have lasted long, for in 1945 the house was sold again to a local farmer, the price having increased by £30.

This new owner installed a septic tank and a "water closet" in 1946, and indeed several improvements seem to have been made over succeeding years. In 1950 a back boiler was installed for hot water and in 1952 the house was connected to the new electricity supply along with the rest of West Scrafton.

1964 saw the house being sold to yet another spinster lady at a price now seven times greater than that paid by the previous owner. She clearly wanted "all mod. cons." as the upstairs bathroom was installed and then the "scullery" extended to form a kitchen. This improvement caused the rateable value to be increased; in 1950 it stood at £5, by 1963 it had increased to £22 and the arrival of the bathroom added another £3, bringing it up to £25. In 1987 this lady bought the cow-byre which is attached to the house, thus essentially completing the building as it stands today.

She remained the owner until 1988 when it was sold to a couple for a sum approximately 32 times greater than she had paid for the house and cow-byre together - inflationary times had set in. The new owners had quite elaborate plans drawn up to build out over the cow-byre and create a holiday cottage, but planning permission was refused and in 1992 they moved on. There are no records of any other improvements made by them, but nevertheless they were able to sell the property for nicely over double the price they had paid for it.

In 1998 the house was sold again to the present owners, Philip and Kate Hudson, at a price which represents an increase of something in excess of 2000 times over the past 100 years. But it is noteworthy that almost all of that increase has occurred since 1945 when the water closet was added - a pivotal event which led to the increase in the value by about £150,000 in half a century.

The house has thus had nine owners in this century and appears to have had several periods when it was occupied by tenants. It is quite intriguing that of those nine owners four of the earlier ones were single women, spinsters or widows. How did they come to be able to afford to be property owners in their own right - surely quite unusual for those times?

The Hudsons had visited the dales on a regular basis since childhood and once their day-to-day family obligations had come to an end, they decided to take the plunge and move to something that they wanted - a quiet rural location with all that that entailed. West Scrafton fitted the bill because they just fell for the house and its position.

Caygill House and Cottage

At the rear of the dwellings along Poverty Street and running up to Caygill Scar is a field having the intriguing name of Bessie Backside, a name which has remained unchanged since at least the 1800s. At the Scar side of the field was a cow byre known as Bessie Barn which was last owned and used as a byre by Tommy Handley.

As a byre it had a hay store in the centre with space for housing five cows at each end. It was sold around 1975 to a Mr and Mrs Hammond whose application for planning permission to convert it into a house was eventually granted in 1977 after a final appeal.

The house was named Caygill House and this was subsequently sold to a Mr Hodgson. who converted it to its present form, making a slightly smaller house together with an attached but self-contained cottage.

The present occupants are Frank Johnstone, a landscape gardener who lives with his family in Caygill House; and Richard Wilson, a botanist, and Sue who are the residents of the cottage.

Chapman's Cottage

$\mathcal{I}$t was the long-established practice until recent times that dwellings in the village were known by the names of their occupants rather than by individual house names. A few of these names still exist, one of them being Chapman's Cottage.

As can be seen from the population records, the Chapman family were living there in the mid-1800s and there were still Chapmans in the village at the end of that century. However, during the early part of the 20th century, the house was given the name of

"Sunningdale" and it was purchased under that name by a Francis William Hogg in 1949. He thought that it would be more in keeping with the local atmosphere to call it by the original name of Chapman's Cottage and it remains under this name today.

It stands towards the northern end of Poverty Street and is believed to have originally been an early 17th century single storey hall, open right up to the roof. It has a lobby entered by a stone quoined doorway, four-paned windows with stone mullions and transoms, and a parlour with a three-paned mullioned window. The first floor was constructed in the early 18th century, also having stone mullioned windows. These were copied in concrete at some later date when additional windows were provided.

The house was purchased from Francis Hogg by Vy Dunford, who had come from Wakefield with her brothers, John and Tom. In 1978, it was sold to Alf and Joan Wight (alias James and Helen Herriot) as their holiday retreat. At the end of the millennium, the house is still in the ownership of the Wight family, Alf's son James having inherited it when his parents died.

Crag View

Although Crag View is in the centre of the village, it is tucked away behind the village green and would remain un-noticed by most visitors. It was built around the end of the 17th century with moulded ashlar window surrounds to the front elevation. It has a projecting porch with a pent roof and an arched doorway. Unusually, the stairway is within an enclosure built on to the front of the building. This appurtenance has a tall narrow window and also supports a pent roof.

In 1897 John Robinson was the local gamekeeper and when he married Ann, a laundress from Stockton, they took up residence in

Crag View. Mrs Robinson, who ultimately ran the village shop in Moor Ghyll, was affectionately known as "Old Ma Rob" and her husband acquired the nick-name of "Father John".

When the Robinsons eventually moved in to Moor Ghyll, Crag View became the home of Joe Bell who sadly committed suicide there. Without being aware of this bit of the house's history, John Watson, when doing some work inside for the then current owners, claims to have had distinct feelings of being watched by someone unseen. He denies it was mice. Slightly uneasy, he finished the job but was happy to be outside again and so coined another embryonic ghost story for the village.

The house is currently used as a holiday home by Bob and Jean Elsby, who have been the owners for over twenty years.

Cullen House

Cullen House was built sometime in the 18th Century and has a date stone showing a weather worn "seventeen something" as possible confirmation. Now home to Charles and June Utley, it has been in the Utley family since the mid-1800s when William Utley first moved in and farmed a few acres which have now changed and been expanded substantially. One thing that has not changed in the intervening years since William's time is the family horn-burn "W.U" used to identify the Utley sheep; his memory therefore lives on and is reputed to be the reason Charles' and June's first son is called Will. It saved having to change the horn-burn mark.

The house itself has of course been subject to frequent amendments, the biggest in early years probably being the removal of a thatched roof and replacement with stone slates. It is impossible to say accurately when this was done, but the oldest part of the building still has the acute angle of a thatching pitch. Moreover, the stone slates now covering that particular roof are amongst the biggest and oldest of any in the village and are probably the ones which immediately replaced the thatch. Another manifestation of its age and amongst the several reasons for it being a grade 2 listed building is the stone mullioned windows on the south wall looking out on to the garden.

It had been occupied by four generations of Utleys before Charles became the fifth following the death of his father Oswald. Ossie as he was known had been gassed in France during the first World War and died relatively young, but in his later years had been very active in the construction of the village's improved water supply.

After the death of Ossie and his wife, the house lay empty for a while until Charles and, June who had been living in Bridge End Farmhouse with the children, were able to rescue it from its deteriorated and sad condition and move into it themselves.

That renovation entailed some significant changes. What had been the trap or cart house with its cobbled floors became the current spacious kitchen (in which much of West Scrafton's information is exchanged), while the kitchen window giving on to the road still retains the distinctive shape of the big original door. The adjacent stable, which had accommodated several horses in its time, became the utility room. Meanwhile the two rooms at the other end of the house were knocked into one to make a larger living room and so by December 1976 the whole structure had been changed into a large. six bedroomed house ready to accommodate the entire family.

Eventually the children flew the coop, Will having married Kath, moved back into Bridge End where he had been born, and Kevin and Clare set up home in Dambreezy, but still all remaining in the farming partnership, while Caroline and Chris moved further afield to Masham and Bedale respectively.

Culverham Farm House
with Barn End and Laneside Cottages

The deeds for Culverham Farm House occupy a largish box, but throw little light on the history of the house itself as they are almost totally concerned with the changing ownership of the land. Since at least the latter part of the 17th century these records give only occasional brief non-descriptive mention of "a messuage" which included out-buildings or "a dwelling" which didn't. On 25th May 1698 it was referred to in an agreement between a Thomas Berwith and Christopher Topham. The date stone over the front door lays claim to an origin nine years earlier and reads somewhat enigmatically "CF 1689 F". It could be the initials of Christopher Forster who had an interest in it by the 1720s; it is unlikely that it signified Culverham Farm as that name doesn't appear to have been coined until fairly recently. But, anyway, such stones are notoriously unreliable indicators of age; builders down the centuries have used material from any convenient source and there are many cases in which date stones have been moved from their original location more than once. As a result the early history of the house remains obscure and can only be reconstructed on thin evidence and reasonable conjecture.

Like practically every house is West Scrafton it has been altered and extended on numerous occasions. There seem to be at least three significant stages in its construction. The largest part of the building is essentially two rooms above a central entrance hall which separates two ground floor rooms and which may once have held a steep narrow staircase. Behind this and dug into the land to the rear is a two story "lean-to" construction which increases the floor area by a good third and boasts a date stone at the northern end saying "FF 1817 Dairy Window", but this merely records the installation of a window by a Francis Forster[3], who occupied the house from 1796; it does not actually date that part of the house which may well in fact be the oldest. A third part was obviously added later to the southern end, the upper part of which was clearly used as a store, but the lower room may have been occupied, possibly by farm hands. Vestiges of a fireplace were uncovered, backing on to the one in the main part of the house.

The style of the whole building as it now stands, with its typical tall rounded window to the staircase, is consistent with that of the late 18th century and a couple of early 18th century keys found a foot or so beneath the flag stone floor of the rear part of the house may confirm the suspicion that the lean-to is in fact the oldest part of the house.

Diagram showing the three stages of build

Since 1698 the ownership of the house and land has changed several times, with up to seven different families in occupation, but by the end of the 19th century, current

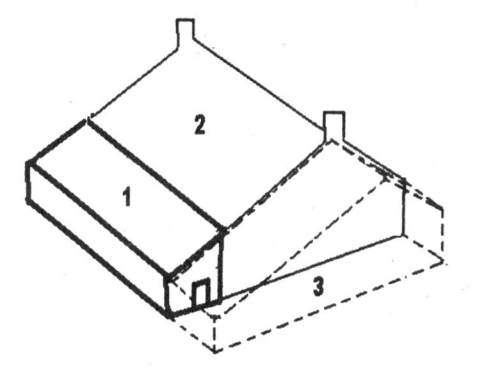

---

[3] The names of Christopher and Francis Forster were taken from the house deeds, but they both appear under the name of Foster in the tax records of 1673.

local names begin to appear in the deeds such as the Handleys and the Utleys. In 1888 Jonas Swales was farming the Culverham property, and on 11th May a William Utley, who had been farming and dealing in cattle near Liverpool and had as mortgagor loaned Swales some £2950, agreed to buy the farm for £3000 and he subsequently moved in to West Scrafton. By doing so he acquired the house, 61 acres of pasture and arable land, together with the right to graze 109 full grown sheep on West Scrafton Moor, all of which he added to parcels of land which he had acquired a few years earlier. When William died in 1908, the farm had been acquired by his brother Thomas Utley, an engineer living in Liverpool. Thomas had made a considerable fortune from the design and production of ventilators for use in cattle ships plying between the USA and this country, while taking the time to father twelve children. The farm was worked first by William's son, Fred, and then later by another son, Dawson Utley, as tenant farmers. In 1920 Thomas Utley sold it out of the family to Joseph Handley whose son Tommy was eventually born there. But in keeping with the historic pattern of fluctuating ownership a large part of the land was brought back into the Utley family in 1979, when Tommy Handley retired and put most of his land up for auction. Gradually over the next few years the farmland was dispersed, leaving as "messuage" the house, some outbuildings and the barn, the latter looking as if it had been there for ever but which in fact had been built much later than any other parts. Until recent years this barn had a date stone inscribed "Thomas Utley, Liverpool 1913", but unfortunately it was defaced when the barn was converted into holiday cottages.

In the 1950s, along with ten other buildings in West Scrafton, the property was given Grade 2 Listed status, but more uniquely perhaps, it achieved status of another kind by being used briefly as a set and an occasional dressing room in the making of the BBC television series "All Creatures Great and Small", and in the process spawned a host of anecdotes which would have done Herriot proud.

After a few years as a holiday let, following the Handley's move to the newly built Culverham House a couple of hundred yards away, they sold it to Philip and Susan Wiles in 1987. The Wiles pursued the planning approval originally held by Tommy Handley and converted the barn into two self-contained holiday cottages, but not without a bruising period of confrontation with the planning authorities. And so, where there had been stalls for 5 cows, stabling for 2 horses and a cart shed, there were now fitted kitchens and sitting and dining rooms, and, where feed had been stored above the animals, were bedrooms, bathrooms, and cosy domesticity. No-one had explained these changes to the swallows, however, and for many subsequent summers they continued to swoop to non-existent nesting sites through any open window or door. The Wiles venture came to an unhappy end following the very sad death of Susan, whereupon the property fell into the hands of a building society and languished there for three years. The barn, having been recently refurbished, withstood the ravishes of the ensuing winters, but the house did not. Unoccupied and damp, it began to lose wallpaper, plaster and ceilings, grow indefinable fungus in dark corners and become a tomb for birds who had fallen down the chimney and patterned the walls with soot before expiring.

It was in this state when Ed & Joan Hullah found it during a pre-retirement reconnaissance on 11th October 1995. Having just returned from a visit to Malaysia a few days earlier, the contrast between lush brilliance and bleak autumn dereliction was too much and they laughed at what seemed a preposterous purchase and walked away. But they came back the following day nevertheless and wandered around in between alternating snow flurries and bright sunshine; the place was beginning to get a grip on them. By November the affair was becoming serious. They reappeared with professional advice in tow; alarming costs for refurbishment of the house were beginning to accrue and give a potential new meaning to the name Poverty Street, the lane by which it stands.

Despite being out of the country for the greater part of the rest of the winter, an offer was made in February and they found they owned it on 29th May 1996. In the preceding months all preparations had been made for work to start on rebuilding the house in June. In the end,

Laneside and Barn End Cottages

September seemed like a reasonable compromise.

Living on site in the cottages was comfortable but of variable value. On the one hand decisions could be made on the spot in concert with the builder, and regular visits from Tommy and Mabel Handley provided useful and amusing guidance around their previous lifelong home; on the other hand watching the enormous amount of destruction before construction was unnerving. The floors were dug out (unearthing the old key), new drains laid, over a hundred flagstones reset, the wall chipped clean and re-plastered, and the old loft was opened up from the house to make an en-suite bathroom and a study. A new bathroom, new central heating, a new staircase and a new downstairs toilet were also added, while the kitchen was rebuilt and windows and ceilings replaced. Moreover, some forty tonnes of stone roof slates were removed and replaced over roofing felt which hitherto had not existed; and then there were the walls outside to be re-pointed. As the builder said, "apart from that there wasn't a lot to do really". And so, surprisingly close to schedule and budget, the place was ready for occupation by August 1997.

The barn then reverted to two busy holiday cottages until one particularly sunny day in the autumn of 1999 Chris and Margaret Schofield, who were staying in the one originally called Swallows Nest, then renamed Lane Side and is now, thanks to them, called Gillside Cottage, expressed an interest in buying the cottage. The idea took off as a third retirement began to look attractive to Joan Hullah. So, in addition, the other cottage, Barn End, was put up for sale and in November, within hours of learning of it, Rob and Kath Hannabuss had hurtled up from Kent to make an offer and so, come March 2000, both were sold.

In five years the changes to Culverham Farm House have probably been more profound in a very short space of time than in any other equivalent period in its long history, but in the end the house, along with the barn, now makes three families and many visitors very comfortable and content with their lot; which may account for the Farm House ghost resting in peace of late. But that is another story.

Culverham House

One of the three houses built in West Scrafton in the last twenty years, Culverham House now occupies what was once a vegetable garden owned by the occupants of Inverburn some fifty yards away. The foundations and some walls up to lower window height were already in place in 1980 when Tommy and Mabel Handley bought the property from a speculative builder. They added substantially to the original planned building and also acquired land to the north and west from Freddie Lawson of Carlton in order to provide what is now the orchard and top lawn. Not surprisingly the new home was called Culverham House after their previous one a hundred yards away down Poverty Street, and as their prize bull Theodor of Culverham was in the offing, the name became even more significant.

Some interesting finds were made during the conversion of Freddie Lawson's land into the garden. One of these finds was particularly useful. The remains of what had been a thatched cottage were unearthed when excavating the foundations for the double garage and this discovery produced sufficient stone to build not only the garage, but also a wood-shed, a conservatory, several lengths of terrace wall and an extension on the first floor above what is now the dining room. Not everything was recycled. A stone-shelved corner cupboard disappeared, as did the remains of the fireplace along with, rather more sadly, stone-mullioned windows which would have been of great value in later years. The cottage itself had apparently burned down and there is a vague memory of someone's grandmother as a small child being carried away from the burning building.

In the process of clearing out the piece of land, an old and dilapidated wooden hut, which at one time had housed hens, calves and other assorted livestock, was dismantled. This revealed twelve bee-boles set in the south-facing wall which were of sufficient interest to warrant their being listed as such by the Department of the Environment and enabling them to join eleven other listed buildings in the village. The bee-boles, shown in fig 24, are recesses built into the dry-stone wall and each would have held a bee-hive. A nearby ancient apple tree may well have played a part in supporting the hives.

Curlew Cottage

We came here in 1996, not long after I had retired. We had been living in the south of Scotland for the last twenty years but had decided to come back to England if an opportunity presented itself. Doreen used to show Afghan hounds and, because we attended various dog shows in the north-east of England, we had a number of friends in the Newcastle and Darlington areas in addition to those we had made in and around the village near Melrose in which we lived. As our son lives in Derbyshire, we had decided that North Yorkshire, and in particular the dales, would be, not only a delightful place in which to spend the rest of our lives, but also a centre of gravity, so to speak, between the various people we wished to visit.

Our first house-hunting expedition included Leyburn where we picked up a number of brochures, Curlew Cottage being one of them. From the photographs it immediately struck Doreen as being the most likely place and we arranged a visit. On our way home she declared that this was the place for her, especially as it had a good garden for the dogs and a magnificent view over Coverdale. Luckily we lived in a place which was "much sought after" and we managed to sell our property quite quickly, keeping our fingers crossed that Curlew Cottage was still available, even though it had been on the market for four years. Luck was on our side and we moved in one foggy January day in 1996.

The building was originally erected as a stone-roofed barn, in 1870 according to the date stone, and had remained as such until 1970 when it had been converted into a two storey dwelling house. Before the barn was built, there had been a couple of single storey cottages running along Poverty Street roughly in line with Chapman's Cottage, but these were demolished towards the end of the 19th century and there are now no remains of them.

The previous owners had made some alterations to Curlew Cottage and, as well as modernising the upstairs bathroom, had added a utility room and a downstairs shower and cloakroom by the addition of a single storey extension finished in the same stone as the barn.

The original conversion had included a wrought iron staircase ascending from the living room to the upper floor landing, but for some reason this had been replaced by a not particularly pleasant wooden structure and we had decided that when we had finished redecorating, fitting out a new kitchen and bedroom, and re-tiling the bathroom, we would look to see what could be done to replace this staircase with something a little more attractive.

The staircase divides the living room, which comprised the main part of the barn, into two sections, the end nearest the kitchen being the dining room, with the opposite end forming the lounge area. There is a large recessed stone flagged fireplace at this end, 3ft deep and 10ft wide with an old wooden breastsummer beam above. I am not sure where this beam originally came from as it has a chiselled cut-out about an inch deep and ten inches long at one end with a one inch diameter hole in the centre; it may have been a support for the hay loft with the cut-out being where part of a winch was attached. However, this fireplace makes the lounge an ideal place in which to listen to music, with a loudspeaker placed one at each end of the recess.

The ceilings of two of the upstairs bedrooms have not been boarded in, thus leaving the original wooden roof trusses exposed. Although this makes cleaning and decorating difficult, it gives these rooms a different atmosphere than the more usual parallel beams which are present elsewhere in the house.

It took us a couple of years to carry out the various changes that we required (apart from the staircase). Sadly Doreen died in 1998, but I could not have been left in a nicer or friendlier place in which to look after the remaining dogs and end my days. The date stone, which is now above the outside door to the utility room, bears the initials TH, which in fact stood for Tristram Hogg, the local farmer whose barn it originally was, but it is nice and fanciful to think that perhaps it can now stand for Tony Harrison!

Dambreezy

Kevin Utley was born in 1965 in Bridge End Cottage and then moved to Cullen House with his parents, Charles and June, when Charles's parents died. He was brought up with farming and stayed with it, although he almost branched out into engineering after college.

Clare Utley is Brenda Thiede's daughter and as the Thiede family had had Great Ghyll Cottage as a holiday home for many years she knew most of the people in the village when she came to live here with Hannah in 1992. She trained as a secretary but found her interest lay in public relations and went on to work in that field in the head office of ICI before she left in order to have Hannah.

Dambreezy was originally a cow byre and hay barn, but in 1989 Kevin obtained planning permission to convert it into a house. He carried out most of the work himself apart from occasional help with the plastering and the electrics.

Kevin wanted to incorporate different levels and a minstrel's gallery and this he achieved, making the lounge rather an unusual and appealing feature of the house. The family moved in on 4th September 1993 and now have three children, Hannah (11), Elizabeth (6) and George (4).

George's favourite animal is a crocodile and in the garden there is a wooden one which Kevin carved with a chain saw!

East Leigh

After years of walking in the dales, Peter and Jane Gower came to West Scrafton for the first time in 1985 to view "The Cottage" as Moor Ghyll was then called. Peter Gower is a geologist and at spends a great deal of his working life in Australia. They had decided to live in the dales and they could hardly believe that there was such a beautiful spot that they had not discovered before. They bought Moor Ghyll and lived there until 1998 when they moved over the road to East Leigh.

East Leigh is a converted barn and was one of the original farm buildings belonging to the Hogg family of farmers of Eastfield Farm. Tristram and Betty Hogg converted the barn to a small house and in 1980 they moved in, selling Eastfield House where they had previously been living, as a separate dwelling. The outside stone steps leading to the hayloft, which were a feature of the majority of the barns in the area, were removed at this time.

The house was bought by Barbara Johnson in the early 1990s and it was extended to the north to give additional accommodation on two storeys. Barbara Johnson kept ponies which at that time were housed in the barn adjoining Eastfield House and which was still part of the East Leigh property. When she moved on, the house was purchased by an architect by the name of Alfred Rigby who soon sold the barn to the Thomases who were now the owners of Eastfield House.

When the Gowers moved across from Moor Ghyll in 1998, they extended the building still further with a utility room and store, thus making the majority of the present house less than ten years old.

Eastfield House

Building of Eastfield House was commenced in 1866 as the plaque on the front wall indicates. The owners were called Pearson, hence the letters CP which are also on the plaque. Unfortunately they ran out of money during building and the house remained as a shell for the next 40 years with only the outside walls standing. This shell was eventually purchased by Tristram Hogg in 1900. He completed the building work and called the house East Field Farm.

The house remained with the Hogg family until 1980 when it was sold to Captain Gavin Hamilton of the Green Howards and his wife Victoria who carried out various internal alterations and renamed it Eastfield House. Unfortunately Captain Hamilton was killed in the Falklands war and Victoria subsequently sold the house in 1983 to a joint ownership of a Mr Firth and a Mrs McKenna who carried out further improvements and used it between them as a holiday retreat. They in turn sold it to a Brian and Jean Kendall who lived in Suffolk., but Brian's mother Elsie was the main occupant. They remained the owners until 1994 during which time Brian carried out further extensive alterations and repairs.

We purchased the house from Brian and Jean in November 1994 when Elsie moved to Suffolk to join her son. Although there is a barn attached to the house, this came under the ownership of the next door property, East Leigh, and so we had to make a separate purchase for this from the then owner, architect Alfred Rigby. A door from the house was put in and the barn is at present used as an all purpose store room, but it came in very useful as a venue for the village millennium party.

One particular feature of the house is the stone gutter to the front, which is apparently unique.

Another interesting fact is that the old name of the nearby field that is now known as Inisher was Ingester (see fig 3). "Ing" means field and "ester" means east. Could this perhaps be a clue as to the origin of the house name? It is a great pity that mispronunciations and mis-spellings throughout the ages have eradicated the true meanings and derivations of our heritage. After all, who could have guessed that there was a meaning to "Inisher" without the old field map?

But what a year 1999 has been! It was good that the weather was so inclement that we were unable to get into the garden.

From April last year Brenda Thiede had her builders working like slaves. The noise was horrendous. There were cement mixers, the high scream of a paving stone cutter and a constant stream of vans and lorries loading and unloading outside causing traffic jams with local farm traffic.

The dust from the cutting caused white clouds to waft over local gardens. Freddie Dobson had to have her car re-sprayed because of it. In addition, she had her house painted and just as the gloss was applied a fresh wave of dust arrived.

Not to be out-done by Brenda, Peter and Jane Gower decided on an extension to their house, so we had confusion from two sides.

All is quiet now and, although the house is not completed, there is only the soft sound of paint brushes.

Still we did get a bottle of vintage port, so all was not lost!

Bridge Cottage

The Old Inn

Curlew Cottage

The Chantry

Forester's Cottage

Chapman's Cottage

Fig 8   A few of the Village Cottages

Page 111

Fell View

John and Liz Watson were living in Blaydon when they first came to West Scrafton on holiday in 1977. They stayed in Fell View, which was then a holiday cottage. They thought that the view of Roova Crag was preferable to the view of the west end of Newcastle-upon-Tyne! At that time, Fell View was owned by Joseph Handley and when in 1981 his son Tommy, who had inherited it in

1979, decided to sell it, the Watsons were given first refusal, an offer which they accepted. John is now a very well established local self-employed builder and Liz is a Family Placement Team Manager for Middlesborough Social Services.

With regard to the house, the earliest date found on the property is inscribed on a stone which was formerly sited in the internal face of the west gable, but has since been transferred to a position in the internal east gable to the right of the fireplace lintel. The stone is inscribed "T.R. 1791".

The earliest date recorded in the deeds is 1796, when some kind of deal was struck between John Spence (mason) of Appletree House and Roland Spence (mason) of Farmley, Otley. The sum mentioned is 2/-. Roland Spence then passed to Thomas Spence, then to Adam Holt, then to James Spence.

After this, there is a gap in the records until 10 November 1877, when Fell View was sold by Will Simpson (labourer) of West Witton, to Christopher Chapman (farmer) of Carlton for £18. Christopher Chapman remained the owner right up until the middle of the Great War as the next transaction recorded is on 1 May 1916 on which date the property was sold by him to Thomas Horner (farmer) of West Scrafton for £20. It then appears to have passed to other members of the Horner family, as on 9 March 1923 it was sold by Leonard Horner (deceased) to Thomas Hogg (farmer) of West Scrafton for £16. It is recorded that the trustees for this particular sale were Thomas Falshaw Harrison of Caldbergh & Simon Thwaite Metcalfe of East Scrafton and it was sold by these trustees on 18 May 1923 to Joseph Handley (farmer) of West Scrafton for £16, although his son Tommy maintains to this day that the sum involved was £29.

In 1979 the building passed to Thomas Handley (farmer) of West Scrafton who sold it on 1 October 1981 to the present owners, John & Elizabeth Watson (Environmental Health Officer and Social Worker) of Blaydon, Gateshead, Tyne and Wear.

Fell View was apparently in existence prior to the house now known as Appletree House, as there is a first floor window in the East gable which is totally obstructed by end wall of Appletree House which butts right up against it.

A 'patten' shoe was discovered when clearing out the stone infill. This shoe is wooden and very worm-eaten (see fig 24) and comes within the present day classification of "concealed shoes". The following information on the subject was gleaned from the Boot and Shoe Collection at the Northampton Museum[4]. It was a common superstitious practice in the post-mediaeval period to deliberately conceal shoes in parts of a building. The earliest known shoe concealment was in the 13th century, but about 45% of discovered hidden shoes have been attributed to the early 19th century. There is no utilitarian reason for this practice yet all the shoes are in inaccessible places which often necessitated building work for them to be hidden. Examples are usually discovered when people start repairing or renovating old houses. The most common places for concealment are up chimneys, within walls, under floorboards and in roofs. Other hiding places are in bricked-up ovens, and around doors, windows and staircases. One reason for hiding shoes in chimneys and around doors may have been because these were openings through which evil spirits could enter the home and the shoe, as a good luck symbol, was intended to warn them off. The high number of shoes hidden in chimneys and ovens, together representing over a quarter of the concealments found, can be attributed to the fact that these were the central places in the home, providing warmth and used for cooking food; therefore it was important for such places to be safeguarded in this way. There are various reasons why shoes should be chosen as a good luck symbol. Almost without exception the hidden shoes have been well-worn, often beyond repair. This is almost certainly an important part of the custom. Unlike other items of clothing, shoes retain the shape of the wearer's body, showing the foot shape, the fit of the shoe and even foot deformities. Because of this, many people think that shoes contain animism or the spirit of the wearer. Because of this one can perhaps see why this custom grew around this particular item of wearing apparel.

It seems likely that the original "Fell View" was a heather-thatched house, with a very steep roof pitch. Three things point to this

---

[4] For more information see "The Archaeology of Ritual & Magic" by Ralph Merrifield · 1987.

assumption; firstly, some stones which are set into the front wall indicate that these would most likely have been at the top as they would have been put there in order to keep the thatch clear of the wall; secondly, while demolishing the rear wall of the original house in 1983, a layer of heather was discovered at an equivalent height to these stones; and thirdly, when the plaster was stripped off the internal walls, a distinct difference in the stonework was revealed, the pattern of which tended to show that there had been a much steeper pitch to the gables at one time.

The earliest stairway was probably a semi-circular set extending out to the rear north-east corner and covered by its own stone flagged roof. This was demolished to make way for the kitchen, bedrooms and bathroom extension which were erected in 1982. It is of interest to note that there was also an access to this stairway from Appletree House.

The original windows were much smaller than the present day ones. It seems that Joseph Handley, Tommy's father, sold the old stone surrounds and the downstairs stone mullioned window openings and had "modern" frames and concrete lintels and sills fitted. These stones may now be incorporated into Deerclose House at Gammersgill together with some from Burnside.

Fords Cottage

Fords Cottage is the newest building in West Scrafton, having been built by Keith and Karin Suttill in 1997. It had not been a long journey for Karin, as she had been born and lived within fifty yards of the site, being the daughter of Bernard and Caroline Harrison of Hilltop Farm.

The name of the house, however, is more interesting than would at first appear. It is built on the site of the Harrison's old sheep dip and originally such troughs were called "fords", a relic of the time when sheep were washed in streams where, no doubt, access was easier at crossing places. In fact, within living memory, it was a common practice for farmers to dam the ghyll on the moor and wash all the peat out of the wool before bringing the sheep down for clipping. The tradition now lives on, in the house name alone of course.

Not surprisingly there is some attractive wrought iron work around the house and garden; that is Kevin's line of business. And, of course, the back of the house overlooks the livery stables and the associated exercise ring, Karin's abiding interest.

Forester's Cottage

We came to West Scrafton first in 1957 and eventually used to rent "Hilltop" for six months every year from October to Easter.

Forester's Cottage was bought by me in 1970 from Bobby Hogg. It had no known name and as far back as can be remembered was always known by the name of the owner, so for at least twenty years we knew it as Bobby's Cottage. The deeds never gave any name and it was referred to as "the derelict cottage at West Scrafton". Bobby used it to store fertiliser and he kept the occasional sick sheep in it. Until the house was emptied, we didn't know that the old original fireplace was in what is now the kitchen. There was no water, electricity or toilet. In the main room (the oldest part) was an iron range which was used for cooking and hot water originally, but it was so rusty that it was literally dropping to pieces.

There was a stone spiral staircase with very worn steps (and it was very narrow) which went to the smaller of the two bedrooms. The other bedroom was quite big. There was no access from the house to the room above the kitchen, but there was a stone staircase outside which went to a door into this room. That, too, had an old original small fireplace which must have been used by the "clogger" when the house was the clog shop for the local coal mine. I wanted the steps kept even though a door was broken through to the main part of the house, but a lorry bringing cement or something for the renovations backed into it and damaged it so badly that it had to be demolished (that's what I was told, anyway). This room was the clog maker's workshop and he made plates for the clogs of the miners who worked in West Scrafton mine. Cut into the beam are the initials and WP, which we were told was Willie Pearson, and my son met a very old man in the pub at Horsehouse who knew who this man was!

Downstairs, what is now the dining room was a glorified pantry. There was a big stone table on which pigs were cured (I was told) and all the far wall had stone shelves for storing jars etc. The window at the back was minuscule so this room was probably quite cold and would store food quite well. I wanted some of the stone shelves kept, but they went the way of the stone outside steps!

The whole of the ground floor was covered with stone flags but these went in order to make the house damp proof. A waterproof membrane was laid and then concrete put on the top.

The original house was one up and one down and the original outside door is still very obvious because it is so big. Then the pantry and second bedroom were built on. The line of the house is cock-eyed and not straight. Lastly, the kitchen and upstairs room were built on adjacent to the road and this is not square to the rest of the building and the angles in both rooms are acute or obtuse which makes floor covering interesting.

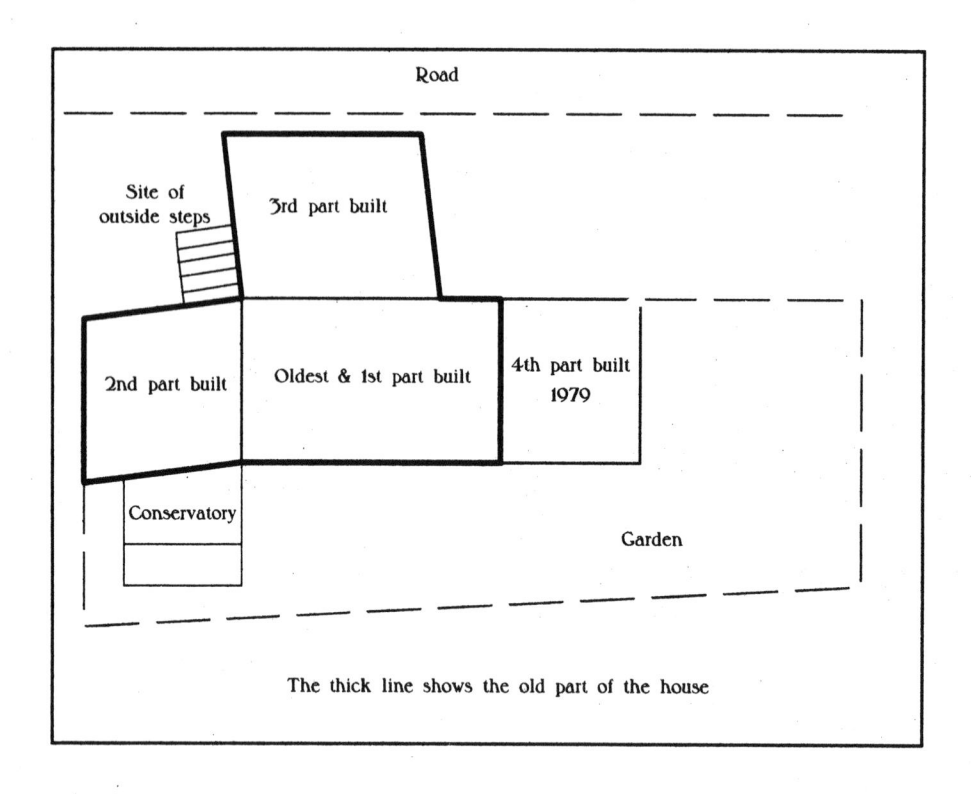

```
                    Road
    ┌─────────────────────────────────┐
    │  Site of    ┌──────────┐        │
    │  outside    │ 3rd part │        │
    │  steps ▨    │  built   │        │
    │         ┌───┴──────────┴──┐     │
    │         │                 │┌───┐│
    │ ┌───────┤ Oldest & 1st    ││4th││
    │ │ 2nd   │   part built    ││part││
    │ │ part  │                 ││built││
    │ │ built │                 ││1979││
    │ └───┬───┴─────────────────┘└───┘│
    │     │Conservatory│              │
    │     └────────────┘      Garden  │
    └─────────────────────────────────┘
       The thick line shows the old part of the house
```

I had an old man called Mr Thistlewaite do some pointing and he was a great expert on stone and could identify the stone of the three parts of the house and which quarries they came from. I didn't record this at the time so I cannot remember this information. The roof was Scrafton stone. All the old part of the house has exposed beams and the upstairs all had wooden ceilings and I still have these. I had the garage and third big bedroom built in 1979 so the house was built in four bits (see above plan).

During the war, the forester who looked after East Witton forest lived here and later Tristram and Betty Hogg moved in. Their son Alan, who is well known in Middleham for his skill with racehorses and who is Mrs Peacock's right-hand man, was born in the middle bedroom. They moved to Eastfield House across the road.

We researched the history of the house and got back to about 1690, but then got bogged down as all the deeds for the last 250 years approximately are in London and tied up in a complicated trust, so we never learnt who actually lived here beyond the "forester". The house had been empty for many years before I bought it.

My garden originally belonged to the two cottages which are now Moor Ghyll and there was a one-holer toilet outside which presumably must have served all three houses. The whitewash is still visible at the back although we had to have the toilet knocked down to gain access from the house at the back to the garden.

The garden was covered completely in six-foot high nettles and about fifteen plum trees which had suckered from an old one, and a few hundred empty oil tins which Alan Hogg had deposited over the years. It was quite a labour of love to get out all the trees and make it into the garden proper. It is not very big but, being walled all round, it is very sheltered and now is usually very pretty. I also had a conservatory built on at the back. This is attractive inside and gets a lot of sun but is very hideous from the moor. I can't think of the way to make it look old and in keeping with the rest of the house. A tree is on the west side and is now much bigger and helps to hide it partially so it looks less conspicuous.

Garth House

Garth House, despite now being part of the Dent farm and only a couple of paces away from the Dent home in Town Head, was until recently part of an entirely different farm, confusingly called Town End Farm. It was not until John and Audrey Bainbridge (née Dent) took up residence in 1981 with their three-year-old son Peter that it was integrated into its present farming unit.. Their daughter Janet was born that same year. Audrey is a farmer as well as being a housewife, while John, who is a fulltime structural steel draughtsman, is equally ambidextrous and can frequently be seen farming as well; and while son, Peter went to the University of Salford where in 1999 he was in his final year studying French, Spanish and Marketing, and his sister Janet commenced her degree course at Preston Agricultural College studying Animal Welfare, there is no basking in academe, for, whenever they come home, they join the family work force.

It is not certain when the house itself was built, but, unlike its neighbour Town Head, it has certainly been extended over the years. The barn which is attached to the house had had a second storey added and now lies under the same roof. The implication is that the roof was renewed over all to accommodate the revised barn height, although there is no clear evidence of earlier thatching. Later still the present cow byre was added to the barn, making yet another extension to the whole, while as a final addition a 'lean-to' extension was appended to the whole length of the northern side giving the gable ends of all three parts of the building their asymmetrical outlines.

There is what looks like a trigonometric height mark cut into one of the lower quoins on the byre but no-one in the family knows its origin or purpose as no benchmark appears on any of the old ordnance maps.

Great Ghyll Cottage

The millennium time was a momentous time for Great Ghyll Cottage. After a long and bitter (but lost) battle with the National Parks Authority over planning details, the alterations began in April 1998 and lasted for over a year. There is absolutely no doubt that it was a year of trials for my neighbours and the village as a whole and a great nuisance and expensive for myself. What started off as an extension turned into almost total demolition and rebuild from foundations up except for the front wall. This was due to the discovery of the weakened structure of the timbers from the previous rebuild in 1970 and it was a great relief that it was not due to the enormous pot-hole under the rock shelf on which the cottage was built early in the nineteenth century. That rock still stands and long may it do so.

We bought the cottage as two derelict buildings - one down two up and a lean-to. They were full of hay and calves. The original privy had been in the garden area of Forester's Cottage opposite and their allotments were what is now the garden of Moor Ghyll. They were built as miner's cottages with smallholdings somewhere and an allowance of gaits on the moor for their livestock. No doubt large families were raised in these buildings when West Scrafton was a busy township on the nineteenth century.

Charles Utley's mother was persuaded to sell them to us in 1970, originally as a holiday home in an area we loved. In the end, after it had been a building site for three long years, it turned out too lovely for occasional use and, as my father had just retired, my parents moved in and created a home for themselves and a welcome retreat for we two GPs on our rare time off! Our children loved visiting us here as do my thirteen grand-children.

After my father died, my mother stayed on for a time; but then my husband died in an accident and my mother moved nearer to me. The cottage then had years of very occasional use until I decided to sell up my home of forty years in Thirsk and make a move up to be near my youngest daughter (who had married Kevin Utley, a farmer in West Scrafton) and three of my grand-children.

The year of building gave me time to plan refurbishment, shop, make curtains and reconcile myself to leaving my lovely home in Thirsk where I had spent two-thirds of my life. I first slept in my new home in my own bed from my old home on April 27th 1999. Local builders, plumbers, joiners, electricians and decorators were here were almost daily and did a wonderful job. The house is exactly as I wanted it. The total destruction of the garden gave me an opportunity to have much of it terraced with local stone and a lovely sunken garden was made by Frank Johnstone, one of our two village landscape gardeners. This is its first spring and the apple and plum blossom have been lashed by frequent storms but the spring flowers are all in bloom. When the sun shines it is glorious to be here to listen to the water of Great Ghyll rushing over the rocks and to look at the sweep of the moor up to Roova Crag; and all from my bed, too! My extended family and lots of visitors come to enjoy the special peace of our far-away village on the moors and take a little away with them to many different far-away places.

Hilltop Cottage

Hilltop Cottage and Town Head vie with one another for being the highest point in West Scrafton proper · excluding Allaker which is some way out · and also for being the oldest. Hilltop Cottage carries a date stone inscribed 1677 making it marginally younger than Town Head which claims 1666. However, there is structural evidence to suggest that Hilltop may in fact be the site of an older building. It has one wall which is five feet thick on the north side which supports the suggestion that it was built on the site of a watch tower, moreover in the west wall there is still a small window with a rounded arch which appears to predate any of the other openings and could have been contemporary with the tower. A number of other windows on the west side have been blocked in, possibly to avoid window tax or perhaps to make them proof against the prevailing weather in its exposed position.

The southern end of the building was obviously added as a second stage and formed a stable with a hayloft above it; the arched cart-house door in the southern gable end and a forking hole for feeding hay to the upper level have been blocked in but are still identifiable.

Further alterations have been carried out in recent years, including the large fireplace which was carved from stone from Roova Crags in the mid-1940s and more modernisation in the early 1980s when the flag stone floor was removed and a damp proof version installed. An inevitable, but sad, loss was the dark pantry with its cool cold slabs which had for decades successfully stored food until the arrival of electricity and refrigerators.

Hilltop Cottage, which has been in the same family for three generations, was originally a farm with land to the north and is now a holiday home for one of the third generation, Gordon Utley and his wife Doreen. Latterly, the farm buildings which abutted to the east and housed cattle and hay storage, have been converted to a farm house, Dambreezy, home to Kevin and Clare Utley.

Hilltop Farm

Bernard and Caroline Harrison have lived in Hilltop since 1976. However, they are not the newcomers that that implies. Bernard's grandfather George had farmed from Hilltop from the late 1800's and when he died one of his sons, Thomas, a lifelong bachelor, took over the house and farm until his death in 1974 when Bernard inherited it. In the intervening time there had been a three farm Harrison partnership for 15 years, with Bernard's father Simon farming at Lane House Farm while Bernard and his brother farmed in West Scrafton and Thornton Rust respectively.

In 1961 he bought Town End farm and married Caroline who was born into a farming family not a million miles away in

Agglethorpe; but on the death of his uncle Thomas, he was able to refurbish the house at Hilltop during the next couple of years and move into it in 1976 along with children Philip and Karin,

At least one of the original features of the house was retained; the old tiled kitchen range is now in what has become the dining room. The oven still works and has been used on occasion when the electricity supply to the village has failed,

The Harrisons have now been in uninterrupted possession of the house for over a century, but nothing is known of its earlier history. However one interesting relic of earlier days is still lying beside an old barn on Granny Banks; the Harrisons' wooden horse-drawn sledge used to lead the scythe-cut bracken down from the moor is still virtually intact, after being redundant for over half a century.

But the inevitable expansion of the property began in 1988 when the barn and the cow byre attached to the house were converted into two cottages for holiday lettings as a way of diversifying the family business to include tourism. Philip, who continues to farm along with his father, married Tracey and naturally they moved into one of them, Bracken cottage. The other, Barn Owl, continued as holiday accommodation. At about the same time, Karin's interest in horses having followed that of Caroline, a livery stable was opened by way of yet further diversification.

Inverburn House

Exactly when the present house known as Inverburn was built is not known, although by the village standards it is reasonably modern. It must have been built during the second half of the 19th century, as the building in its present form is shown on the ordnance maps surveyed in 1891, but a building of quite a different shape is depicted on the maps of 1851. At that time the site was occupied by at least two cottages owned by a cattle trader who frequently dealt in Scotland. In the intervening years, the cottage burnt down and gave rise to the perhaps unlikely story that, as the owner was in Inverness at the time, Inverburn would be a suitable name for the house built on the ashes.

It is constructed of random stone with dressed stone front and has a double-fronted four square up and down flagged roof. The out-buildings consist of a two storey barn incorporating a carriage house, a stable and an attached two-hole earth toilet. Attached to the house is a fuel store, a laundry and a pig sty.

Norman Oddy and his wife, Irene, came to live in the house in January 1977, before he retired as a merchant navy captain on bulk carriers. They formerly lived in Goathland in a house which Norman says was far too large and for various reasons decided to move from the Moors to the Dales. They lived in a rented house in Middleham for a while during which time they looked for something permanent. They eventually found Inverburn House and liked it even in the depths of winter, so they decided to move in. Norman, now a widower, lives there with his dog which he regularly walks up the East Scrafton road twice a day.

Lane End Cottage

Working as a professional gardener covering the areas around Redmire, Preston-under-Scar, Wensley, Leyburn, Middleham and Coverdale, West Scrafton is centrally placed for me to get to all these places.

It is not known when Lane End Cottage was originally built but when I was clearing out the barn shortly after I took up residence, I found a stone which read "EY 1834". This stone may have been above the front door before the porch was added, or it may have come from a farm sale! It now resides above the front door between the upstairs windows.

By looking closely at the external stonework and internal walls, the evolutionary growth of the building can be worked out. There is a join to the left of the front door and also one to the left of the back door. A further join can be seen running down the south gable end and there is a blocked in doorway from the upper floor.

The oldest part of the building is what is now the right-hand side through to the back. Stone flagged steps occupied what is now half of the kitchen. The dining room and second bedroom, with an outside door and external steps, were added later, and the kitchen and bathroom later still.

Many years ago the building was used as a local school house, particularly necessary when the 1851 records show that there were as many as 48 children under the age of 10 living in the village

I bought Lane End Cottage on December 8th 1997 and the builders moved in. They moved the stairs into the living room to make the kitchen twice the size it was. An Esse cooker was put in with an internal flue leading into the chimney from the fireplace in the dining room which was blocked off. I took out the other tiled fireplace in the living-room and built a stone one using two steps from outside for the hearth and mantelpiece. Internal doors were stripped of years of paint back to natural pine and the covered oak beams were exposed. A large airing cupboard was made upstairs where the old stairs had come up. The bathroom suite was shuffled around to accommodate the cooker flue on its way to the chimney and the bath was moved from under the lowest part of the sloping roof.

Outside a lot of the earth was moved to make a level hard standing area. The following summer the outbuilding was renovated with new floors, doors and windows. Part of the front wall of this outbuilding nearest the cottage was rebuilt before a small porch was put over the back door. A pair of large stone gate posts were brought back from a cottage in East Witton for the rear entrance and the dry-stone wall beside the footpath known as Back Lane was rebuilt using stone from a wall on the other side of the garden which in turn was replaced by a fence and a hedge.

Before me, Fred and Charlotte Utley moved here from what is now the garage of the Manor House with their children Thomas, Jim

Nancy, Eva and Arthur Mickle, the latter being Charlotte's child before she was married. Fred and Charlotte died, Nancy and Thomas moved away but Eva, Jim and Arthur stayed. Jim, like his father before him, was a lengthman working for the Council keeping roads and verges, ditches and hedges clear and tidy around West Scrafton. Eva and Arthur both worked at the old Coverham dairy. Eva outlived them both and ended her days as a cleaner and caretaker of the many holiday cottages and second homes in the village including Alf Wight's next door.

Lane Farm House

Paul and Joy French initially came to the village of West Scrafton with their three children, living in Garth House for three years before purchasing Lane Farm House in 1980.

Paul was born in Kent where he lived on the family farm before branching out into golf course construction and maintenance.

Joy was from Kirkby Malzeard near Ripon but left to teach for one year in Kent where she met Paul and married him. Their three children were born while they were still living there. However, Paul's work eventually brought him to Bedale golf course and the family moved to the Bedale area in 1972.

In 1981 Paul left the golf course, becoming self employed to work in general agricultural repairs in the dale, while Joy taught at the Spennithorne primary school. Their three children moved away from the area for employment when they left school.

At Lane Farm House Paul planted many trees and made a large garden from part of the four-acre field which went with the farmhouse, the surrounding farmland being kept by the East Scrafton estate when the farmhouse was sold in 1980. Paul has been a keen gardener, keeping the family in vegetables for most of the year.

The house itself is a 17th century longhouse, originally built as a single storey dwelling. Some time later the roof was raised and an upper floor added, access to which is by way of an internal stone stairway. Outside there was a barn which was converted into further accommodation. A byre was added and a flight of stone steps at the end of the house leads up to a loft over this byre.

In 1999 Paul and Joy built a "consumption dyke", a wall containing currently unwanted stone from around the site. It is situated on the west side of the large modern farm building. They put inside it a "time capsule" containing mementoes from life at the end of this millennium in an aluminium saucepan!

Manor House

This maybe the smallest of manor houses but it is certainly one of the more intriguing buildings in West Scrafton. The current deeds go back to January 1756 when a Thomas Butterfield owned it, but the building is certainly older than that. Indeed the Old Inn which is attached to the southern side of the Manor House is reputed to have been built in 1590 and is obviously of a later vintage as the Manor House external chimney is incorporated into its internal joining wall. There is a long held local belief that in 1545 it was the birth place of Henry Lord Darnley, the future husband of Mary Queen of Scots. Although his birth is officially recorded as having been in the Leeds area - not a geographically precise description - this does not necessarily rule out the possibility of his being born in West Scrafton Manor House, a more specific locale. Further support for this legend comes from the fact, his father, the Earl of Lennox, owned West Scrafton properties at the time.

Whatever its date of origin, it seems to have been built as a single storey house with a steep thatch, probably of bracken. However, there may have been a sleeping area in an attic under the steepest pitch of the roof accessed by an internal stone staircase, the latter being a fairly unique feature which is still in use. In the mid-18th century the roof was replaced with a shallower pitched stone slate roof and mullioned windows were installed. There was also a two-storey cottage to the north side of the main building.

The property seems to have been occupied and eventually owned by James Stubbs (labourer) from about 1850 and by Paul Stubbs from 1909. The Stubbs' occupation lasted for some seventy years until 1920 when the house was sold to Dawson Utley. It appears that he sold it a mere two months later to Mrs Betty Handley in December of the same year. However, the then two-storey building at right angles to Manor House remained in the Stubbs family. This building was described as "all that dwelling house built upon the site of the old building formerly occupied by John Harrison known as Dwelling House with Peat House adjoining" and Paul Stubbs made it over to his daughter Elizabath Bell in 1923. For a time it was rented to William Palfreyman, a cripple who walked with the assistance of two sticks. He lived alone, but despite his infirmity managed the house well. He died in the late 1940s and Elizabeth Bell thereupon sold it to Oswold Utley in 1953.

Neither the Manor House nor its adjunct was particularly salubrious by present day standards and a measure of this can be seen from the fact that Betty Handley's daughter Annie who inherited the Manor House sold it in 1959 for the princely sum of £250 and that when Ossie Utley acquired "John Harrison's house" he immediately used it as a convenient place in which to keep chickens.

There had been very few significant improvements made for some considerable time. Alderman Harry Watson, the ex-mayor of

Wakefield who had parted with the £250 in return for ownership, had to spend considerably more than that in refurbishing Manor House and providing it with a new roof. Three years later he bought the hen filled two story "dwelling house with peat house", reduced it to a single storey garage and returned the whole entity to single ownership once more. It was in this enhanced condition when a senior police officer serving in the area, Dick Hall and his wife, bought it in 1977. He continued to live there after retirement, but when his wife died he decided it was too big for him, moved across the road to the cottage in Bridge End Farmhouse and sold the Manor House in 1997 to Mrs Juliet Elliott, a farmer's wife from Nottinghamshire whose family uses it as a country retreat.

Moor Ghyll

Moor Ghyll is a descriptive name. The house abuts West Scrafton Moor and lies close to Great Ghyll that runs through the village. The name is also recent, some 15 years old. Ordnance Survey maps refer to the house as "The Cottage". It is, however, still widely known as the old shop from which Mrs Robinson sold her wares between 1897 and 1954. For much of that period, and earlier, the house was owned by the Falshaw family. The Title Commutation Award of 1846 shows John Falshaw as owner and occupier of both the house and the present day garden. The 1851 census shows that John was born in 1791 and was then a widower and farmer of 20 acres. Living with him were his son Thomas, aged 14; his brother James Falshaw, agricultural labourer, aged 50; Elizabeth Blackbird, housekeeper, aged 26, and her son William, aged 9. All were born in West Scrafton.

By the 1881 census, Thomas had taken over the running of the farm, then expanded to 30 acres, and was living with his wife, Ann, who was born in Melmerby, and their two children, Thomas Law, born in 1871, and Mary Grace, born in 1874. Thomas died in 1889 and Ann in 1913 when the property passed to their two children. By then, however, Thomas Law was farming at Caldbergh Ings, his sister Mary Grace was married to John Horner of Ings Farm and "The Cottage" was a shop and home to the Robinsons (see page 243). The house remained in the Falshaw family until Thomas Law Falshaw's death in 1951 when it was sold, along with a couple of fields off Low Lane and 16 sheep gaits, to local farmer Thomas Hogg. It was not long before the shop closed when Mrs Robinson left the village for North Cowton in 1954, her husband having died seven years earlier.

Having been in the ownership of one family for a century and maybe longer, the house, now divested of land, was to pass through five families in fifty years. In 1960 Robert Hogg sold the then unoccupied house to John Dunford of Wakefield. In 1979 it passed to Ian and Mary Sutcliffe of Middleham; then in 1985 Peter and Jane Gower from Wakefield acquired it. While the Gowers were in the throes of renovations they discovered hidden away three cheques written by a Mr E Pugh for various sums "for partners and self". One of these cheques is shown in the photograph below, but it has not been discovered who Mr Pugh was or for what the cheques were in payment.

Although it is not obvious from this sample when they were dated, the other two are clearly marked 1795.

In 1998, when Peter and Jane moved across the road to East Leigh, the house was bought by Ian and Jenny Brotherton. Ian and Jenny both originate from Leeds, but came here from the slightly larger but still small village of Over Haddon near Bakewell in Derbyshire. From there, Ian worked at Sheffield University full time until 1997 but since then part time, thus enabling the move here. As winter approaches and we sleep in what was the hay loft, we appreciate the improvements made by previous owners, particularly the Gowers working with Paul French and John Watson.

Moorhen Farm

It was in 1975 that the first brand new dwelling in West Scrafton for nearly a century was built by Bobby and Hazel Hogg. It was a a single storey building and to this day it remains the only bungalow in West Scrafton. Bobby and Hazel moved into their new abode to the east of the village from what is now known as The Old Inn, but since the 1920s when the alcohol licence lapsed. it had been known as Moorhen Farm House.

When they moved they inevitably took the old name with them and Moorhen Farm House remains but with a different location. The bungalow is about half a mile from the village and not only does it provide for more immediate access to the farm, being adjacent to it, but it has beautiful views over the dale to the west.

The Old Inn

The Old Inn was recently taken over by John and Liz Sheehan when Leone Neale, the previous owner who had used it as a rural retreat for very many years, decided to sell it. They came to the village because it was a "beautiful, unspoilt dales village, off the beaten track and near Middleham and Leyburn" to use their words.

The building had several names during its lifetime as an inn. It was originally known as "The Partridge" and then, sometime in the

1840s, John Horner its licensee, changed its name to "The Grouse Inn". It subsequently had another change, not this time of bird species but of sex, to "The Moorhen Inn", a name which it retained until it was bought by Bobby Hogg's father, Tommy, in about 1922 when the innkeeper was Joe Stubbs. Tommy also worked the largest smallholding in West Scrafton as a tenant farmer. But, with the local mine eventually turning from decline to closure and the departure of the mine workers, the inn was no longer viable and in 1925 the licence was allowed to lapse. The inn then reverted to what it had in part always been, a farm house, and subsequent tenants (the Guys, Frank and Mary Robinson, and Harry and Mary Gatenby) farmed from the renamed Moorhen Farm House until Tommy Hogg died in 1953 when Bobby inherited it.,

The building has its origins in 1590, but the main part of what exists today was added in the early 18th century. It was originally built around the external chimney-stack of Manor House. The main roof is interesting in that it has purlins of tree trunks, some of which still have the bark intact. Above the outside stable is a room that contains a fireplace and this is said to have been a separate dwelling at some time in the dim and distant past. In addition there were one or two other cottages attached to the west side which were removed by Mrs Dean, a subsequent owner, many years later. and traces of a flagstone floor, a fireplace and some stone steps still remain. Inside the house there are two further stone staircases. The kitchen contains a beehive oven. There are flag floors in what was the bar area, and in the cellar in which one can see where the house is built on solid rock.

One Friday sometime in 1983, a cloudburst up towards the south-east brought torrents of water roaring down the steep road from Swineside and the brown foaming flood poured into West Scrafton en route for Great Ghyll. Cullen Ghyll, which is a frequently dry tributary to Great Ghyll and a natural channel for this mass of water from the Swineside road, runs under the outbuildings of Moorhen Inn through a culvert, but this soon proved inadequate. In minutes the whole area was inundated and the store, which at that time had a floor some three feet below ground level, was soon awash and animal feed, boxes of tools, wire netting and a couple of buckets of eggs were swirling around in the flood.

Les Brown was visiting and, not one to miss a little excitement, he joined Hazel to see the drama unfold, but none expected the second act. As they watched the chaos amongst the swirling water, everything suddenly disappeared; boxes, feed, implements. virtually everything in the store. A hole about five feet in diameter had swallowed the lot. To say that they all stepped back is probably something of an understatement.

The flood from a cloudburst is short lived and when the water subsided the third act of the drama unfolded. The sides of the hole were revealed to be stone built. It was not, after all, organic rock that had given way, but the cover to some kind of store or perhaps an old well. It had been laid down at some time long past when the store was re-floored. Possibly a combination of the weight of the flood water and the erosion of the fissures beneath caused it to fail. But on a busy farm there is no time for lengthy investigation and so no one is sure as to what purpose the large stone-lined hole originally served, although Hazel says she could have sold tickets to people who came to gaze and made a small fortune. The hole was filled in unceremoniously with several cart loads of rubble, entombing the contents of the store and forming the base for a new concrete floor, some three feet higher at ground level this time. But as the building had been two storeys this left precious little headroom in what had been a room with a low ceiling in the first place and so the floor to the upper level was sacrificed, making it single storey, as it is now.

Some residents in the village with houses sited above the Scrafton Pot draw comfort from the story, as it was a man-made structure that had failed.

But during the renovation work carried out by John and Liz Sheehan, they noticed that in the walls either side of, and in line with the erstwhile famous hole and the conduit, there had once been low openings, now closed in and too small to have been old doorways. They developed the theory that perhaps the hole had once housed a water wheel driven by water entering at the upstream side opening and exiting at the other. The configuration of land, water and building would certainly seem to support the idea, but there are no records or memories to confirm it.

Allaker

The Manor House

Culverham Farm House

Cullen House

Crag View

Hilltop Farm

Fig 9   Some More of the Cottages

Quarry Lodge and Gilbert Scar Lodge

The name given to the building comprising the two properties now known as Quarry Lodge and Gilbert Scar Lodge seems to have been subject to change in the past. The deeds mention Quarry Farm, Quarry Lodge Farm and Gilbert Scar Lodge Farm at various times. The 1850 ordnance map refers to the building on the site as Gilbert Scar Lodge and this is presumably the same house and cow byre referred to in the deeds before conversion to two houses. The part of the building now known as Quarry Lodge was originally the living accommodation and Gilbert Scar Lodge the byre. Until 1970 the house and byre and the surrounding land were owned by a local charity known as the Foster Trust (see page 51) and let to tenants as a farm.

In 1970 the cottage, cow byre and land were sold by the charity and Quarry Lodge ceased to be a farm house. The cow byre was converted into a holiday cottage by Terry and Ann Clegg who still own the property. Quarry Lodge was more than doubled in size in 1985 when the owners Mike and Cynthia Ryde built an extension containing a bathroom, hallway, two bedrooms and an additional living room.

Quarry Lodge was purchased in 1999 by Liz and Ian Fobbester from Fairford in Gloucestershire. At some time in the past Quarry Lodge must have been associated with local slate mining operations as there is a spoil heap of stone chippings underlying the garden lawns. The 1850 Ordnance Survey map shows three mining levels driven into the slope on the left hand side of the track leading to Quarry Lodge and an additional level is still visible adjacent to Nathwaite Bridge.

Roova Barn

The Forrests came to West Scrafton in 1982 at a time when they needed long term rented accommodation and Bridge End Farm was available. They rented it for four years during which time they fell in love with the village, bought the barn associated with the farm and renovated it over a period of two years.

The barn was originally built in the 18th century as the barn for Bridge End Farm across the shared yard. It originally had a heather thatched roof as did many of the buildings in the village. Being a typical dales barn, it had its hayloft upstairs and animal quarters below. An interesting and unique feature to the roof is the use of scroll end style kneelers, markedly different to the normal dales design. The building was used as a barn by the Utley family until they sold it to the Forrests in 1984. Because of the lovely views from the first floor, the Forrests have made their living quarters (kitchen, living room and study) up there, with the bedrooms downstairs.

All the original forking holes and doorways have been retained and new windows added to match the original openings with stone architraves. The end stairs outside originally descended in to the yard, but now go down in to the garden.

Geoff and Julie Forrest have three children, Thomas, Joe and Hannah who have contributed to this book elsewhere. Geoff is a builder by trade and Julie is the Town Clerk at Leyburn. They not only love the village, but they like the people, the setting and especially the freedom that it has given to their children who have all grown up here.

The Chantry

The Chantry has been known by a number of names during its long history, the name even being corrupted to "The Shanty" at one time! Its other well known name, used in the books on Yorkshire by James Herriot, was "Grange Cottage".

It is thought that the house itself was originally built around the 15th century, possibly as a grange of Coverham Abbey. This grange may have included a chantry chapel, but this is not recorded in the register of chantries which was commissioned by Henry VIII. One of the original walls has a lancet window with Perpendicular tracery over two trefoiled panes and stretches from the kitchen to the upstairs rooms. Although this is a very interesting and rather unique feature of the house, one drawback is that all sounds and smells from the kitchen travel to the upstairs bedrooms!

The entrance doorway has an architrave of stone with the letters FAB inscribed on the lintel. There are two main rooms on the ground floor each containing 18th century stone fireplaces, while in between there is a stone staircase.

Outside there is an old coach house standing right on the edge of Great Ghyll and in real peril of falling in to it as flood erosion eats into its foundations. It is a two storey building erected around 1800 with stone architraves both to the coach entrance and to the stable door. There is a flight of steps leading up to the hayloft. This building was more recently used as a garage.

Thirty or more years ago Alf Wight (James Herriot) and his family used to rent the cottage from the then owner Dr Dubberley as their rural retreat (see page 61) and they obviously thought that it was very cosy in spite of the local age-old story about strange lights being seen in the windows.

Town Head

Town Head Farmhouse has been the Dent family home since 1939 when the late Tommy Dent married and took a tenancy on the farm, but following the death of his parents Alan Dent is now sole occupant.

The farm is unique in effectively having two farm houses, the other being the adjacent Garth House where his sister Audrey lives and shares the farming with him. It is unusual in another respect in that, unlike the majority of buildings in West Scrafton, Town Head has not been radically extended, although at some time in the far past it has shared the experience of many others by being converted from thatch to stone slated roof. The gable end gives some evidence of this as the line of the original lower steeply-pitched roof can be seen. The main building has early 19th century sash windows, but the rear elevation has 18th century side-sliding sash windows on the upper floor.

If date stones are anything to go by it marginally predates Hilltop Cottage and makes it the oldest building in the village. A fairly clear (considering its age) raised inscription over the back door says "IG 1666 GG" set in a curved lintel as part of a well proportioned, and obviously old, stone surround to the door. From there the view is down the hill and over the village which no doubt accounts for the name.

The Women's Institute

The Women's Institute is well represented by the women of West Scrafton as seven of the ladies are members of the Coverdale branch and regularly attend the meetings which are held each month in the village hall in Carlton. As is usual in most local organisations, these meetings normally take the form of talks or demonstrations followed by tea and a chat.

The Display at Leyburn

In 1999, the end of the second millennium was marked by the Coverdale branch winning the much coveted "gong" at the Leyburn handicraft exhibition that was held in May. Some of the items on display were chosen to be shown at an exhibition that was to be held at a later date in Grassington and some were picked to be exhibited alongside others selected from the whole country at a national exhibition to be held at Tatton Park. Clare Utley was lucky enough to have a wreath of fruit, which she had modelled from salt dough, chosen.

In August the local branches held a Craft Fayre at which food was served and cakes were sold. There were demonstrations of various crafts and the whole day went off very well. Later that month a trip to Ripon was organised so that the local members could visit their area headquarters located there. Those who who attended that trip were treated to a delicious supper and this was followed by a demonstration of stamp art and a tour of the building.

The Leyburn branch held a show on the 28th August. Coverdale won the second prize for "A Cricket Tea" display, one concerning "A Nursery" and for a very artistic display entitled "A Fairy Tale". First prizes were won by several local people and again Clare Utley was in luck as she got a first prize for a display of her hen's eggs!

During October the Coverdale branch was given a superb slide show that was especially fascinating as it was in 3D. Later that month there were celebrations to commemorate the Institute's 70th birthday. It was a great evening and for a change the food was provided by outside caterers, thus relieving members from one of their usual chores.

Many of the members have, of course, very full working days and the Women's Institute provides a welcome opportunity to share what leisure hours they have.

Schooling

In the 19th century the children of West Scrafton had their own village school which was situated in what is now Lane End Cottage. It was run for a time by Mary Whitfield who lived at Bridge End Farm House. As time went on, however, there was an increasing trend towards centralisation and during the first part of the 20th century, in fact right up until the mid-1970s, the school in Carlton was the source of primary education for all children under the age of eleven who lived in the many villages in Coverdale. It used to have connections with a small church group that was known as "The Good Shepherd".

For a long time children from West Scrafton had to walk over to Carlton each day as there was no transport available, although during the war Charles Utley's father ran a taxi and provided transport for those children in the dale who had to walk more than two miles to school. Unfortunately West Scrafton, being nearer to Carlton than this, did not get this luxury. In 1961 a school car service began operating, which was free for those children who lived more than two miles from the school, but West Scrafton children were allowed to use it on payment of a fee. Audrey Bainbridge (then Audrey Dent) once won a prize for not having missed a single day's school in a full year; and she always walked!

Mrs Annie Weatherall from Horsehouse taught at the school for many years, teaching both the Hogg's and the Handley's families from West Scrafton. She took a short break from teaching after she got married but then returned to Carlton school and carried on to teach the offspring of both these families some twenty years later. Unfortunately, the school closed in 1976 when the government policy of the day was to close local schools and to concentrate teaching resources in much larger urban establishments. From then on, the primary education for the area was the responsibility of the school at Middleham, while the older children had to go to Leyburn. As the distances from West Scrafton to these schools are well over the two mile limit, free transport was provided in the shape of special school buses which collected the children from the various villages in the dale and brought them safely back home after school had finished for the day. This facility is still continuing at the beginning of the 21st century.

Four particular children from the West Scrafton families mentioned above attended Carlton school between 1962 and 1967. All four eventually went on to gain places at university, being the first pupils from the village to do so. Sheena and Linda Handley went to Manchester and Cambridge respectively. Sheena, after gaining an honours BSc degree in physics, obtained a post with British Nuclear Fuels at Ruislep near Warrington and became Senior Safety Controller. Linda left Cambridge with a BEd degree and, after starting work as a senior house-mistress at the Royal Russell school in Croydon, went on to become Head Teacher at Springfield Park school in Horsham in West Sussex. Janice Hogg gained an honours BSc degree in Agricultural and Food Marketing at Newcastle and now works at Harlow-Carr near Harrogate. Freda Handley studied geography also at Newcastle and followed this up with Hotel Management at Manchester University. Her first job was in London as Catering Manager at Olympia. Perhaps this high success rate in one small village is an indication of the high standard of groundwork laid down in the local village school.

As mentioned above, after the school in Carlton closed, children from West Scrafton had to travel to Middleham and Leyburn for their education, where Peter and Janet Bainbridge from the village both gained places for higher education. Peter went to the University of Salford where in 1999 he was in his final year studying French, Spanish and Marketing. In that last year of the millennium, Janet commenced her degree course at Preston Agricultural College where she studied Animal Welfare.

At the turn of the millennium, with twelve children in the village, it seemed highly likely that more of these would aspire to higher education and do well for themselves in the twenty-first century.

Some Children's Stories

There is a quality to the life of the children of West Scrafton that is rare. It is redolent of the Huckleberry Finn stories, with its freedom to roam at will day or night, to be free to build spectacular forts and dams, to ride shotgun on tractors and to take a few risks of knocks and bruises. To be immersed in

The "Fort" by Great Ghyll built by the children

the life of farms and animals, never to find the immediate world boring and to be surrounded by none but friendly people is a rare benefit indeed.

The two pieces which follow were written by the offspring of Julie and Geoff Forrest and Kath and Will Utley respectively.

* * * * *

It's autumn 1999 and I'm Thomas Forrest aged 13; I'm Joe Forrest aged 10½ and I'm Hannah Forrest aged 8. We have lived in this village all our lives and we live in Roova Barn which is behind Bridge End Farm. We like living in that house because we have a stile that leads over the wall to the stream. In winter the stream always ices over and we like breaking the ice. We don't get much snow but we still go sledging on Goose Bank on plastic bags or plastic sledges. We've all got bikes and we cycle around the village a lot but we have to be careful because there are lots of windey corners in the village and some cars come through the village too fast. Sometimes we go up the moor with our bikes.

We go to school at Middleham (Primary School) and Leyburn (Wensleydale School). Every day we wait at The Old Inn for the Handley's school bus. If it's raining we shelter in the phone box or under the arch at The Old Inn. Now there are seven children who wait for the bus; Thomas is the oldest and Beth Utley is the youngest. If we get bored while we're waiting we play football or just talk to each other. The bus comes at about half past eight and we get back at twenty-five to four every day. We like going to school on the minibus.

There are other children of our age in Coverdale who we play with. Hannah's best friends are Hannah Utley and Rosie Bostock from Gammersgill. Joe's friends are Ian Rounce from Swineside and Geoff Southgate from near East Scrafton. There aren't any boys of Thomas's age in Coverdale but he has a friend called Tom Peacock who lives near Jervaulx. Our mum takes us in the car to see our friends. When Hannah plays with the other Hannah they like to play in the hay bales up at the farm and they like roller-skating on the tarmac near the stream and they go to Brownies at Leyburn every Thursday.

When other children come to West Scrafton for their holidays we often play with them too. We usually meet them at the stream because they always love to play there. They always think that we are lucky to live next to a stream (and we are).

Inside the fort

I'm Joe and I like helping on the farm. I like it best in spring, summer and autumn. In spring I help with the lambing and sometimes I help with the dipping and milking and rounding up sheep. I like going with Charles (Utley) to check the sheep that he has in other places in

Coverdale. I also enjoy making dens and dams and going fishing down to the River Cover.

We get taken to the cinema at Leyburn quite a lot, which we like. We go swimming to Richmond swimming pool and if we have a day out we usually go to Sandsend and Whitby. We quite like visiting big towns for a day but we like living in this small village.

* * * * *

I'm Bret William Utley and I was born on 5th November 1992. My brother Liam John was born one minute after me and we both have blue eyes and blond hair, but my mum says we are not identical twins. A lot of people think we are though; you can see they don't know which name to use.

We have a sister called Kim Ruth and she wasn't born until 24th November 1996. She has blue eyes and blond hair too, but Dad says its a good job there's only one of her.

We all live at Bridge End Farm along with Scooby (Mum's black Labrador) and we have some ducks that live on the moor outside our back gate. There's one black duck, two grey ones and a grey drake.

Me and Liam go to Middleham on the school bus at 8.30 in the morning and come back at 3.40 in the afternoon, but Kim goes to the play group in Middleham just for the morning, so Mum has to take her in the car. But when we're not at school we can ride our bikes all over the place and play a bit of football, but Kim still has little wheels on her bike so she can't ride on the grass like we can. If it's raining we watch TV or read our comics; we get Dandy and Beano. Dad often takes us round the farm on the quad-bike. Kim always wants to come with us, but Dad can't always manage the three of us on the bike so she goes when we are at school. She also gets taken swimming with Mum while we are at school, so maybe she's glad to see us go there.

Saturdays, Mum takes Liam and me to Richmond in the morning for our swimming lessons; we can swim 25 metres. It's great fun and sometimes in the school holidays they put big rafts in the pool for us all to play on. Then on Saturday afternoons we go to Nanna's at Wensley. It's good because we can ride our bikes to Bolton Hall, throw stones in the river and sometimes Nanna plays football with me and Liam. Kim goes there on Thursdays so Mum can get her shopping done.

The dam on Great Ghyll made by the children

FARMING

Hay Raking by Hand

Hay Raking in the 1930s

Bringing Home the Hay

The Traditional Haymaking Picnic

Sheep Shearing

Lateral Thinking?

Fig 10   Some Farming Pictures from the Past

Farming in West Scrafton

In the considerable stretch of time since the land was first scratched and animals husbanded on it West Scrafton has been a farming community and has rarely housed any other than farmers and those closely involved with them. People not directly involved in farming have had a relatively brief appearance and that almost entirely in the last couple of centuries. Even when the number of farms has reduced from the ten or so in the early 1900s to a mere four farms and seven houses now, and while the number of homes occupied by families with no connection with the land has increased to around twenty, it staunchly remains a farming community. The "incomers" may only live on the edge of farming, but the gathering of sheep, the constant to and fro of farm machinery, tractors and cows, the pungent smell of slurry and muck as well as the varying fortunes of farming itself are a part of their lives. It is too small a place for them not to be.

The four farms (there were five until Tommy Handley sold up and divided his holding among the remaining four) cover some 1500 acres, including moorland, within the parish boundaries which stretch from the River Cover in the north to the foot of Roova crag in the south and from the boundary with East Scrafton to the edge of Swineside in the west. All of them have some parcels of land which touch the southern bank of the river, as well as others beyond the parish boundary and all have grazing rights on the moor through ownership of gaits, an ancient entitlement based on a number of grazing animals and their "followers" or offspring for each gait. An extract from the minutes of the village meeting held in 1843 are shown here to provide an insight in to the apparently arbitrary and parochial way in which gaits were "sized".

> At a meeting of the Inhabitants of West Scrafton held at the house of Mr Joseph Horner Inn Keeper pursuant to Notice on the thirteenth day of November One thousand eight hundred and forty three it was unanimously agreed that for the Bye Law men five sheep for each man was allowed for their service for one year and that the bye Law men be elected yearly. Resolved that 4 ewes and their lambs to be equal to five geld sheep & the four lambs to be taken from their dams on the 20th day of August. Agreed
> Resolved that 1 horse is equal to 8 ewes and lambs, or 10 geld sheep; and that a year old horse is equal to 6 ewes and lambs or 8 geld sheep, and that 1 cow is equal to 4 ewes and lambs, and three two years old Beasts is equal to 2 gaits and two one year old Beasts is equal to one gait; and that one goose and 10 goslings is 1 gait; and that 2 asses is equal to 1 gait and that each man take possession from this date; as witness our hands this 13th day of November 1843.

From pasture to moorland a variety of grazing land supports a little under 3000 sheep and 700 cattle along with a small and variable number of horses. Pigs, once kept to provide a private meat supply for most households, are now never seen. Probably the last in the village were kept at Town Head purely at the request of the Bainbridge's daughter Janet when she was a child. However, to complete the rural picture, a number of hens range very freely through the village while more territorial ducks occupy the small pools on Great Ghyll above the bridge.

The Hoggs, who have owned land here since the 19th century, occupy the bulk of the land to the east while the Utleys have the central tract running south to north and which has increased fivefold since Cullen Farm and its seventy acres was first purchased seven generations ago. The Harrisons farm generally to the west of the Utleys, but further to the west, on the other side of the road to Nathwaite Bridge the land is a mosaic of Dent and Harrison holdings. Moreover they both have lots on the other side of Utley's land, quite remote from their main holdings, all of which is indicative of the historic need to buy land as and when it became available. Still further west, however, where the land rises towards Swineside and Arkleside moor, both the Dent and Harrison holdings form two broad and clearly defined swathes of grazing. A map showing the four farm holdings within the parish boundaries is on page 171.

Much of the land has changed hands innumerable times; the present pattern of ownership bears little resemblance to that of a generation ago and now extends across the river and beyond the boundaries of the parish where all four have land, one as far away as Middleham. On the other hand, the parish plan produced in 1849 is still an accurate record of current field boundaries and many field names remain unchanged, albeit with variations in spelling. Although the land may be widespread and intermingled, the axis around which farming revolves is of course the small cluster of farmhouses, byres, milk parlours and sheep dip troughs that is West Scrafton: and it is to these that the livestock ebbs and flows to and from pastures on a daily basis for milking, seasonally for lambing and wintering, and to a varying schedule for general husbandry, vaccination and dipping. Throughout the year there is a constant movement of livestock, sometimes individually, other times in great numbers and it is this that gives the village a pulse.

To the south, West Scrafton Moor forms a long narrow wedge between the ghyll and the track (which in earlier days led to the coal mine) as it descends in broad folds, nears and eventually touches the southern edge of the village. This rough land is owned by Martin Vallance who exercises his shooting rights over it, while the West Scrafton farmers simultaneously exercise their grazing rights over the same land. It is the moor's heather which not only defines the difference between the interests of the farmers and the owners of the moors, but also represents a conservation issue. Grazing sheep gradually eliminate the heather essential for the grouse for which the land and shooting rights were acquired and the limitations on grazing inherent in the allocation of gaits, as well as conserving feed, was an early method of keeping a rough balance between these two conflicting needs. However its effectiveness in conserving the moorland heather was not successful; today there are only childhood memories of the heather thick on the village edge along Great Ghyll. Dense heather growth now starts on the skyline and stretches beyond but out of sight.

Against this background, typical of many upland farming areas, the Countryside Stewardship Scheme has, amongst other options, provided the basis for an agreement between farmers and landowners which over the next ten years will gradually reduce the number of sheep on the moor to allow regeneration of the heather. West Scrafton Moor is classified as a "white ground" moor, not as heavily heathered as "black ground" and producing richer grass in the summer. The cut back in grazing is therefore greater for the winter months to encourage winter heather growth while the optimum use is made of summer grazing on the grass. Gait holdings will decrease in line with this pattern and compensating subsidies are provided from Countryside Stewardship Scheme funds.

Novel co-operative ventures in conservation in recent years included the use of helicopters to spray and kill off bracken which was spreading out of control, a bane to sheep and heather. It had been cut for use, along with rushes, as bedding for livestock until the 1950s, but when that ceased because it was arduous scythe work and less economic than straw, it spread unhindered until its extent called for remedy. The cost was shared between government and farmers over the two consecutive years in which the operation took place and another step was made towards the aims of the countryside stewardship and control of the land which could not have been imagined by previous generations.

Fig 11 Map showing present Farmers' Holdings within West Scrafton

But perhaps one of the greatest changes in farming practice in recent years came with the formation of the Milk Marketing Board in 1932 and its guarantee to take all milk from producers large and small and market it for them. By the 1970s the filling of milk churns and the heaving of their not inconsiderable weight off and on to stands and trucks, the risk of the contents going sour in summer while they awaited collection, the scalding and sterilising of the empty churns and the uncertainty of the selling; all disappeared to be replaced with a regular call from a refrigerated bulk tanker. Production of milk rose six or seven fold when freed from the churn's restrictions and moreover that part of farming became incomparably easier.

However, the pendulum swings, and in the last couple of years of the 20th century, first the Hoggs, then the Harrisons and finally the Dents found that milk was no longer a viable commodity for them despite the acknowledged benefits of bulk collection and marketing. They withdrew from the scheme, thereby almost immediately converting their herds from milk to beef, leaving only the Utleys still being visited by the refrigerated tanker.

National and international issues have of course had an impact to varying degrees on this small close community. Wars brought a degree of prosperity when food production was critical to national survival, while imbalances within European agriculture and its resultant Common Agricultural Policy helped to produce a regime of subsidies which afforded some protection against the declining viability of (amongst others) these small hill farms. On the other hand there has been no escape from the escalating and all pervading bureaucracy allied not only to the not unwelcome subsidies, but also to the increasing governmental control of health and environmental matters. "When the weight of paper is equal to the weight of the beast, it's ready for sale" is a tired jest.

Gone are the days when many a deal was made on the shake of hands, receipts were rare and the closest thing to a universal record for reference was the "Sheep Marks Guide" published every decade or so for "Mashamshire and Fountain's Earth", an area which covered Coverdale, Colsterdale, Moorheads, Ilton, and Dallowgill, all once touching the Fountains Abbey land. This publication contained each farmer's individual sheep marks. Pictures of a sheep facing both left and right show the ears punched, nicked or

THE SHEEP MARKS GUIDE

IN WHICH IS DESCRIBED

THE SEVERAL MARKS AND LETTERS

ON THE

SHEEP

BELONGING TO THE FARMERS

JAMES WALLS, West Scrafton
Marked with W on the far ribs, JW on the horn. Lambs O far shoulder.

THOMAS HARRISON, West Scrafton
Marked with a prop on the near fore shank and near loin, with TH. on the horn. Lambs tar mark same as ewes.

THOMAS F. HARRISON, West Scrafton
Marked with O on the near loin, H far buttock, with TFH. on the near horn. Lambs near ear under-bit, prop near shank and far shoulder.

THOMAS HORNER, West Scrafton
Ewes and shearlings marked with L on the near and H on the far loin, LH on the far horn. Lambs H on far loin, rud across loin.

THOMAS HOGG, West Scrafton
Marked with H on the near loin, a prop on the far huggon, with I·H on the horn. Lambs H near loin, hole through far ear.

JOSEPH STUBBS, Moor Hen Inn, West Scrafton.
Marked with JS on the near loin, rud down near shoulder, with JS on the near horn. Lambs two holes through near ear with prop on near shoulder and S. on near ribs.

WILLIAM T. CHAPMAN, West Scrafton,
Marked with C on the far buttock and C near horn. Lambs prop far buttock.

PAUL STUBBS, West Close House, West Scrafton,
Marked with P on the near ribs and PS on the far horn.

HENRY GUY, West Scrafton
Marked with a + on the far ribs, blue far huggon, with HG on both horns. Lambs + on far ribs, under-bit far ear.

Mrs. BELL, Town Head Farm, West Scrafton,
Marked with a prop on the near huggon and far ribs, blue far rib, with RB on the horn. Lambs prop near huggon.

clipped and the wool marked with the owner's cypher. The Dents, for example, clip the tip off the Swaledale ear, mark the horn with a number 1 to 5, have TD as identity and mark the wool with a blue D on the ribs and a red on the shoulder. The 1913 edition, from which the extracts on the previous page are taken, has a delightful biblical quotation on the title page: "What man of you having an hundred sheep, if he loses one of them, doth not leave the ninety and nine in the wilderness, and go after that which is lost until he find it? And when he hath found it he layeth it on his shoulder rejoicing". The sentiments remain, but the shoulder is now a quad-bike. Charles Utley remembers in his youth exchanging stray sheep at the half way point with a distant owner who had been identified in the Sheep Mark Book and the arrangement, in the absence of telephones, being set up by post card.

In its way it was a precursor to the elaborate control routines in place today. Movement of livestock on and off farms have to be reported. The Bovine Spongiform Encephalitis outbreak in the 1990s has enforced the strictest recording and tagging of all beasts. Livestock and acreage returns have to be made, the use of sheep-dip is now regularly monitored by the Department of the Environment and many other checks and reports now form a burdensome, but sometimes essential, part of farming routine.

But, despite its greatly varying fortunes, West Scrafton farming remains a committed way of life as much as a business. Its long and arduous hours, often in harsh weather, and its uncertain returns have been endured for a very long time by many generations and those roots are still good today. No doubt they will survive any coming changes to farming and the countryside.

A Farming Diary of 1971

As a school project, Tommy Handley's daughter, Linda, kept a brief diary of events on their farm for the year 1971. She kept such a diary for three consecutive years, this being the last of them. It is reproduced here to enable a superficial comparison to be made with the diaries compiled just on thirty years later at the end of the millennium.

For non-farming readers, a brief list of livestock terms is given below:

Sheep

Ewe (or gimmer)	Female sheep
Ram	Male sheep
Lamb	Young sheep up to December, then known as hogg or tup
Hogg	Virgin ewe
Tup	Yearling ram
Wether (or geld sheep)	Castrated ram (usually sold at 6 months)
Mule	A crossbreed (in West Scrafton a Blue-faced Leicester tup on a Swaledale ewe)
Shearling	Sheep after its first shear
Draft ewe	Elderly ewe to be sold out of stock as unsuitable for hill farming

Cattle

Bull	Mature male cow
Bullock	Immature male cow
Heifer	Virgin cow
Suckler cow	Cow with calf requiring milk
Stirk	Male or female 1 year old
Lim heifer	Heifer of the Limousin breed

FARM DIARY OF 1971

As a farmer's daughter, one of the things I've done now for three years is to keep a record of events on our own farm, which comes in useful for reference the next year. This is my diary for the year 1971.

January 2nd	Brought the hoggs back from their winter quarters.
January 11th	One of the bullocks we're fattening for beef has developed pneumonia · the rest seem all right so far.
January 20th	Bullock has recovered. All are in a fine condition.
March 25th	Got our first lamb today.
March 29th	1st pair of twins today. All the sheep have been moved to Inisha.
April 6th	Thirty four lambs now. Sold the bullocks today.
May 1st	Been marking the lambs. Low May 2 calved a heifer.
May 2nd	Only 3 sheep left to lamb.
May 6th	The cows went out for the first time today since last November.
May 27th	Our young puppy was killed today · run over by a Landrover.
June 1st	Cut the Stripe (first hay field) today.
June 10th	Baled the hay from the Stripe.
June 16th	Gathered the sheep in from the moor for clipping.
June 23rd	Cut the Low West field.
June 25th	Sold Diane 3 today at Leyburn.
June 28th	Cut top West field, also the Ewbank and Bessie.
July 2nd	Baled the Low West field.

July 3rd	Baled Bessie today. Cut the Borivins and B's field.
July 5th	Baled the top West field and the Ewbank.
July 6th	Cut the Far Borivins and Inisha.
July 7th	Cut B's field.
July 8th	Mown off (finished cutting grass for hay).
July 9th	Baled Little field and the Butt.
July 10th	Baled the Long fields.
July 12th	Baled the lower part of Inisha.
July 13th	Finished baling Inisha.
July 14th	Finished Hay time.
July 30th	Sold forty lambs (half breeds) at Leyburn auction.
August 2nd	Fern Sunshine 2 calved by accident - she was crushed against a wall. The bull calf is dead. Had to take calf down to Thirsk for brucellosis tests as a formality.
August 3rd	Tests proved negative. No brucellosis.
August 31st	Have got nineteen calves this month, have lost 3 calves from heifers because they were too big for the heifers.
September 1st	Lost a cow today - trod on a sewer and went in head first. Found her this morning drowned.
September 30th	A further nine calves this month, only one heifer's calf has been born dead.
October 30th	Only two calves this month.

This is the end of my 1971 diary, which also includes a bale count of every field. This year we had about a thousand more bales than last year, due to a rather late Summer and long Spring.

One thing that is noticeable about this diary is the apparent change in field names over the last one hundred and fifty years since the 1849 map shown in fig 4 was produced. The changes are slight (for example, "Ingester" seems to have become "Inisha") and are no doubt due to verbal mispronunciations over the period without the documents containing the original field names being available for reference. It may be remembered that the ancient word "ing" meant field and "ester" meant east, so that the 19th century "Ingester" could still be translated to "Eastfield", but this translation is now unfortunately lost. This is a good example of how names (and spellings) evolve, even over a comparatively short space of time.

A good many of the present day fields are known by their owner's names, such as "Tommy's Stripe", and the next section mentions some of these. It is left to the reader to puzzle out which fields on the old map are being referred to, bearing in mind that some of the old field boundaries have been removed.

The Farming Calendar Today

January

New Year's day and only essential work is done. Animals have to be given their silage and the cows milked, so the day starts at six in the morning as will every successive day for the rest of the year. It is getting on for eight-thirty before breakfast can be taken. Moreover, by five in the evening there is another two hours of milking to put in. But at least this year started with an abnormally warm and wet month which seemed almost without precedent. Temperatures as high as 11°C were recorded; the average maximum was an unseasonable 6°C and at no time did the thermometer read below -2°C. However, there were some light falls of snow amounting to a couple of inches on one or two days which stayed in the gulleys on the high ground for some time; otherwise the bland conditions were tempered by the dale's customary high winds which gusted to 50mph on occasions; and, of course, there was the rain!

About 8 inches fell in January which is some 3 inches more than normal and resulted in the moor and fell becoming very water-logged despite the plethora of drainage runnels; and Great Ghyll itself was frequently in spate, wiping its channel clear of detritus and then subsiding to an almost dry course below the pothole which always takes the bulk of the flow. The continuous wetness underfoot took its toll on the sheep and some of the lame were brought down to be treated and rested up under cover before being put back on the moor.

Meanwhile the steady round of milking, feeding and trading of livestock continued almost without regard to the weather. On really wet days the sheep sheds were cleaned out ready for the lambing sheep to be brought in, but otherwise there was little excuse to be inside! Blocks of sheep-feed, dubbed as "smarties" and made of molasses, the by-product of the sugar industry, were dropped off on the moor where they were greeted by streams of sheep sweeping down the shoulders of the fell anxious to get to the feast. Across the dale in the pasture known as Mount Allotment, Will Utley sorted out the horned wethers and put 70 into the sheep house. He de-horned some calves and brought a Limousin heifer back for calving. Just under three weeks later it calved a bull calf and four days after that a red Limousin heifer produced a heifer calf, continuing another of the steady patterns that last throughout the year.

On one sharp cold morning Charles Utley took the Landrover and trailer up on to the moor with hay for feed and Joe Forrest, like any 12 year old, couldn't resist riding in the trailer where the sheer fun of it quite outweighed the cold and the marked discomfort of being bounced violently over the open moor.

But the short cold snap claimed its first victim when a ewe dropped a lamb up by Great Ghyll during the night and Ed Hullah came across it frozen solid during an early morning walk. At first it seemed as if it was premature despite its full term appearance, but later surviving births in February, hitherto unknown so early, marked it as the first of the phenomena. These Swaledale ewes must have come in season in September up on Arkleside moor where the air is obviously very good.

In between times, fences were repaired around Inisher and Handley's Stripe and some dry stone walling was repaired behind Bridge End Farm.

Early in the month, Will took a couple of bulls to Northallerton and a further two a week later during a brief snow storm. He got a reasonable price but, at 95p per kilogram, it seemed thin compared to around 140p which could have been obtained three years earlier. Similarly the sheep (twenty mules on the 6th and sixteen on the 13th to Leyburn, together with fifty-four draft ewes to Middleham and twenty-six lambs to Leyburn) brought in nearer £20 each rather than the £40 of a couple of years previously. The cold wind continued to blow through the livestock price market and the future seemed more uncertain than usual, but at least the MAFF inspection of the tags and records of calves born in 1998 presented no problem; the inspection merely served as a reminder of the BSE disaster now virtually past.

February

On a day of wild winds at the beginning of the month, Mrs Mary Dent died almost exactly a year to the day after the death of her husband, Tommy, a man of remarkable stamina and courage who had farmed in the hills for nearly half a century despite having lost the use of both legs to poliomyelitis in 1948.

By the middle of the month sheep are being brought down from the fell in anticipation of lambing due in March and April. A couple of them surprised Will Utley by dropping a horned gimmer lamb and a horned tup up on the moor ahead of the gather; a somewhat unusual event as horned lambs are not born this early in the year. It was the "Arkleside effect" noticed in January.

The Hogg, Harrison and Utley sheep were gathered in on 17th and sorted out into respective ownership in the pens at the end of Poverty Street before being dosed with fluke drench and put back on the moor. A few more lambs were discovered up there, including a pair of horned twins, and brought back to shelter. By the following Wednesday the first of the Utley's sheep due to lamb (the ones marked with yellow) were brought down from the fell and injected with an all encompassing "7-in-1" vaccine before being put into the sheep houses where the pens had been set up in readiness a little earlier. Individual maternity wards are a sign of the times; a generation ago it was rather more spartan work for sheep as well as for farmers. At the month's end the final tally was sorted out and Alan Dent found twelve missing Utley sheep on the moor, allowing them to join their proper owner.

At this stage a Department of the Environment inspector appeared on the scene to test West Scrafton farmers' compliance with the sheep-dipping regulations now in force. This was the first time the Department had carried out such an inspection and used the Harrisons' Hill Top Farm dip as its "test centre" for the dipping of the Utley's, the Hogg's and the Dent/Bainbridge sheep. The animals, of course, performed to order as they have done for generations, but it was the owners who were subject for the first time to a critical examination of the way this essentially toxic process is handled. Not everyone passed first time.

By way of a light interlude before the onset of the totally absorbing lambing season, Bernard Harrison took to a little pheasant shooting; an activity which he shares with like-minded friends every winter. A bag of thirty-five birds made a good day's shooting.

Meanwhile, the more mundane work of wall and fence repair competed with the spreading of slurry for available daylight hours. With the frost-hardened ground able to take the weight of the slurry tankers, they were coupled up to tractors and driven between slurry tank and field while any bystander was well advised to avoid inhaling. Years of exposure still doesn't make it a sweet smell. In a matter of three days Will Utley managed to cover Ewe Bank, Handley's Pasture, Pasture Meadow, The Croft, Stripe, East Pasture, Shed Fields, Joe Allotment, Neddies, Bessy Banks and East Low Field before the slurry store was empty and he could write "Thank God" in the farm diary.

March

Lambing attracts snow as every hill farmer knows and this month was no exception; none of it was very significant, although it lay around for the greater part of the third week. But there was a good measure of rain for more than two thirds of the month and while lambs can stand cold and they can stand the wet, a combination of the two is not good. Apart from the needs of land conservation, this is another reason for there being an agreement between farmers to keep the moor clear of sheep from the first day of this month until 6th April. During this fallow period the land has time to recover and the sheep are able to be lambed and generally husbanded in the relative comfort of sheds or pastures nearby. Lambing started in earnest around 20th of the month, although a Masham ewe and a black mule both lambed triplets a couple of weeks earlier, thus starting the season a little too bountifully for their good.

The shearlings due to be shorn of their wool in June or July were injected with the "7-in-1" vaccine and those that had been coloured to identify them as being due to lamb in the third week were segregated.

With most slurry stores now empty and the ground softening in the rain, attention turned to "muck-spreading", a process which, with a little imagination, can be said to be a sweeter operation. Muck is marginally kinder on the nose than slurry, its more liquid and nutrient filled equivalent, and has a longer tradition which could be said to give it status. And, of course, the spreading of artificial fertiliser (generally nitrous phosphate and potash) which is also going on at this time is positively benign in this respect, although many people harbour doubts about its effect on wild life in general and fish in particular when it becomes a significant element in the run-off from land to water. Later in the month a number of, fields were rolled and seeded which, as much as the lambing, seems to give an indication of spring.

Despite an indoor life all winter one of the Utley's Limousin cows gave birth to a dead bull calf. However, three of their bullocks were cleaned up ready for market in Northallerton the following day and were duly transported to auction; and several Friesian heifers were freeze branded with their passport numbers.

The controlling hand of the Environment Department extends to the use of dip in sheep farming and it made an appearance on an extremely wet Tuesday early in the month to examine the sheep-dip tubs of West Scrafton following on from the visit last month. Control of the run-off and collection of the used toxic dip met the standard in all cases this time.

Bobby and Tommy Hogg dipping sheep

April
Lambing was in full spate and occupied the greater part of every day and many a night.

The first few days were fine and warm and two first week

shearlings down on the Middleham fields had lambed, so, thanks to the benign weather and there being no room for them in the big shed, they were put out on Pasture Bottom. Second and third week shearlings were brought in from outlying pastures and by the middle of the month Will Utley was crying "they're lambing like mad" and was then too busy with them night and day to do little else. It was no different on the three other farms.

Showery days turned to snow and Roova Crag was greyed over with it, and as it dissipated and turned again to rain those sheep which had just lambed were kept back in the shed for a few more days before being turned out to pasture. As a result, lambing sheds were full until the first dry day, when over a hundred sheep and lambs were turned out to graze, the castrated male lambs now officially wethers. By the 18th only 76 of Utley's sheep were still to lamb and by 24th it was down to 33. The end was in sight.

The virgin hoggs had their number burnt into their horns, each farmer with his own system to identify the year of birth. The Dents, for example, merely use the numbers 1 to 5 unrelated to the year (1999 is TD3), whereas the Utleys and Hoggs use the last digit of the year, 1999 being WU9 and JH9 respectively. The Harrison's sheep, however, will wait until their first shearing before being horn-burnt with a TH and the year of the shearing. They were then dosed, injected and turned out on to the moor which presented them with a spread of fresh growth for them to feed on, as by this time the moor had been devoid of sheep and ungrazed since the beginning of March,

Unlike sheep, cattle have a fairly level reproductive regime imposed on them and had been calving steadily during the winter, at least sufficiently to maintain milking levels. On 20th a Limousin heifer in the Utley's herd calved a heifer to maintain the pace and a couple of days later two Angus calves and two Limousin heifers went to the Leyburn auction; one up and two down on the livestock count this week.

But the great day for cattle fell early this year thanks to the warmer weather. Within a week all the cows and calves had their first release when they were turned out of the sheds in which they had spent the long winter and now they showed something akin to jubilation as they took in the mild fresh air and freedom like prisoners released; but only for the day; as at nightfall they were back inside and it would be several weeks and better weather before they were totally free of the sheds.

Will later "turned 37 stirks into the Strip for a gallop", a phrase which epitomises this seasonal event. There is something incongruous about frisky cows, but it is a pleasure to watch. The Handleys have treasured film footage, taken several years ago, of their Charolais herd leaping about like lambs on being turned out.

May

The warmer weather managed to produce thunder on the day that a start was made on marking lambs with their owner's colours against the time when they have to be sorted again from the common flock. They were also drenched for worms and vaccinated against pneumonia before being let out, along with their dams, on to the moor to feed on the fresh growth and to join the hoggs released last month. Meanwhile the young stock is out to grass, some of them having been castrated beforehand. On Sunday 2nd May, according to Will's diary, "Crofty came up and nipped some Lim bull calves", a surprisingly delicate way of reporting the modification. Each day the weather continued to warm up and culminated in a heavy thunderstorm at end of the month.

June

Flaming June started with thundery weather and the flaming digger needed a new cylinder head. Kevin Utley therefore had to make a trip to Northallerton for a replacement and he took the opportunity to pick up some pipe and silage sheets while he was there. As he has a strong engineering bent (every generation of Utleys seems to have produced at least one engineer) this sort of maintenance is not beyond the farm's capacity and in any case there is no shortage of help; Will and John Watson are, amongst others, competent in most things mechanical and electrical. Machinery is everywhere; even this month's spraying of thistles in Handley's pasture is done from the quad-bike and, as a break from farming, Kevin Utley joined John Watson in the mechanical digging in of the electrical cable to supply the village's new water filtration system.

In the main the weather was fine and warm; both the longest day and Midsummer day were beautifully clear and hot, the sheep and their lambs grew fatter off the richer feed on the moor and the cows, no longer confined to the sheds at night, made the most of the fresh green grass. However, in other fields that fresh green grass gradually found itself under another attack. In one hot week it was mowed and then "dashed out" to dry by the spinners before being mechanically raked into wide rows. Happily there was no rain in West Scrafton during those critical days, although some fell in Carlton. On 10th of the month the "Silage Queen" arrived to make the first silage cut of the year. A massive piece of mobile machinery, it is contracted in with its operator to trundle down the rows, picking up the dry silage and chopping it into half inch lengths before blowing it into the trailer which is then taken to the silage pit or clamp. Within a couple of days the silaging was finished and the clamp was full, sheeted over with the edges secured with old vehicle tyres where it will probably remain until needed for winter feed (see photograph of silage gathering on page 189). Elsewhere another piece of clattering machinery, the baler, magically produced, at regular intervals behind it, massive shiny airtight black bales, looking like a collection of semi-inflated wheels for some vast amphibious vehicle. They were then collected and loaded on to a trailer which was "led home" by a tractor and the bales stacked to await use when summer's green grazing was gone.

Sheep and lambs were due for dosing and injecting against a range of diseases, so they were gathered up from the moor, brought down and duly treated in the pens. The hoggs amongst them were clipped and piles of wool filled the big wool-sheets, work which would continue well into next month.

Dosing sheep

Almost exactly four weeks after last month's storm another one rolled through the night and once again knocked out West Scrafton's electricity, but at least the silage was in and dry.

July

It is the height of summer, but fog and steamy mist appeared on a couple of mornings at the beginning and end of the month, soon to be followed by more thunderstorms and confirming the infinite variety of the parochial weather in what was in fact the sunniest month of the year.

By the middle of the month the air was filled with that most evocative of sounds, the multiple pitched bleating, the baritone, contralto and of course castrati, of hundreds of sheep being gathered off the moor in order to be clipped of their wool. As. the shearing continued apace the sheds, vacated by the cattle now feeding in the open pastures, began to fill with bulging wool-sheets, They will be stored there until October when the cows will be ready to re-occupy the sheds and the wool sold.

Meanwhile, milking continued mornings and evenings, cows were moved between pastures and mowing of the still lush grass in others was interspersed with a few day's muck spreading and cleaning out of sheds. And by the end of the month it was time for the second silage cut to be led away, sheeted under the great tarpaulins and held secure under the weight of old tyres.

August

This was the month when the Harrisons finally got out of the milk business. It had become less and less viable and the moving of cows up and down the road to and from the milk parlour had become too onerous. From now on it would be sheep and suckler cows only on their land.

Those fields which had had the second cut of silage were now spread with fertiliser and the slurry spreader was once again a regular sight. It was also the time to buy in straw for bedding.

About the middle of August the lambs, having been "spained" or weaned were separated from their dams to a chorus of bleating which continued through the night. Each has an individual voice which would be distinguishable to the human ear if there were not so many of them calling at the same time. Oddly enough they seem to be silent if the night is wet, but it was dry this year. It is not a lengthy trauma for either ewe or lamb. The mothers are let out on the moor while the lambs are put on to the green pasture grass to fatten them up and both are immediately, purposefully and silently grazing.

Everyone's sheep have been sheared and now they were being sorted out and gathered in for dipping. The days were punctuated by the protesting bleats of sheep and the slamming of sheep dip gates as they were ushered in batches to the dip and forcibly immersed. The air is sharpened by the sweet pungent smell of sheep dip, a mixture of organophosphates.

On the 11th of the month, at about eleven o'clock, as Will Utley was walking sheep back to West Scrafton from Highfield on the way to a dipping session the almost total eclipse of the sun occurred. A number of people had been musing on the possibility of any reaction from the livestock or indeed wild animals and birds at this brief unscheduled nightfall, but apparently the sheep disappointingly lived up to their reputation for single-mindedness, ignored the phenomenon and trotted on. No one seems to have recorded the reactions of any other animals; but then it was only a like a dark cloud in this part of the country.

Meanwhile, there was drain work to be done. The ground below Roova Crag had become waterlogged from the springs up there and so a long herring-bone system of drainage was installed to relieve it. A 3-ton Hi-Mac was hired to help the work and it took two loads of gravel from Masham and several days work over a couple of weeks to finish it, but it no doubt made a pleasant change from dipping sheep.

The first batches of lambs were taken to the sales in Hawes and Leyburn, a routine which would continue steadily into February.

September
The month turned out to be one of the warmest Septembers since Coverdale records began in 1977, but it was very wet. Around thirty per cent more rain fell than in an average September and the third cut of silage needed a careful eye on the weather to get it dried successfully and baled or stowed in the clamps. Between dry

Muck spreading in January

Showing the teamwork required in Silage Gathering

Fig 12   A couple of Farming Activities

days of silage work the muck spreading went on. Some fields were rotovated, mixing the manure into the damp ground which a day or so later was harrowed, seeded and rolled, all of which should result in lush grazing next year. About the 17th the last of the slurry was spread on Handley's Pasture and part of Long Fields before the slurry tank was quite empty. However the pungent work didn't end there. The tank itself had to be cleared of the residue and scraped out, a job made even more unattractive by the onset of very wet weather.

It was now time for the ritual of smartening up sheep for market, Their faces were washed, their wool dyed a faint light brown and their back ends cleaned up. Everyone does it and everyone knows what they looked like the previous week, but quite properly the product of all that labour and attention has to be presented in its best form. Once again, when the lambs have been sorted out, the bleating trailers head off to the markets in Leyburn and Hawes.

Meanwhile a routine visit by the vet to take blood tests on the horned tups gave them a clear bill of health; importantly they were free of scrapie.

October

After a family debate lasting several weeks Alan Dent decided to get out of milk by the end of the quota season in March next year. The returns for the endless round of feeding, moving the herd to and from the milking parlour and the milking itself looked worse by the month. Until recently they had used the milk shed at the end of Low Lane to milk some cows in the remote pastures down by the river. It was easier to move the churns up through the village to Town Head every day than the cows, and as Alan so succinctly says "cows and villages don't mix". Better to stick with sheep and beef.

Meanwhile regular trips to Leyburn and Hawes with heifers and lambs for sale is interspersed with moving more sheep off the moor, dipping and tailing them, de-horning calves and mucking out the calf sheds.

The year end was in sight, it was "getting back-endish" and loads of sugar beet and brewers grain were brought in and stored for winter feed. Towards the end of the month the cows were brought into the sheds each night, signalling the beginning of their winter incarceration which would be complete when they ceased to be let out during the day. It was also time to think of next year's lambing and the gimmers were due to have their back ends shaved to give the tups a chance of success when the time comes for them to sire next Spring's new generation. A few tups had already been moved to strategic fields.

But still the weather was relatively dry and pleasant and on 15th Will Utley had his annual invitation to join one of Martin Vallance's grouse shoots along with a few neighbours. They had a reasonable bag, some twenty five brace all told. Will's six birds from eleven shots was very satisfying, particularly in what has been a sparse season for grouse.

November

In the first week of the month the Bainbridge Bros. truck arrived to load the wool which had been stored in sheds and took it to Bradford. Swaledale wool is not of great value these days and it will end up as carpet or even insulation for buildings, a fact which is reflected in the price paid, of course. But at least it clears space in the sheds for wintering livestock.

Another gather off the moor brings the bleating streams of sheep down to be sorted, dosed and injected. Several days throughout the month are occupied in going round the tups daubing their bellies with a mix of coloured powder and oil which will identify those ewes that have been served. The colour is changed roughly every ten days, so there will hopefully be a clear idea of when each ewe will lamb next year. But by way of encouragement the ewes have been gathered round the tups. No-one wants a number of ewes to miss out through not having been properly introduced and by no means all of them are certain to have read the invitation card correctly.

A whole day of fog on 12th and again on 14th seemed to signal the end of autumn and Monday 15th saw the last day of pasture grazing for at least some of the cows and calves. They were brought into the sheds the night before but from now they will not be let out to graze in the mornings and will remain inside, feeding on winter fodder until the Spring. Other cattle were brought home from outlying pastures and by the end of the month all herds would be inside for the winter.

There had been a little time available to spread yet more slurry and repair fencing and walls, but now there was a chill in the air and several days and nights of ground frost. In the latter part of the month snow flurries gave the first notice of winter proper.

December

The month started wet and cold with snow falling on the first Sunday followed by flooding in the dips and hollows of land and on roads, but nevertheless over the first weeks the Swaledales were turned out on to the moor where for generations they have stoically weathered the winters and the tups were changed around to give variety to their flock. The Blue-faced Leicester sheep on the other hand, not being of a similar hardy strain, were brought inside where they would stay until mid-February. The fattening lambs were also favoured by being brought into the sheep houses where they joined the general assault on the stock of winter feed.

It is time for more cattle to be injected against worm, lice and mange and some of their pastures get yet another dose of slurry spread on to the thin layer of snow to ensure that next year the grass will make lush grazing once again. It is hard to imagine today's stretches of cold wet muddy ground ever reverting to summer pasture.

And still, despite the rapid approach of Christmas and the New Year, the steady trading of stock continues. Nearly every Tuesday the market in Hawes receives another batch of lambs for sale and on most Wednesdays the Leyburn Market sees more lambs and cattle arrive from West Scrafton. And when those holidays arrive, some time is taken for traditional family celebrations, but only by judicious juggling of tasks and hours. The cows must be milked on time and the stock in the sheds must be fed. It may be New Year's Eve again, but the immutable needs of the farms continue year in and year out and that instant of change from one calendar year to the next has no significance for the land or the animals on it; they move to a longer slower rhythm.

Tommy Handley's Charolais Bulls

Eighty years ago, in 1920 to be precise, Tommy Handley's father, Joseph, who until then had been farming rented land in Swineside, bought Culverham Farm, which consisted of the farmhouse and a number of acres of farmland including Ewebank, for £5000. This was a not inconsiderable amount in those days as is borne out by the story of Joseph Handley's wish to borrow £16 from the bank in order to buy the cottage next door, which is now the much enlarged and enhanced Fell View. The bank manager apparently drew his breath in and refused on the grounds that the overdraft was big enough already.

Tommy Handley took over the farm where he had been born on his father's retirement in 1954. Land exchanges made to rationalise holdings between farmers had changed the shape of the farm map a little since his father's day but it remained a mix of sheep and cattle; some two hundred Swaledales and a pedigree herd of Freisians. The Freisians were sold in 1974 (they "sold well") and herd of suckler cows and a bull replaced them over the next three months, only to be sold when standing at about fifty head in 1979. It was in that year when changes in the milk industry, increased regulation and the conversion to bulk distribution from the age old system of churns, persuaded him to "get out of milk".

Hill sheep farming may have its moments of satisfaction but they don't occur during the winter and rarely at lambing time. In the severe winter of 1979 seventy lambs were consigned to the same pit having perished in the bleak weather. Coupled with the onset of rheumatism and a bad back this was close to being the last straw and the Handleys nearly dropped out of farming altogether and moved away; but West Scrafton kept a hold on them and almost simultaneously Culverham Farm was put to auction in 1979 and the partially built Culverham House was bought. Charles Utley got the greater part of the farm at the auction, with three of the fields at the west going to the Dents.

However, the fields known as the Stripe, Ewe Bank, the Cow Pasture and Bull Garth did not go to auction and, with the proceeds of the auction in hand, Tommy launched into breeding Charolais cattle, a breed which had always intrigued him. So by 1980 he had a new house and the start of a new herd.

A reduction sale at Perth in Scotland of a herd of Charolais gave him a cow for £2600 which eventually calved the famous "Theodor" which three years later brought him a remarkable sum at the same Perth auction. Theodor was unmistakably a valuable bull and at Perth there was a considerable amount of pressure to make a private sale before the auction was held. After a fair amount of whisky hospitably supplied by an interested buyer at the Waverley Hotel he was offered £3,000. An offer of £10,000 might have made him give in to a private sale with or without whisky, but come the auction and a well paraded Theodor, a Mr Frank Bowley parted with 28,000gns and led the bull away. As it turned out, this sum was a joint Charolais and European record. The bull's offspring in a subsequent sale made a total of £133,000, a pretty spectacular escalation in value from the original cow's £2,600. The rest of the Charolais herd was sold in 1987 to a Mr Robert Montague. Meanwhile Theodor was bought by a Texan in 1988 before he ended up in Mexico where he died in 1994, a well travelled beast with progeny both live and as straws of semen spread even further around the world..

A couple of years after the record sale of Theodor, Tommy decided to take another of his Charolais bulls to the fatstock auction at Bedale as he thought that this one was not good enough for the pedigree market. Unfortunately, it turned out that the bull had other ideas. The side door of the trailer measured only 22" x 36"

Two Charolais Calves

Young Theodor

Tommy at the Perth Show with Charolais "Culverham Theodor"

Fig 13   Tommy Handley's Charolais Bull

and as Tommy opened it at the auction ground, all 14cwt of bull came hurtling out, made a mad rush at his master, who just managed to side-step in time, and careered on up Emgate to the centre of Bedale, knocking over an unfortunate woman in the process. Luckily the woman was not hurt. However, one poor man, who was painting a second floor window at the time, had his ladder knocked away and he was left hanging on to the window-ledge by his fingers. He, also, had a lucky escape.

The bull then made his way further up the road with Tommy and many other people in pursuit and eventually turned in to the golf course. He was rounded up in due course, but not until he had made many deep footprints in the soft grass. A very much relieved and shaky Tommy was only too pleased to hear the gunshot and very thankful that no-one was hurt.

Tommy Handley continues to judge Charolais at shows around the country; his first invitation to do so of course followed the celebrated sale of Theodor.

GAMEKEEPING

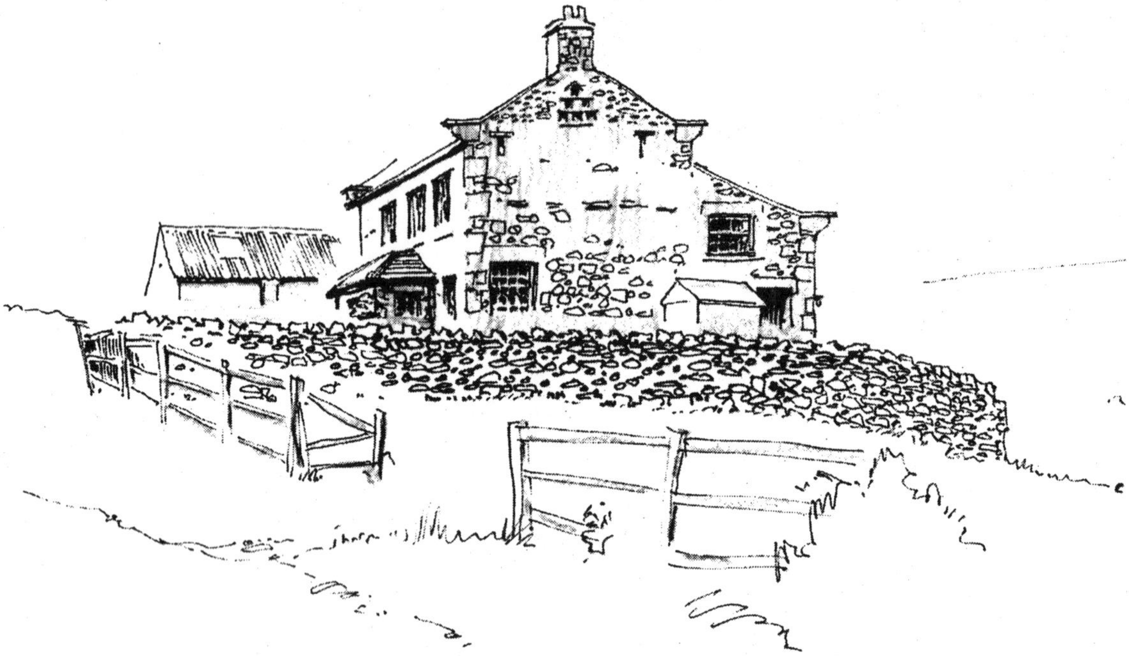

The Gamekeeper's Story

The Southgate family has lived in Lane House since 1990. At that time it was converted by Mick's employer, Neil Corner, from the original cow-byre on what, until 1980, had been Harrison land. The conversion to the present house was carried out specifically to provide Mick and his family with a home on the estate of which he was the gamekeeper. One of three full-time keepers in Coverdale, his own territory is made up of three parts; the first part stretches from Thorow Ghyll just east of Moorhen Farm to Caldbergh Ghyll and, following a gap to beyond Caldbergh, a second patch is in Coverham, while the third, being Melmerby Moor on Penhill, is rather more remote. Lane House is actually outside the West Scrafton parish boundary (as is Joy and Paul French's Lane Farm House) but, as both the Southgates and the Frenches are so obviously a part of the West Scrafton community, the boundary has by common consent been expanded to include them for the purposes of this record.

A gamekeeper's job is of course to produce a "harvestable surplus" of game; essentially feeding it and protecting if from vermin in order to provide sufficient numbers for a couple of shoots a month in the season, while at the same time maintaining a healthy stock for the future. The grouse are truly wild birds, but pheasants are bought in from game farms as chicks and raised to fly over the guns where some 45% of them will eventually be shot.

The shooting seasons therefore represent the culmination of the year-round work. The open season for grouse is from 12th August to 10th December and that for pheasants is between 1st October and 1st February. Within those seasons there will be around twelve days of grouse and eight or nine days pheasant shooting. Lesser game have a variety of less memorable dates; the duck and partridge seasons are about the same with 1st September to 31st January and 1st February respectively, while snipe stand uniquely with their long season extending from 12th August right through to 1st February. An important secondary benefit of the vermin control is that not only are game bird eggs and chicks protected, but all wild birds' offspring are saved from excessive exposure to predatory birds as well. Controlled burning of the moor to encourage healthy heather growth is likewise beneficial to all wild life which is reliant on it in any way for food and cover.

Nevertheless, there is a cautious concern, a sensitivity, about the image of gamekeeping and its associated shooting as being a cruel sport practised by the privileged few. The emotive arguments raised in support of the current and proposed countryside legislation, the "right to roam" and fox hunting in particular having raised public awareness, are understandably seen as an irritating spotlight shone by politicians, "townies" and sentimental activists on a part of rural life which is in the main no more cruel than the raising and slaughtering of calves and lambs; birds and beasts all end up on the table after all.

The shooting season covers the greater part of six months and preparation for it fills the other six pretty readily, so not surprisingly Karen and the children end up holidaying on their own often enough. Mick would no doubt refuse to admit that the work was so satisfying that holidays for him are really not necessary, but he does speak most eloquently of the times between April and June when the game eggs and broods are most at risk from predators and he would rise at two or three in the morning on a couple of nights a week in order to sit out on the moor before dawn to listen. At that time bird sounds give away the presence of vermin and ultimately provide him with guidance for shooting and trapping. Come the dawn and fuller daylight, a view over several hundred acres allows bird activity to provide an added dimension to the search. Curlews and lapwings swoop and turn to harass foxes, stoats, weasels, ferrets (the latter generally feral, tame ones turned wild), and carrion crows do likewise as they attempt to protect their nest or brood and in the process give a clear indication of any predator's whereabouts. As a result there is a chance, but only a chance, that a well laid snare or a good shot will add another entry or two to the "vermin list" recorded in the back of the Game Book. Snares can be used year round but traps, for stoats and weasels in the main, can only be used in winter when the rabbit-meat bait will remain fresh.

One time in particular he recalled when he was on Penhill, sitting in one of his regular sites at around 4.30 in the morning and found himself about 40 yards from a pair of grouse and their newly hatched chicks, when a fox appeared. The cock and hen frantically tried to distract the fox but it was as determined as they were. As one chick bounced into the air the fox took it with practised ease and obvious satisfaction. Mick then shot the fox with equal ease and satisfaction. He uses a Ruger .22-250 with more clout than a .22 and it made a clean kill.

In addition to a couple of guns, his "tools of the trade" include a pair of labradors, two terriers and a lurcher. A certain amount of time is spent training the labradors to flush out game and pick up the killed or injured; he finds labradors easier to train than spaniels. The terriers, of course, accompany him on his campaign against vermin, while the lurcher is able to catch the faster specimens including foxes. However, guns and dogs are all employed in the reduction of rabbit numbers; foxes and stoats in particular are, to a degree, dependent upon rabbits as a source of food and so the fewer there are, the fewer their predators.

Apart from being somewhere in which to put the immutable dates of the shooting seasons, a monthly calendar doesn't properly accommodate the record of a gamekeeper's work any more than it does for any form of land and livestock farming, but the sequence of work throughout the year (and January is as good a month to start as any) looks rather like what follows.

Page 202

A Gamekeeper's Year

January

The grouse season is over, but two or three pheasant or duck shoots are held although the numbers are thinning out a bit towards the end of the season, but there are still enough to provide work for beating teams, loading for the guns and picking up shot birds. Much of the remainder of the time is spent in controlled burning of heather when it is dry enough, putting out straw and feed for the game and keeping up the endless attrition of vermin.

Game husbandry continues between shoots, of course. Pheasant sections (wire enclosures holding around 40 birds in the less wooded areas and up to 150 where there is plenty of cover) have to be maintained, brought in, repaired and stored along with the feeding hoppers.

Grouse are out of season shortly before Christmas (10th December) but throughout January and into February and March they attract a certain amount of ingenious attention when they are treated for strongyle worm (*trichostongylus tenuis*). In previous years when winters were hard, the frost would kill the worm and the weaker birds carrying it as well, but with several successive mild winters the pest has flourished. The birds excrete the worm eggs which eventually become larvae making their way up to the heather tips and are then picked up by other birds during their foraging; and the cycle accelerates.

So an attempt is made, prior to the breeding season, to dose them by hand, a practice that only started in the mid-1980s. On a dry night, when it's not too frosty, a searchlight on the moor is more likely to be Mick at his work than poachers at their's. But he reckons that "the generation of gamekeepers before him would be turning in their graves if they thought that he was catching grouse at night and dosing them". The light is used to dazzle and immobilise the birds which are then netted, grabbed and dosed using a dosing gun, similar to that used on sheep but with a smaller nozzle, which is pushed over the tongue and into the gullet. Knowing where to be and where to look is no doubt the true knack, but chance plays a part as well in the success or otherwise of the job. On a good night forty to fifty grouse can be treated this way. The target is to catch and dose about 65% of the known stock, but with a lot of luck perhaps half will be treated and the spread of the worm may be contained.

Rather less intensive work, which also takes place during good weather in the first three months of the year, entails putting out medicated grit for the grouse to accumulate in their crops. Grit improves their digestion and the medication is a secondary attack on the strongyle worm.

February & March

The shooting season is over, but otherwise the routines of January carry on throughout the next two months, although the burning of heather in March when it is usually drier is more intense than in earlier months; again dependent on the weather, some track maintenance can begin at the latter end of the month. The game crops (mostly kale) alongside woodland or other game cover have to be mown and tended in order to provide feed for pheasants, while straw has to be put out for the birds to scratch amongst as they feed on the grain.

Trapping and shooting vermin continues unabated as does the worming and gritting of grouse.

April & May

Ad hoc track maintenance proceeds when feasible and burning continues up to 14th April at the latest. Beyond that date, fire would disturb nesting birds or early chicks which are already under increased threat from hungry vermin with their own progeny to feed. Carrion crows are a particular threat at this time. By about 12th May the first grouse chicks are out but the main hatching is more likely to be around 22nd to 24th May. At this stage the chicks are at their most vulnerable while the vermin, particularly carrion crows, and vixen and their cubs, are at their most voracious, a juxtaposition which concentrates a gamekeeper's mind.

June

Better weather allows further track maintenance, fencing and some work on the butts, either building new ones or repairing last winter's damage; but the most significant task is the building of pens in anticipation of the arrival of an order of six-week old pheasant chick due to be delivered in July.

July

The recently bought pheasant chicks arrive and require feeding three times a day in the big pens which have been erected in the low woods and hold up to 150 birds. From here they are trained to feed further and further up the hill side by spreading the feed and whistling so that the birds will eventually fly to the whistle. They can then be positioned in the best location ready to be flushed out on a shooting day later in the year. Meanwhile, water butts have to be filled, straw and corn put out and turf added to the outer walls of the shooting butts to make them less obtrusive.

August

The 10ft x 10ft sections for about 40 twelve-week old pheasants have been erected in the more open locations and into these go the twelve-week old chicks which have just been delivered. They are released gradually in batches and fed from hoppers, but to stop them roaming too far they are driven back to the pens sometimes up to three times a day by the dogs which gives them less contact with humans and so become a wilder bird. The "dogging" can go on well into September before they are totally conditioned and go back to the pens of their own accord.

The "glorious twelfth" sees the start of grouse shooting and a few days employment for beaters, good sport for eight or nine guns and maybe a bag of 150 birds each day. Each gun is often supported by a loader who hands his boss a freshly loaded gun immediately both left and right barrels of the first have been fired. The West Scrafton shoot uses about twenty or so beaters, flankers and dog-men to drive the game towards the butts in a vast flag-waving arc between the two flankers with half a dozen dogs, some flushing up the birds and the others retrieving the fallen ones.

A shoot is followed next day by a sweep-up of the detritus. Empty cartridge cases litter the butts, the occasional bird lies undetected by the dogs on the day and the lunch huts have their own debris. All has to be picked up and cleared away.

This is also the time when the wild ducks are fed on the ponds which have been created on the moor's edge specifically to attract them. The Scrafton pond is shallow and out of sight in the rough-pastured dip between Scrafton Moor and Caldbergh; there is another at Melmerby. The stock of wild duck is getting low and so some forty reared birds were bought for the first time this year to restore the balance, but with some misgivings.

Shooting reared birds seems pitiful, but without some fresh stock the numbers are certain to decline, and hopefully the inter-breeding will produce a generation of wild birds.

September

Grouse shooting continues, as do the preparations for the pheasants in October. The pheasants have been gradually conditioned to perform correctly on the days of the shoot. Pens where they roost, furnished with grain hoppers and nearby water butts, have been positioned on the lower ground and the birds have been encouraged to browse on the higher ground beyond the line where the guns will be positioned. These habituating arrangements take several weeks to become effective, and yet the ambushes sprung in November and onwards are nowhere near as lethal as would be expected. The wily birds in the main get through, and more than half survive the season.

Meanwhile, the rides in the woods and the game crops still have to be mown, the feed hoppers and water troughs filled and an eye kept on vermin.

October

On the first of the month the pheasant season open, although shooting is unlikely to start much before November.

And, of course, the grouse season continues through to

mid-December, and between shooting days the care of both pheasant and grouse goes on with the same demanding routines, putting out medicated grit, filling feed hoppers and water butts and spreading straw with the grain.

However, the onset of colder weather heralds a change in the campaign against stoats and weasels. Trapping becomes more effective as these creatures are averse to any but the freshest meat and the rabbit- meat bait set in the traps takes much longer to decay at the lower temperatures. These traps are set in tunnels made of stones to prevent injury to other wild or even domestic creatures, and are a humane version of the old and now illegal gin trap, with a trigger plate and heavily sprung bar.

Foxes on the other hand will eat anything but they have to be taken by snare or, more rarely, shot. Mick remembered lamping a fox one night last October, but they are more astute than a grouse in a lamp's glare and this one, like so many, ducked and he missed. There is never a chance for a second shot.

November

The first pheasant shoot of the season. Unlike the open moorland venue for grouse with its butts, treeless horizons and the arc of flag waving beaters fifty yards apart, pheasant is shot in more cultivated surroundings amongst fields, hedges and copses. In place of the moorland butts pegged lines are set up for the guns to position themselves across the likely line of flight, which, if the earlier induced habits hold good on the day, is overhead en-route to the feeding pens, the birds being driven by the shouting beaters (rarely more than 20 yards apart in this case) with sticks and dogs.

November is also a time to tackle some fencing and gate repairs, a bit of creosoting along with the usual trapping and shooting of vermin.

December

The grouse season is over by the 10th of the month, but there are a couple of pheasant shoots still to go before Christmas; however, Boxing Day is a traditional fixture with a nine o'clock start, abandoning the normal lunch break but going through until two o'clock in time for a truly festive lunch instead. A short day but a merry one.

A hard frost or snow will draw the birds to the feeds, making it necessary to disperse them prior to the arrival of the guns. On the other hand, they are then more inclined to return to the feed when driven by the beaters, over-flying the guns and thereby fulfilling the whole purpose of their existence. Two or even three shoots may take place before Christmas and on many an occasion during the school holidays the two boys, Geoff and Joe along with their sister Becky, will take sticks and join their father and the beaters to thrash the trees and undergrowth while they shout and wave in order to flush the birds before the advancing line; great sport on a clear dry day, but less so when everything is cold and wet.

By the year's end about twelve days of grouse and eight or nine days of pheasant shooting will have been completed and depending on the continued success of his gamekeeping and vermin control, the year's climate, the absence of disease and any other external factors, Mick Southgate will oversee a similar programme next year.

VILLAGE RECORDS

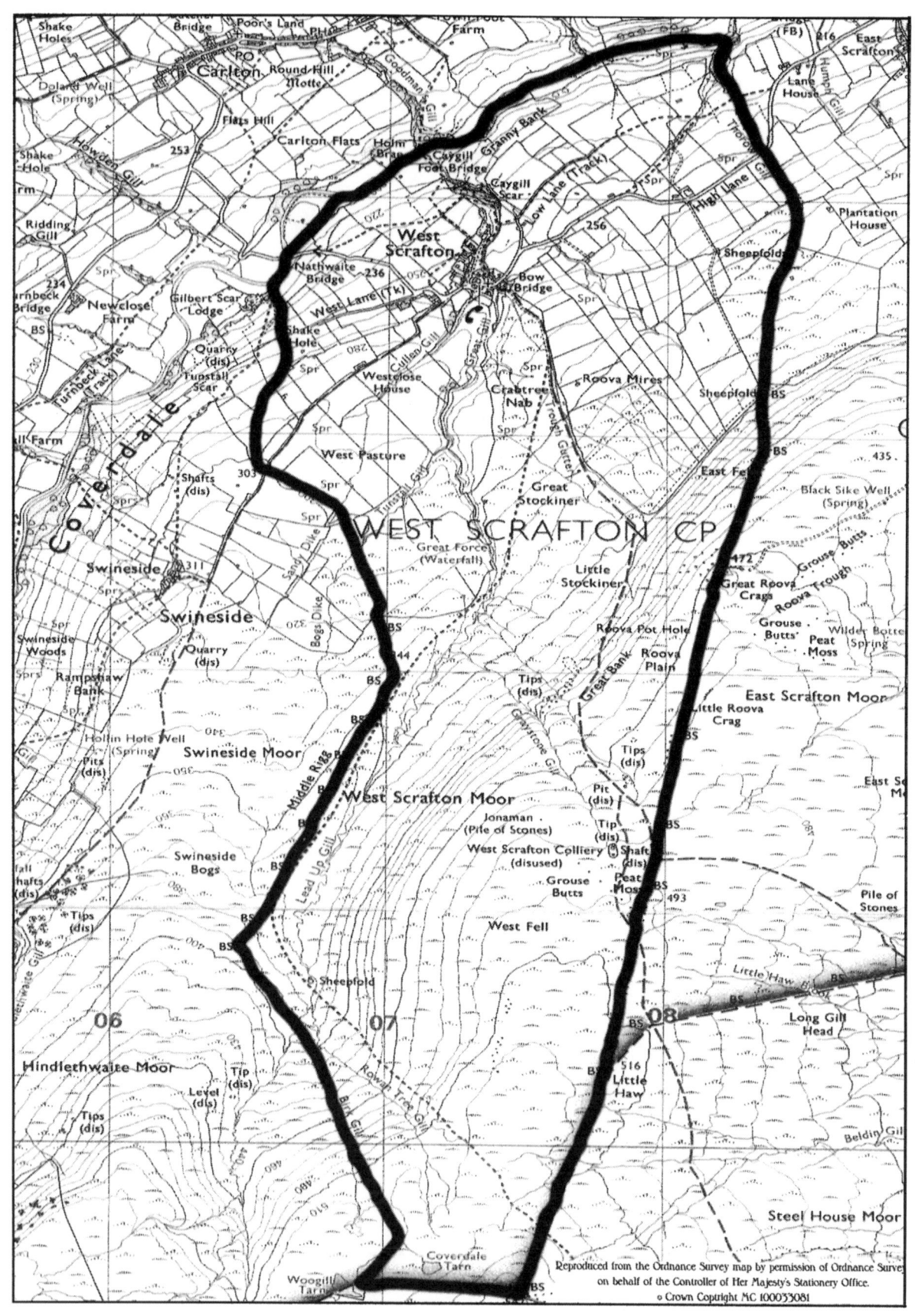

Fig 14   Map showing Civil Parish Boundary

Page 210

Civil Parish Meeting

There are sadly too few occasions in the year when West Scrafton folk can get together and have a good chat but one of them is the Annual Parish Meeting. It would be fascinating to go back in time and listen to the banter and conversation that must have taken place at the Parish Meetings of old. Meetings were minuted only from 1909 and details are unfortunately sparse. Attendance was usually only about ten to fourteen people (men only of course!). The only business conducted at these early meetings which was deemed worthy of note seemed to be the voting in of the Chairman, the bye-law men and the overseer and his assistant (the latter recorded as having been paid the sum of £2 per annum in 1909). The bye-law men took care of fence and track repairs, etc. The other item minuted annually until 1918 was the payment of the sum of 2/- (10p) "for the use of heat and light" at the Moorhen Inn (now known as the Old Inn) where the meetings were then held.

It is not certain what qualities were required of the Chairman, except perhaps the name "Thomas", which seems to have belonged to all the Chairmen voted in between 1909 and the 1940s! Little other detail was noted but the following items have been picked out which might be of interest.

In 1910 the Meeting agreed to give permission to the West Scrafton Coal Company for it to use the lime kiln which at that time was situated on Goose Bank. In 1923 the first details appear of repairs to village amenities such as the mending of village stand-pipe taps, the renovation of fences and repairs undertaken to the moor road, etc.

In 1930 a special meeting was held at which it was agreed to "write to all those with poultry hen huts and all other wooden structures to be removed out of the village within 14 days". It was in that same year that members arranged to "survey the water supply from source".

In 1932 it was agreed that "a general rate be laid for the purpose of any account against the township", and a precept of £7 "was sent to the Leyburn Rural Rating Authority". For the first time the village elected a Treasurer.

In 1933 the Meeting agreed to "send a letter approving Carlton Parish Council's purchase of a trailer hearse for £23 and the disposal of the old one". In that same year the various gait holders met to discuss the putting up of a fence between Swineside Moor and West Scrafton Moor and the fencing in of Goose Bank. The money was raised by means of a loan from the Midland Bank and the letting of 100 sheep gaits.

From 1933 onwards the meetings were held in the ex-Wesleyan Chapel, having been held in members' homes from the time when the Moor Hen Inn closed down in 1918.

Action was never rapid and when villagers decided to request a telephone box for the village from the General Post Office at Northallerton in 1935, it was not provided until after the war and it took until 1954 to decide that a light in it would be useful, partly, of course, because there was no source of electric power in the village until 1952! It was in 1943 that an afternoon postal collection was requested and this service still remains at the end of the millennium.

In 1947 the meeting was discussing the conditions attached to the "taking over of the water supply by Leyburn Parish Council" and this was still a topic two years later.

In 1949 the village Meeting asked the Education Committee to supply "conveyance to and from school for West Scrafton children", but this does not appear to have happened until many years later in the 1960s; and some three years later in 1952 the "Electric Board" was asked to supply "electric" to the village. The community was gradually getting itself equipped with up-to-date services; these were added to when Leyburn District Council was requested to arrange refuse collections from the village in 1955. In 1957 the topic of rubbish deposited in the ghyll was raised yet again, this time concerning the removal of an old car dumped there!

Street lighting has been discussed several times, first in 1959 (at a proposed cost to the village of £181) and again in 1968; in 1981 a specific request was actually made to the District Council but nothing materialised. However, most recently, in 1998, an offer from the Council for the installation of a few street lights was discussed at a special meeting but this time the idea was rejected by the current inhabitants, as the desire to become more "urbanised" no longer had an appeal.

West Scrafton won a tree for the green in the Best Kept Village competition in 1961 and in 1962 it was decided to further improve that area. Harry Watson is the man responsible for the attractive small green; he donated £100 of his own money towards the scheme.

The mobile library began to visit every second week in 1967 and this was also the year that Tommy Handley became the Treasurer. Thirty-two years later in 1999 he is still faithfully doing that task!

In 1975 the village registered its claim for the ownership of all the village greens with the Common Land Commission. In 1978 a very long and drawn-out task began, namely the registering of the ownership of West Scrafton moor. This is minuted over the next few years. Its progress was slow and a lot of hard work was put in (a copy of the proposed submission is shown over the page). However, it all appeared to have been in vain when the moor suddenly had a new private owner with, it seemed, a legitimate claim.

In 1978 the District Council recommended that West Scrafton merged its Parish Meeting with that of East Scrafton and Caldbergh. Happily this was never made official!

Meetings of the last twenty years or so have repeatedly highlighted the same complaints each year and these, no doubt, will still be made well into the next millennium. These include the inadequate gritting of the road in winter, the tardy arrival of the snow plough (snow; just a memory now?), water flooding over the road, overgrown junctions and blocked-up passing places. . . . . .

As the end of this century is approached we should be proud of the Civil Parish Meeting. Its annual gatherings are well-attended and generally good-natured. European funding has awarded the village £9,000 allowing a clean, bacteria-free waters supply to be finally achieved, thus keeping the European Union bureaucrats happy. The village can surely boast one of the best organised and most efficient Water Committees in the Yorkshire Dales!

*****

The following is a copy of the proposed submission for ownership of West Scrafton moor.

West Scrafton was originally a moorland a village and there were no fences or gates preventing free access to the moor. In those days sheep and cattle grazed within the boundaries of the village and on the village wastes and verges. There is no record of when gates walls and fences were erected but there is now no free access to the moor.

West Scrafton moor appears to have been without any ownership for over a hundred years. A survey of 1843 shows its area to be 913 acres and it was not subject to a valuation. According to the county archives there have been no enclosure awards of the moor since then. Indeed, there are no enclosures recorded at West Scrafton.

Inhabitants of the village had gaits on the moor, the village appointed byelaw men, and still does, and inhabitants had rights to the cutting of bracken. There is a record of a Lord of the Manor in 1831 when, according to the History Gazetteer Directory East and North Ridings 1840, the Lord of the Manor was James Deardon. There is also an agreement dated 1898 in connection with the village water supply which was entered into between the village and Mrs Agnes A Wright, tenant for life of the Manor of West Scrafton.

At the turn of the century there was a coal mine on West Scrafton moor but there is no record of the payment of royalties to an owner. It seems that the coal mine ceased operating about 1910 following a second disaster including the loss of life in the pit.

Shooting rights on the moor are held by Mr H St J Coghlan who acquired them before the 1939/45 war but they were at that time disputed rights and certain farmers in the village claimed independent rights to shoot on the moor.

The village has accepted responsibility for fencing the moor for a very long time. The mine shaft represents a hazard both to humans and to animals and it is fenced and the fence is maintained by the gait holders. The boundary fence of the moor has been renewed on many occasions and is maintained by the gait holders. The fence of that section of boundary with the Swinton estate was last renewed in 1973 the materials being supplied by the Swinton estate and the erection undertaken by the gait holders. The boundary between West Scrafton moor and East Scrafton moor which is owned by the Chaytor estate requires renewal and is at the present time subject to negotiation. It is apparent, therefore, that the inhabitants of West Scrafton have not only accepted the responsibilities of owners but have exercised the rights of owners for a very considerable period of time.

According to War Agricultural records West Scrafton moor was a gated pasture administered by a moor committee. There is no moor committee at the present time but it is proposed to set up a moor committee at the next Parish Meeting.

I produce a survey of 1843 which was undertaken on behalf of the village's Commissioners for the Poor, and minutes of the Village Meeting, extracts of which prove the steps which have been taken over the years to fence and maintain the moor. I submit that these records prove the assumption by the village of rights of ownership and acceptance of responsibility.

Apart from the fact that the moor is an essential ingredient to the life of the village in that it provides grazing for animals essential for the livelihood of local farmers, there are two other important reasons why ownership of the moor should be vested in the village. The first is to prevent conflict of interests which has recently occurred when the owner of the shooting rights deep ploughed part of the moor with a view to improving the growth of heather and the increase in the population of grouse. This is in conflict with the interests of the farmers who need improvement in grazing rather than heather. The second is the need to control the use of the moor by outside interests. There is a growing tendency for visitors to enjoy the amenities of the countryside and whilst no one wants to limit their enjoyment that enjoyment has to be tailored to the needs of the local community. It is important that dogs on the moor should always be under control, that such sports as motor cycling motocross and similar pastimes should not be allowed to become unrestricted to the detriment of the grazing and sheep farming interests of the local community. Rights of way across the moor will, of course, be preserved by the village if they are awarded ownership of the land. However, if they are not awarded ownership of the land the control of undesirable activities will be made very much more difficult. It is the intention of the village meeting if ownership of West Scrafton moor is awarded to the village to appoint trustees as provided for in the Local Government Acts, namely the Chief Executive of the Richmondshire District Council and the chairman of the Village Meeting.

Chapel Records

Methodism came to West Scrafton during the time of the Wesley brothers, John and Charles, in the latter part of the 18th century. Meetings were originally held in either the Moorhen Inn or in one of the member's homes. The Wesleyan Society grew and in 1866 two chapels were built in the village, a Wesleyan

The Present Methodist Chapel

chapel in Poverty Street and a Primitive Methodist chapel by the bridge. They were needed because it was some distance to travel from West Scrafton to either Horsehouse or Coverham, and Methodism was strong in the village as it had been a mining area and non-conformity seems to have been linked with such an industry.

There was a family called Swales in the village and one of their children was the Reverend William Swales who left but who used to come back every year to organise a Christian Camp at West Scrafton. This was a notable dales event and, in addition to the preaching of the Reverend Swales, there would be boiled ham and other things to eat.

The old Wesleyan chapel has not been used as a place of worship for a considerable length of time. It was originally closed in 1930 when the union of the two branches of Methodism took place and the local society chose to use the Primitive chapel because the "feel" was good, even though the site and building were not considered as accommodating as the Wesleyan chapel. The Primitive chapel is still in use, but the Wesleyan building was eventually sold for £300 in 1966 to the 15th Airedale troop of

Boy Scouts from Yeadon near Leeds. The conveyancing documents were signed by some twenty villagers including Messrs Hogg, Dent and Robinson. Some time later it was sold again and has more recently been converted into a holiday home.

However, the remaining Primitive Methodist chapel is still going strong and in fact it celebrated its centenary in 1966, the same year in which the Wesleyan chapel was sold. During the 1998 anniversary meeting, some old documents

The Old Wesleyan Chapel

were discovered which gave a few additional clues as to the history of the building. From these documents it was gleaned that the building originally cost £300 to build and that half of this money was donated by a certain Mrs Hogg who apparently lived at Bridge End. This lady is said to have made money by rearing male chickens, dressing them and then taking them on foot to Middleham where she used to sell them. It must have been quite a remunerative venture to have been able to afford such a donation!

Not a single christening had been held in the chapel until 1947, but since then there have been fifteen up until 1998. Those who have been christened there are Alan Dent, the twins Sheena and Linda Handley, Freda Handley, William Utley, Kevin Utley, Caroline Utley, Christopher Utley, Peter Bainbridge, Janet Bainbridge, Robbie Phillips, Daniel Croft, Emily Watson, Kim Utley, George Utley and Nathan Suttill. The reason that the chapel had not been used for christening before 1947 was that it had been the local village custom for the children to be christened in their own homes.

In 1994, a survey showed that the building needed a considerable amount of maintenance work done on it, so in the following three years the members set about raising funds for its renovation. The work was completed in 1998 at a cost of £10,538 and included waterproof-rendering, insulating and dry-lining one external wall, pointing all the others, complete re-roofing, rewiring and adding niceties such as a new pine storage bench and making the pulpit movable. These renovations were carried out by John Watson and Paul French and were partly paid for by a grant of £2,000 from a Methodist millennium scheme known as Vision 2000. The not inconsiderable remaining amount was raised by gifts, donations including various embroidered items, two sponsored walks, a "sponsor a slate" scheme for the roof, a performance by the East Layton Singers (an old-time music hall troupe), a table-top sale, a Christmas Nativity event and a concert held in Leyburn. In addition, some money was withdrawn from the West Scrafton chapel's building society account.

Chapel cleaners with Joe Bell in the 1930s

A re-opening celebration was held in the June of that year. The sponsored walks, one in 1995 and the second in 1997, in particular proved to be very successful fund raisers and there may well be another in the new millennium to help pay for further finishing touches such as pew cushions.

During this time, two of the Chapel's faithful members, Tommy and Mary Dent, died and are greatly missed. Mary Dent was very good at remembering all that needed to be done and doing a great deal of it herself.

At the present time four special services are held each year; these are on Good Friday and the chapel anniversary, and also there are the Harvest Festival and the Candlelight Carol services, the latter being held in aid of a local charity. Normal services are held each week on Sunday mornings at 10.30am with the attendance ranging from anything between four and thirty people. On one Sunday in each month a family service is held and up to ten young people with ages ranging from 2 to 17 can take part in the worship and activities.

In the millennium year the Good Friday service was held on April 2nd at 7.30pm. There was a full house and the chapel funds were augmented by the sum of £128 which was taken at the collection. The Gunnerside Choir took the service which was thoroughly enjoyed by all, as indeed was the supper served at the close of the event.

On June 13th two chapel anniversary services were held at 10.30am and 6.30pm. The morning service, which was attended by 28 people, was conducted by Ruth and John Dent from Barnard Castle. The East Witton Male Voice Choir conducted by Mrs Taylor from Preston-under-Scar gave a concert of sacred music in the evening. It was deemed to be an excellent performance and the chapel was two-thirds full. Tea, biscuits and scones were served to round off a very pleasant evening.

The Harvest Festival was held on Sunday October 3rd at 2.30pm. Angela Foster from Quernhow took the family service in which children from the village took part. They also took the traditional gifts of fruit and vegetables. The Festival was continued on the Tuesday night when the Uredales took the service with songs and readings. A supper was served and the evening ended with a sale of produce.

The villagers again filled the chapel for the Candlelight Carol service, together with many people from surrounding places. The chapel was decorated with holly and candles which when lit produced a very suitable atmosphere. There were twelve people reading the nine lessons and there were also poems, duets and various musical instruments to help make it an occasion to be remembered. Alf Suttill, who had taken the Candlelight service for many years, was unfortunately indisposed and so Joy French and June Utley stepped into the breach. Tea and mince pies ended a really friendly evening and the collection amounted to £130, of which £30 went towards the newly formed SALT club for children and £100 was donated to the local fund for breast cancer. The SALT (Sharing And Learning Together) club was started in

November 1999 with between eight and twelve children. They join in games, activities and Bible stories under the leadership of Susan Pearson from Caldbergh and Joy French. New Year's Eve saw another service led by Joy and Paul French, and a number of the people attending went on to the millennium party that was being held in the Thomas's barn.

To finish with an anecdote from the past, it is a local story that in 1823 West Scrafton was included in the Middleham Primitive Methodist Circuit; then, after the new Wesleyan society came on to the scene, the two chapels were subsequently built, and it was arranged that the services would never be held at the same time. The story that was reported in order to show the kind of opposition that the new sect had had to encounter, relates that years before the chapels were built a Nicholas Manners was preaching in a hired room over one of the two public houses in the village and the hymn "Vain delusive world, Adieu" was being sung when the floor gave way and the congregation was precipitated into the ale casks below. It was later discovered that one of the supporting beams had been sawn almost in two by a member of the "opposition". It was apparently very many years before the Methodists ventured to set foot in West Scrafton again.

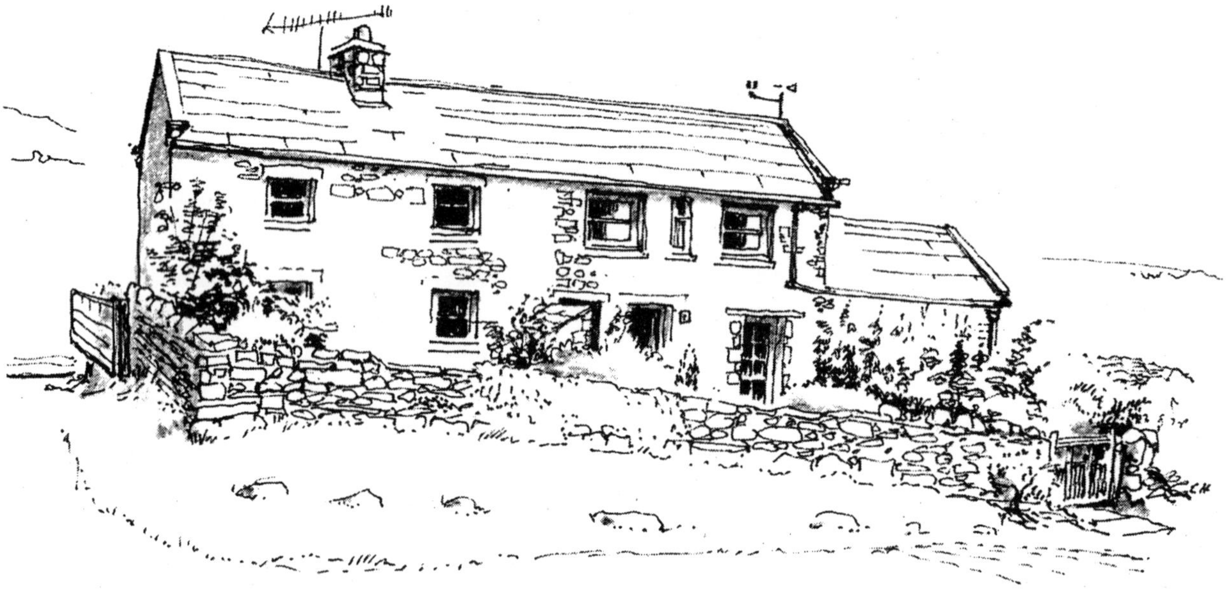

Weather Records of 1999

The weather records for West Scrafton are carried out at Lane Farm House on the West Scrafton to Caldbergh road where Joy French has a number of instruments recording many of the aspects of the weather. This weather station, which is depicted in fig 24, is situated at latitude 54°15′, longitude 1°52′ and altitude 225 metres and comprises the instruments which are described below.

Rain Gauge. This is a 5" diameter gauge of a meteorological office pattern, the rim of which stands 12" above ground level in order to avoid any splash-back during heavy rain.

Tapered Glass Measure. This is again of meteorological office pattern and is calibrated in millimetres for use with the above rain gauge.

Hygrometer. This measures the humidity from 0% to 100% and is a hair type instrument with a 4" dial (real hair!).

Barometer. This is 4" diameter aneroid instrument which measures atmospheric pressure in millibars.

Maximum and Minimum Thermometers. These are both of a meteorological office pattern for use within the Stevenson screen. The maximum one has a range from -20°C to +55°C and the minimum one extends from -35°C to +45°C.

Grass Thermometer. This is an ordinary maximum/minimum thermometer laid permanently on the grass.

Anemometer. This instrument measures the wind speed and direction and is mounted on a pole above the apex of the roof. Joy was put in touch with a lady from Swaledale who was looking for a good home for her father's anemometer which had been lying in her garden for several years. Her father had been employed by Munro Instruments in London from his youth and was involved in manufacturing precision instruments of all descriptions for both ministry and civilian use. This particular anemometer is identical to the one that was used on the meteorological office roof until it was superseded by more recent technology. After retrieving it, Joy's husband, Paul, repaired and serviced it and mounted it on its roof pole where it does an excellent job creating much interest and excitement, especially during gales! The maximum gust it has so far recorded was 93mph on Boxing Day 1998.

The weather station is pictured in fig 24.

The following tables show the various weather parameters measured on a month by month basis during 1999.

Barometric Pressure

Month	Highest	Lowest	Average
January	1033mb (31st)	991mb (2nd)	1008.0mb
February	1034mb (2nd)	1000mb (21st)	1008.0mb
March	1024mb (17th)	986mb (3rd)	1009.0mb
April	1036mb (28th)	984mb (21st)	1009.3mb
May	1022mb (31st)	1006mb (21st)	1013.7mb
June	1025mb (11th)	1000mb (27th)	1015.1mb
July	1028mb (8th)	1003mb (20th)	1016mb
August	1024mb (21st)	999mb (18th)	1012mb
September	1025mb (9th)	986mb (20th)	1004mb
October	1027mb (12th)	991mb (23rd)	1013.2mb
November	1042mb (11th)	998mb (5th)	1017mb
December	1022mb (20th)	975mb (25th)	1000.5mb

Humidity

Month	Highest	Lowest	Average
January	88% (5th)	57% (4th)	74.1%
February	91% (13th)	53% (16th)	69.2%
March	100% (10th)	52% (22nd)	81.3%
April	100% (27th)	56% (14th)	88.4%
May	100% (4th)	52% (20th)	80.3%
June	96% (7th)	43% (22nd)	71.0%
July	93% (18th)	50% (25th)	74.8%
August	97% (25th)	51.5% (21st)	78.5%
September	98% (27th)	47% (5th)	93.2%
October	99% (24th)	67% 911th)	86.4%
November	100% (12th)	58.5% (26th)	83.5%
December	100% (11th)	58.5% (24th)	81%

Maximum Temperature

Month	Highest	Lowest	Average
January	11.5°C (20th)	2.5°C (12th)	5.98°C
February	9.5°C (18th)	0.5°C (9th)	6.2°C
March	13.0°C (31st)	2.5°C (9th)	8.0°C
April	18.8°C (29th)	2.6°C (16th)	11.2°C
May	19°C (3rd)	11°C (21st)	13.9°C
June	20°C (15th)	11.4°C (2nd)	16.0°C
July	25.2°C (31st)	12.3°C (21st)	19.5°C
August	28°C (2nd)	12°C (9th)	18.1°C
September	25.8°C (5th)	14.3°C (30th)	18.1°C
October	15.9°C (10th)	8.2°C (20th)	12.1°C
November	13.1°C (26th)	5.4°C (17th)	9.6°C
December	11°C (3rd)	0.6°C (19th)	6.0°C

Minimum Temperature

Month	Highest	Lowest	Average
January	6.5°C (20th)	-2.0°C (14th)	2.08°C
February	8.5°C (4th)	-3.0°C (8th)	2.1°C
March	7.7°C (30th)	-1.5°C (28th)	3.8°C
April	10.2°C (6th)	-2.5°C (15th)	4.0°C
May	11°C (24th)	3.5°C (15th)	7.9°C
June	14.4°C (19th)	6.3°C (22nd)	9.4°C
July	18.1°C (8th)	6.5°C (30th)	11.8°C
August	15.5°C (5th)	1.8°C (22nd)	10.4°C
September	16.1°C (2nd)	5.1°C (14th)	10.1°C
October	13.2°C (10th)	-1.8°C (5th)	5.7°C
November	9.3°C (4th)	-3°C (21st)	4.2°C
December	5.8°C (1st)	-7.1°C (20th)	0.8°C

Wind Direction and Force   (Beaufort scale)

January

Prevailing winds: Westerlies.
SW: 12 days.   W: 8 days.   NW: 3 days.   E: 1 day.   S: 1 day.   Calm: 6 days.
Wind force: Highest 9am: force 5 (4th 12th 15th).   Highest 9pm: force 6 (14th 24th).
Lowest 9am: calm (10th 11th 21st 29th 30th 31st).   Lowest 9pm: calm (10th to 29th 30th 31st).
Average 9am: force 2.06.   Average 9pm: force 2.45.
Combined average: force 2.2 (5mph).
Gusts to force 8 (40mph) on 4th 5th 13th 19th 24th 25th.
Gusts to force 9 (50mph) on 14th 15th 18th.
High winds on 9 days - all westerlies.

February

Prevailing winds: Westerlies.
SW: 2 days.   W: 18 days.   NW: 5 days.   E: 1 day.   Calm: 2 days.
Wind force: Highest 9am: force 7 (4th).   Highest 9pm: force 7 (3rd 4th).
Lowest 9am: calm (8th 13th).   Lowest 9pm: calm (10th 12th 17th 23rd).
Average 9am: force 2.7.   Average 9pm: force 2.7.
Combined average: force 2.7.
Gusts to force 8 (40mph) on 16th 21st.
Gusts to force 9 (50mph) on 15th 20th.
Gusts to force 10 (60mph) on 3rd 4th 20th.
Winds of force 5 or over on 9 days.   Highest gust of force 12 (80mph) on 3rd/4th.

March

Prevailing winds: Westerlies.
SW: 7 days.   W: 8 days.   NW: 5 days.   N: 3 days.   E: 3 days.   S: 2 days.
Wind force: Highest 9am: force 4 (19th).   Highest 9pm: force 5 (2nd 28th).
Lowest 9am: calm (10th 17th 25th).   Lowest 9pm: calm (12th 13th 14th 24th 25th 27th 30th).
Average 9am: force 2.1.   Average 9pm: force 1.7.
Combined average: force 1.9.
No gusts above 35mph.

April

Prevailing winds: Westerlies.
SW: 2 days.   W: 5 days.   NW: 4 days.   N: 1 day.   E: 6 days.   S: 2 days.
Wind force: Highest 9am: force 5 (6th).   Highest 9pm: force 4 (21st 22nd).
Lowest 9 am: calm (1st 2nd 3rd 4th 14th 19th 18th 19th 24th 28th).
Lowest 9pm: calm (1st 2nd 3rd 8th 15th 17th).
Average 9am: force 1.6.   Average 9pm: force 1.6.
Combined average: force 1.6.
Winds below 20mph all month apart from 6th when gusts reached force 6.

May

Prevailing winds: Westerlies.
SW: 7 days.   W: 7 days.   N: 1 day.   NE: 5 days.   E: 5 days.   SE: 2 days.   S: 1 day.
Wind force: Highest 9am: force 4 (18th 22rd 25th).   Highest 9pm: force 4 (28th).
Lowest 9am: calm (6th 20th 31st).   Lowest 9pm: calm (26th 27th 31st).
Average 9am: force 1.6.   Average 9pm: force 1.6.
Combined average: force 1.6.
Winds reached force 4 or 5 on 9 consecutive days (18th - 26th) and were blowing most of each day.

June

Prevailing winds: Westerlies.
SW: 9 days.   W: 10 days.   NW: 3 days.   N: 1 day.   NE: 4 days.   E: 1 day.   SE: 1 day.
S: 1 day.   Calm: 1 day.
Wind force: Highest 9am: force 3 (8th).   Highest 9pm: force 4 (15th).
Lowest 9am: calm (10th).   Lowest 9pm: calm (10th 11th 14th 24th).
Average 9am: force 1.26.   Average 9pm: force 1.3.
Combined average: force 1.3.
Highest wind was up to force 5 (18th).

July

Prervailing winds: Westerlies.
SW: 2 days.   W: 11 days.   NW: 2 days.   N: 2 days.   NE: 8 days.   E: 2 days.   SE: 1 day.
Calm: 3 days.
Wind force: Highest 9am: force 3 (17th 21st).   Highest 9pm: force 5 (21st).
Lowest 9pm: calm (1st 2nd 30th).   Lowest 9pm: calm (1st 2nd 4th 5th 15th 22nd 26th).
Average 9am: force 1.6.   Average 9pm: force 1.09.
Combined average: force 1.13.
Winds up to force 5 during 15th 17th 20th 21st 24th.
Highest gust: force 7 (17th).   On 22 days only force 1 was recorded, on 8 of which recording was only just possible.

August.

Prevailing Winds: Easterlies.
N: 5 days.   NE: 10 days.   E: 2 days.   S: 1 day.   SW: 6 days.   W: 3 days.   NW: 1 day.
Calm: 3 days.
Wind force: Highest 9am: force 2 on 13 days.   Highest 9pm: force 2 on 9 days.
Lowest 9am: calm (3rd 4th 6th).   Lowest 9pm: calm (3rd 21st 25th).
Average 9am: force 1.3   Average 9pm: force 1.2.
Combined average: force 1.25.
Highest gust: 24mph (9th).   For the first 9 days the winds were predominantly NE; also NE from 17th to 25th.

September

Prevailing Winds: Westerlies. (Records only available from 15th to 30th)
SW: 5 days.   W: 2 days.   NW: 1 day.   NE: 2 days.   SE: 4 days.   Calm: 2 days.
Wind force: Highest 9am: force 3 (18th 19th).   Highest 9pm: force 3 (18th 19th).
Lowest 9am: calm (22nd 26th).   Lowest 9pm: calm (21st 22nd 23rd 26th 29th).
Average 9am: force 1.1.   Average 9pm: force 1.3.
Combined average: force 1.2.
Highest gust: force 7 (35mph) (8th).   In whole month 9 days calm and very light winds often rising in afternoon (data from Carlton records).

October

Prevailing Winds: Westerlies.
SW: 4 days.   W: 8 days.   NW: 2 days.   NE: 3 days.   E: 3 days.   SE: 2 days.   S: 2 days.
Calm: 7 days.
Wind force: Highest 9am: force 6 (31st).   Highest 9pm: force 4 (27th 30th 31st)
Lowest 9am: calm (7 days).   Lowest 9pm: calm (29th).
Average 9am: force 1.5.   Average 9pm: force 1.7.
Combined average: force 1.6
Easterlies were between 14th and 24th.
During 30th many gusts to force 7 and one to force 8, but 17 quiet days of calm or force 1.

November

Prevailing Winds: Westerlies.
N: 2 days.   NE: 4 days.   S: 2 days.   SW: 7 days.   W: 5 days.   NW: 4 days.
Calm: 6 days.
Wind force: Highest 9am: force 7 (28th).   Highest 9pm: force 6 (27th 28th 30th).
Lowest 9am: calm (6 days).   Lowest 9pm: calm (4 days).
Average 9am: force 2.   Average 9pm: force 1.9.
Combined average: force 2.
Gusts up to force 8 on 30th.
Gusts to force 9 on 28th and to force 10 on 30th, but calm or only force 1 on 18 days.

December

Prevailing Winds: Westerlies.
N: 2 days.   SW: 6 days.   W: 16 days.   NW: 4 days.   Calm: 3 days.
Wind force: Highest 9am: force 10 (3rd).   Highest 9pm: force 7 (23rd).
Lowest 9am: calm (11th 18th 20th).   Lowest 9pm: calm (6 days).
Average 9am: force 2.4.   Average 9pm: force 1.9.
Combined average: force 2.2.
Gusts to 80mph during night of 2nd.
Gusts above force 7 on 9 days.

Cloud Amounts (measured in Oktas at 9am)

January
Highest: 8 oktas on 9 days.   Lowest: 1 okta on 4 days.   Average: 5.54 oktas.

February
Highest: 8 oktas on 6 days.   Lowest: 1 okta on 2 days.   Average: 5.6 oktas.

March
Highest: 8 oktas on 17 days.   Lowest: 1 okta on 1 day.   Average: 6.3 oktas.
Note: From 1st to 9th, 6 days were sunless; there were only 3½ hours sun in the 9 days.

April
Highest: 8 oktas on 13 days.   Lowest: 1 okta on 4 days.   Average: 5.9 oktas.
Note: Fog recorded 9 otkas on 1 day (as sky and cloud are not visible).

May
Highest: 8 oktas on 11 days.   Lowest: 0 oktas on 1 day (20th).   Average: 6.0 oktas.

June
Highest: 8 oktas on 12 days.   Lowest: 0 oktas on 1 day (25th).   Average: 5.96 oktas.

July
Highest: 8 oktas on 10 days.   Lowest: 0 oktas on 1 day (31st).   Average: 5.8 oktas.
Note: Fog recorded 9 oktas on 1 day (3rd).

August
Highest: 8 oktas on 9 days.   Lowest: 1 okta on 1 day (2nd).   Average: 6.4 oktas.
Note: 9 oktas (fog) on 3 days. It was 1 okta cloudier than average for August.

September
Highest: 8 oktas on 7 days.   Lowest: 1 okta on 5 days.   Average: 5.2 oktas.
Note: 9 oktas (fog) on 2 days (22nd 29th). Least cloudy month so far this year.

October
Highest: 8 oktas on 10 days.   Lowest: 1 okta on 4 days (2nd 4th 5th 29th).
Average: 5.8 oktas.
Note: 9 oktas (fog) on 2 days.

November
Highest: 8 oktas on 13 days.   Lowest: 1 okta (6th 20th).   Average: 5.9 oktas.
Note: 9 otkas (fog) on 2 days (12th 14th).

December
Highest: 8 oktas on 10 days.   Lowest: 1 okta on 4 days.   Average: 5.3 oktas.

Rainfall

January

Highest daily reading: 34.0mm in 20 hrs (15th).   Lowest daily reading: Nil on 1 day (22nd).
Average per day: 6.5mm.   Total for month: 201.9mm.

February

Highest daily reading: 18.5mm (28th).   Lowest daily reading: Nil on 10 days.
Wet days (over 0.1mm): 11.   Trace of rain: 7 days.   Total for month: 42mm.

March

Highest daily reading: 26.6mm (2nd).   Lowest daily reading: Nil on 8 days.
Wet days (over 0.1mm): 22.   Trace of rain: 1 day.   Total for month: 89.2mm.
Note: 64.5mm fell in first 9 days.

April

Highest daily reading: 20.9mm (20th).   Lowest daily reading: Nil on 10 days.
Wet days (over 0.1mm): 19.   Trace of rain: 1 day.   Total for month: 52.9mm.

May

Highest daily reading: 16.0mm (7th).   Lowest daily reading: Nil on 14 days.
Wet days (over 0.1mm): 16.   Trace of rain: 1 day.   Total for month: 61.3mm.

June

Highest daily reading: 34.0mm (7th).   Lowest daily reading: Nil on 11 days.
Very wet days (over 1mm): 10 days.   Wet days (over 0.1mm): 2 days.
Trace of rain: 7 days.   Total for month: 105.3mm.

July

Highest daily reading: 5.6mm (2nd).   Lowest daily reading: Nil on 19 days.
Very wet days (over 1mm): 4 days.   Wet days (over 0.1mm): 5 days.
Trace of rain: 3 days.   Total for month: 14.9mm.

August

Highest daily reading: 12.1mm (9th).   Lowest daily reading: Nil on 10 days.
Very wet days (over 1 mm): 12 days.   Wet days (over 0.1mm): 2 days.
Trace of rain: 7 days.   Total for month: 59.2mm.
Note:- 20mm less than average for August; other parts of country had wettest August for years.

September

Highest daily reading: 32.5mm (19th).   Lowest daily reading: Nil on 12 days.
Very wet days (over 1 mm): 16 days (13 in second half of month).
Trace of rain: 2 days.   Total for month: 108.1mm.
Note: 30mm more than September average.

October

Highest daily reading: 35mm (1st).　　Lowest daily reading: Nil on 11 days.
Very wet days (over 1mm): 10 days.　　Wet days (over 0.1mm): 5 days.
Trace of rain: 5 days.　　Total for month: 104.1mm.

November

Highest daily reading: 15.1mm (5th).　　Lowest daily reading: Nil on 7 days.
Very wet days (over 1mm): 16 days.　　Wet days (over 0.1mm): 4 days.
Trace of rain: 3 days.　　Total for month: 68.2mm.

December

Highest daily reading: 44.8mm (2nd).　　Lowest daily reading: Nil on 5 days.
Very wet days (over 1mm): 21 days.　　Wet days (over 0.1mm): 2 days.
Trace of rain: 3 days.　　Total for month: 248.8mm.

Sunshine

January　　No record taken.

February　　Most in a day: 6.31 hours (7th 8th 9th 22nd).　　Sunless days: 2 (5th 25th).
Total for month: 67 hours.

March　　Most in a day: 11 hours (17th).　　Sunless days: 7.
Total for month: 86 hours.

April　　Most in a day: 11.5 hours (28th).　　Sunless days: 3 (16th 20th 26th).
Total for month: 105.5 hours.

May　　Total for month (approx.): 147.25 hours.

June　　Most in a day: 12.25 hours (1st).　　Sunless days: 4.
Total for month (approx.): 153.25 hours.

July　　Most in a day: 12.5 hours (31st).　　Sunless days: 1.
Total for month: 209.75 hours.

August　　Most in a day: 10.75 hours (2nd).　　Sunless days: 6.
Total for month: 123.75 hours.　　(Approx. record).

September　　Most in a day: 12 hours (5th).　　Sunless days: 3.
Total for month: 160 hours.　　(Approx. record).

October　　Most in a day: 10.5 hours (5th).　　Sunless days: 6.
Total for month: 84 hours.　　(Approx. record).

November　　Most in a day: 7.75 hours (6th).　　Sunless days: 10.
Total for month: 61 hours.

December　　Most in a day: 6.25 hours (19th).　　Sunless days: 9.
Total for month: 62 hours.

Notable Weather Phenomena

January
Snow on ground: 50mm (10th 11th 12th).   Snow laying on 18th.
Fog on 30th.   Rainbows on 3rd 13th 17th 20th 21st 25th 26th.

February
Snow fell on 8th 21st 23rd.   Snow laying on 21st 22nd 23rd 24th.
Fog on 13th.   Rainbows on 4th 21st.   Hail on 27th.

March
Snow fell on 5th 6th 9th 10th.   Snow laying on 6th.   Dense fog on 31st: early mist on 12th. Rainbows on 3rd 21st 29th.

April
Snow fell on 13th 14th 15th.   Fog on 3rd; early mist on 1st 2nd.

May
Thunder on 10th. Thunderstorm on night of 27/28th.

June
Thunder in afternoon of 2nd.   Storm during night of 26/27th (electricity failed).
Longest day (21st): lovely day, clear evening with sunset.
Midsummer's day (24th): beautiful, hot.

July
Fog and steamy mist persisted till midday on 3rd. Fog on morning of 30th. Thunder on 5th.

August
84% eclipse of the sun at 11.20am on 11th.
Fog on 4 days (4th 5th 13th 25th).   Thunder on 13th.

September
Thunder storms on 19th 20th 22nd.   Warmest September since Coverdale records began in 1977 and highest max. and min. readings.
Lowest pressure readings recorded for September.

October
Fog on 23rd clearing later.   Thick fog on 24th remaining all day.
Strong wind force 6 to 7 (30th 31st).

November
Fog on 12th (all day) and 14th.   Air frost on 3 days; ground frost on 8 days. Snowflakes on 18th.

December
Moon nearest to earth for 70 years.   Snow falling on 8 days.   Lying snow on 16 days. Hail on 4 days. Fog on 1 day.
Flooding of River Cover on 2nd.

Summary of Monthly Parameters

Month	Barometric Pressure	Average Humidity	Average Max. Temp.	Average Min. Temp.	Average Wind Force	Average Cloud	Total Rainfall	Total Sunshine
January	1008.0mb	74.1%	5.98°C	2.08°C	2 (4 - 7mph)	2.5 oktas	201.9mm	N/A
February	1015.0mb	69.2%	6.2°C	2.1°C	2.7	5.6 oktas	42.0mm	67 hours
March	1009.0mb	81.3%	8.0°C	3.8°C	2.1	6.3 oktas	89.2mm	86 hours
April	1009.3mb	88.4%	11.2°C	4.0°C	1.6	5.9 oktas	52.9mm	105.5 hours
May	1013.7mb	80.3%	13.9°C	7.9°C	1.6	6.0 oktas	61.3mm	147.25 hours
June	1015.1mb	71.0%	16.0°C	9.4°C	1.3	6.0 oktas	105.3mm	153.25 hours
July	1016.5mb	74.8%	19.5°C	11.8°C	1.2	5.8 oktas	14.9mm	209.75 hours
August	1012.0mb	78.5%	18.1°C	10.4°C	1.25	6.4 oktas	59.2mm	123.75 hours
September	1004.0mb	93.2%	18.1°C	10.1°C	1.2	5.2 oktas	108.1mm	160 hours
October	1013.2mb	86.4%	12.1°C	5.7°C	1.7	5.8 oktas	104.1mm	84 hours
November	1017.8mb	83.5%	9.6°C	4.2°C	1.95	5.9 oktas	68.2mm	61 hours
December	1000.5mb	81%	6.0°C	0.8°C	2.2	5.3 oktas	248.8mm	62 Hours
Year's Values	1011.2mb	80.1%	11.5°C	6.0°C	1.7	5.8 oktas	1155.9mm	1308.5 hours

It is interesting to compare the above values with the same parameters averaged over the last twenty years in Carlton on the other side of the dale but only ¾ mile away as the crow flies (or the weather blows). This shows either that the weather in 1999 was somewhat different from the average of the last twenty years or that Carlton experiences weather that is not quite the same as that in West Scrafton.

Here are the same two tables showing the twenty year Carlton values.

Month	Barometric Pressure	Average Humidity	Average Max. Temp.	Average Min. Temp.	Average Wind Force	Average Cloud	Total Rainfall	Total Sunshine
January	1011.0mb	87.5%	4.6°C	-0.2°C	2.8	5.9 oktas	133.7mm	31.48 hours
February	1012.0mb	87.4%	4.9°C	0.0°C	2.8	6.1 oktas	104.6mm	56.53 hours
March	1010.0mb	85.3%	7.5°C	1.4°C	2.8	5.9 oktas	108.3mm	88.35 hours
April	1013.5mb	86.9%	9.9°C	2.4°C	2.3	5.6 oktas	75.4mm	92.83 hours
May	1015.0mb	84.1%	13.6°C	4.8°C	2.1	5.3 oktas	68.0mm	114.26 hours
June	1015.0mb	83.1%	16.4°C	7.6°C	2.2	5.6 oktas	70.6mm	117.91 hours
July	1016.0mb	81.7%	19.0°C	9.9°C	2.2	5.5 oktas	49.8mm	137.87 hours
August	1015.0mb	83.7%	18.3°C	9.9°C	2.2	5.4 oktas	81.0mm	133.61 hours
September	1014.5mb	86.0%	15.5°C	7.9°C	2.6	5.4 oktas	76.7mm	90.70 hours
October	1010.5mb	86.9%	11.9°C	5.5°C	2.6	5.7 oktas	106.3mm	85.10 hours
November	1011.5mb	88.2%	7.8°C	2.6°C	2.8	5.8 oktas	108.1mm	48.83 hours
December	1009.5mb	87.2%	5.4°C	0.8°C	2.9	6.0 oktas	140.7mm	33.91 hours
Total Values	1012.8mb	85.7%	11.2°C	4.8°C	2.5	5.2 oktas	1125.2mm	1031.8 hours

Note: The sunshine figures are averaged only between 1993 and 1998.

Three of these parameters, those of minimum temperature, maximum temperature and rainfall are shown below in the form of graphs where it can be seen that the year's averages are not all that different from past history. The rainfall is rather more erratic and the temperatures seem to be between 1°C and 2°C higher than in the past.

In all three graphs the dotted line represents the 20-year average and the solid line is the 1999 West Scrafton reading.

Minimum Temperatures

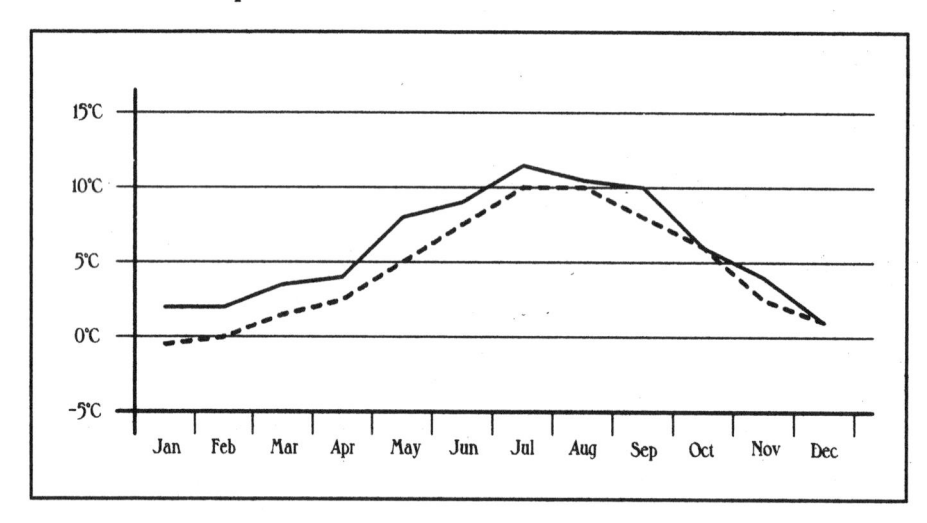

Maximum Temperatures

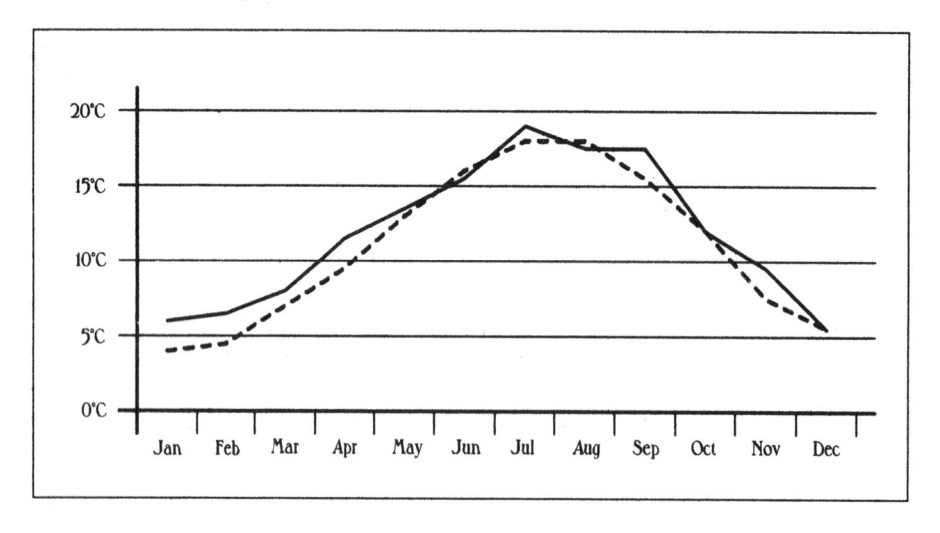

Rainfall

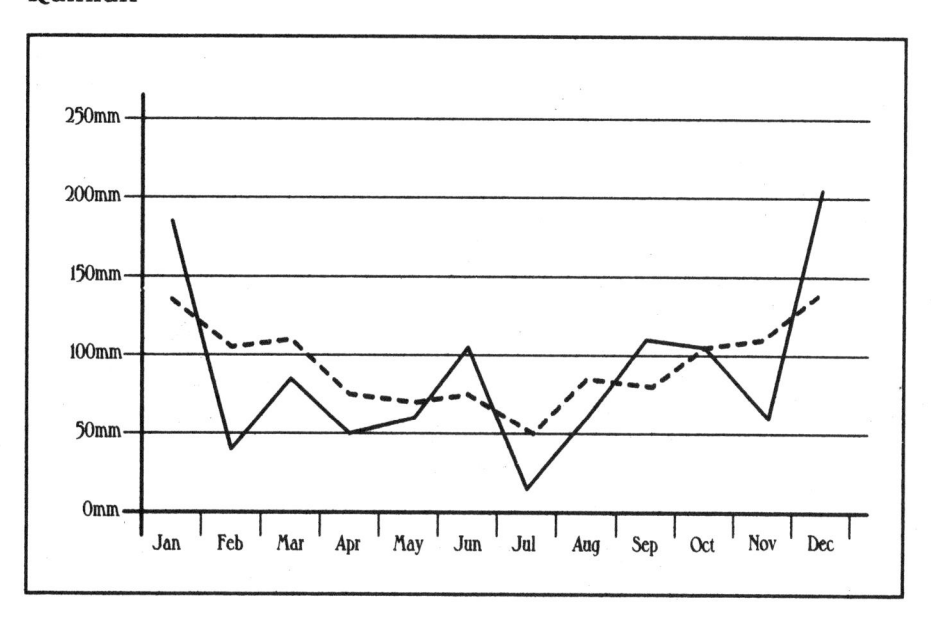

Three Winter's Tales

The winter of 1979 is reputed to have been the worst winter around these parts within living memory; West Scrafton was isolated by snow nine times.

It started just after the New Year on January 2nd when there were very keen frosts with the temperature staying a long way below zero even during the daytime, causing many of the houses to be without water as the pipes were frozen solid. Culverham Farm was frozen up for five weeks and there was only one tap running on the farm. In order to get water to the cattle and the farmhouse, a hundred metre length of alkathene pipe was connected to the tap, but at one stage it was so cold that the water that was running through the pipe froze and the whole length had to be coiled up and taken into the farmhouse kitchen where it was left overnight to thaw out.

As though the intense cold was not enough, there were dreadful blizzards at that time which brought the overhead electricity lines down and the village was without any power for thirty-one hours at a spell.

The bad weather continued and February 15th was recorded as the worst day in living memory. The blizzard was so strong that it was not safe to be out in the open. Quarry Lane was completely blocked by snow for ten days and even the postman could not get through for over a week. Farmers had to transport milk to the local dairy at Coverham in churns on their tractors and they brought back the mail and some provisions on their return journeys.

It snowed heavily again on March 16th and once more West Scrafton was isolated from the outside world, this time for another six days. Even in April there were further snowfalls and snow could still be seen on the fells at the end of May.

Living in a place like West Scrafton, perhaps we can be forgiven for seeing the positive side of any global warming that might be taking place.

* * * * *

David and Felicity Thomas were returning early from Beverley, where they had stayed with friends for the weekend, because snow had started to fall at around three o'clock. Having negotiated York and eventually come through East Witton to Coverham, they made slow progress up the hill to home. Just beyond Nick Southgate's house they found the Sahara-type drifts too much to take and they ground to a halt. David backed down to Mick's house and parked in his drive. He went to the front door where a pair of recently used Wellington boots was dripping in the porch. Through the window he saw that Mick had his stockinged feet to the roaring fire and was a reclining position.

David knocked tentatively on the door and Mick came and instantly realised their predicament. They tried a tow, but this failed. Mick eventually said that he would take the Thomases home in the Land Rover together with their luggage. This he did with the Land Rover in low gear all the way. David went down to see him when the weather permitted and offered him a bottle of whisky which he at first declined, but eventually accepted with the words "I hope you get stuck again and again"!

Incidentally, Ruth Burgess also got stuck, but below Mick's house. She, being a game girl, walked back with the dogs. This is the last time that David can recall snow of this amount in this area, as West Scrafton seems to keep pretty clear up here. They have only been snowed in that once in the five years since they have been here.

* * * * *

Bobby Hogg and Charles Utley in reminiscent mood fell to comparing this mild January with their childhood memories of the dramatic winter of 1947 when the whole country was still recovering from its war wounds with food and fuel still rationed and disaffected miners railing against their new employer, the Coal Board, which had been set up on the first day of the year.

In the middle of the month temperatures fell and it began to snow; on 29th January the temperature fell to minus 16°F and the whole country froze to a standstill. The weather was not to improve until the middle of March. West Scrafton was soon cut off from normal access and Les Brown's father, who owned the only lorry in the area, positioned it down at Coverham where the chances of getting to and from civilisation were somewhat better.

There were no other mechanical vehicles and any snow removal was by shovel alone. The sole wooden snow-plough owned by Ossie Utley was pulled by two horses and was quite unable to cope with the deep fall, and, with the lane being much narrower than it is today, the drifting was more marked making the clearing of the route progressively more difficult. Nevertheless, people did get in and out of the village, sometimes using a horse-drawn peat-hod as a snow-sledge as far as Caldbergh where the road was often reasonably clear, and sometimes on horseback or on foot. Bobby Hogg remembers as a 20-year-old being sent up the moor on his father's white pony to rescue five sheep stranded in waist deep snow and hefting them on to the pony to carry them back individually to the sheds. But amongst all the farmers' holdings, in those days about 8 in all, there were some severe losses and more than 50 sheep died in the cold.

But in some ways the people of West Scrafton may have coped more readily than others. The nation's power-cuts left them unmoved as there was no electricity to lose. Moreover, the horses could probably out-perform any mechanical vehicles in those conditions; there was a fair degree of self-sufficiency for food and fuel and a substantial body of strong manpower available which was largely inured to hardship and made light of it. Certainly the children did as the School in Carlton was closed.

On the other hand, half a century's passing may have blunted their memories of the harsher reality.

LOCAL AMENITIES

Past and Present

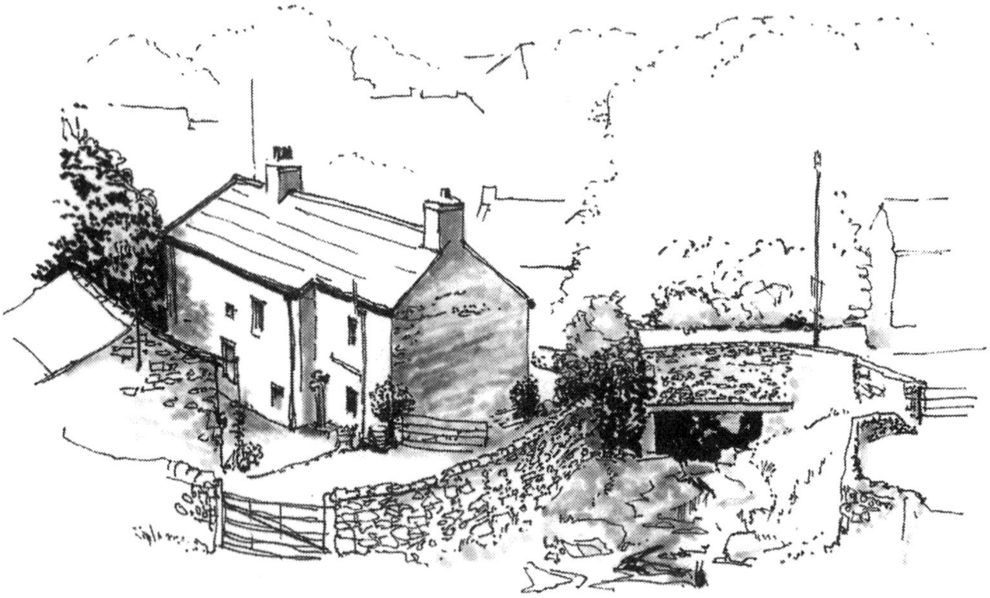

The Village Shop

A few decades ago, before the car became the normal mode of transport with which to fetch and carry provisions and other household goods, rural villages were of necessity self-sustaining. At one time West Scrafton boasted a couple of shops of its own, one of them being in the front room of the house now known as Moor Ghyll and currently occupied by Ian and Jenny Brotherton. The wife of the house was a lady going by the name of Mrs Ann Robinson and she ran the shop from the late 1800s right up to the 1950s, while her husband, who was the gamekeeper for the Coverham estates, went about his business. She was known affectionately as "Old Ma Rob".

Her establishment was one of the life supports for the village as she produced and sold all kinds of food, ranging from buns and cakes to meat and vegetables. Apart from selling the normal groceries, Mrs Robinson made bread for the village and would do special baking on request. Her stock also included cigarettes, paraffin and home-made hen mash, in fact all the necessities of village life. She was known for being good-natured and would provide a free bag of sweets on a Saturday to each customer household with children. She even provided midwifery and "laying-out" services.

At one end of her kitchen table she would be preparing fruit and flour and various other ingredients for making her buns, while at the other end there would be a newly caught rabbit being prepared for making her famous rabbit pies. There was, of course, no thought that this mix of foodstuffs might not be a very healthy way of doing things, but in those days people's immune systems were much more used to dealing with any infections that might have been transmitted by means that we nowadays would call unhygienic. Anyway, as far as history or memory can tell, no-one seemed to suffer from her "delicacies"; in fact, when she died in the 1960s, she herself was well over 90 years old. Imagine the convenience of having a shop in West Scrafton today!

During renovations at Moor Ghyll, one of her shop weights was found under the concrete floor where a 2oz weight had fallen between two flagstones. It was stamped with the dates of its 'Weights and Measures' inspections, the last one being 1954. To say that the shop was her living room was literally so, as it was the only room. There are recollections of a young customer finding Old Ma Rob taking a bath in front of the fire behind an oilcloth curtain. His purchases were made under instruction from behind the curtain!

"Old Ma Rob"

In those days the building consisted of a "two up, one down" cottage in the centre portion of what is now Moor Ghyll. There was a store at the eastern end and, at the western end, a barn with a hay loft above and a peat store and wagon shed below.

A History of the Water Supply

Until late in the nineteenth century, West Scrafton's household water, that essential element of modern living, came from a trough behind Cullen House into which flowed spring water off Goose Bank. Then, at the turn of the century, an agreement was made between the owner of West Scrafton Moor, Mrs Annie Agnes

The Water Tanks on the Moor

Wright of Coverham Abbey, and the people of the village for them to take water from springs on the moor for household use only. Although the countryside in these parts is mainly limestone, which is normally associated with hard water, the water from these springs is quite soft as the soil near the crags is of millstone grit. Four stand-pipes were erected in the village, two of which still exist, one by The Old Inn (see fig 24) and one by Lane End House; the one which was near the moor gate by Bow Bridge and the one opposite Culverham Farm have since been removed. A holding tank of 620 gallons capacity was sited on the moor at the top of the first bank through the gate to the moor by Bow Bridge. There were those, of course, that were of the opinion that the quality of the water from this new piped supply was inferior to that from the old spring! Town Head continued to use its own supply at that time which was located within its garth.

This situation continued for some time and normally the supply was reasonably satisfactory, but eventually one of the farmers broke ranks by using this village household water for farming purposes and then some of the others naturally followed suit. It followed that in periods of drought during dry summers there were repeated problems of insufficient supply; in particular the two farms at Town Head, which by now had decided to use the village supply, occasionally ran out of water completely. This caused friction between neighbours and families to such an extent that the two farmers insisted on having separate pipes from the village main to their respective premises.

After the first World War, Oswald Utley took responsibility for the village water supply and he took it upon himself to maintain the springs and the pipes. He was, in fact, a very skilled and efficient village water engineer, and the system remained as originally laid out in the early nineteen hundreds until well into the years after the Second World War.

In the late 1950s Manor House acquired a new owner, an Alderman Harry Watson who was an ex-mayor of Wakefield, and it was not long before he made his presence felt. He obtained the services of the craftsmen from the Wakefield based West Yorkshire Omnibus Company, of which he had been the ex-officio head, to help him to modernise and restore Manor House and within a short period of time he was elected as the clerk to the West Scrafton parish meeting.

The need for and the use of water increased dramatically in the sixties and seventies. For one thing, domestic water-using equipment became commonplace. Villagers acquired such items as washing machines and dishwashers which were duly installed in people's houses and the use of immersion heaters enabled more frequent baths and showers to be taken. The numbers of livestock on the farms also increased enormously, particularly dairy herds and sheep. All these things caused the existing system to become seriously deficient. There were several very dry summers in the early seventies, during which time the inadequacy of the supply became even more apparent, and the parish meeting decided that improvements were essential. Harry Watson was very much involved in the planning of the improvements and in the financial implications. At that time the contribution paid by the villagers for the distribution of the water was still only £3 per household per annum and nothing had been done to build up funds for improvements or emergencies.

In 1976 plans for a new 10,000 gallon holding tank on a much higher site on the moor were finally drawn up and put out to tender. It was hoped that the increased altitude and size of the tank would solve all the problems of lack of water at Town Head and would also mean that village water would reach Allaker and most of the field troughs up the Swineside road. The lowest tender was accepted but the cost could not be covered by the funds available in the Water Committee's account. An appeal was therefore made for loans and a number of residents made interest free loans to enable the tank to be built. The last of these loans was repaid to Mrs Neil in 1981. Harry Watson sold the Manor House and left the village in 1977 at the age of eighty. However, he left the maps of the water distribution system with his successor and they are still available.

The new 10,000 gallon holding tank was an enormous step forward in the village water supply, but in the ensuing years there were other unwanted developments, and new problems inevitably arose. The first of these was probably due to the construction of the tank itself. The acceptance of the lowest tender unfortunately meant that the work was not of a particularly high standard. The tank was built of concrete blocks with significant gaps between them and the only lining was a cement rendering which proved to be inadequate for the job. It was fine when the tank was full but, as the inside water level fell in dry periods or at times of maximum consumption, contaminated water was able to penetrate through the walls. This meant that the tank itself could be a source of impure water and by the 1970s it had become illegal for any water supply to contain more than a regulated amount of impurities. The post-war nationalisation of water meant that water had become a national resource under the Water Resources Act and all water supplies became subject to quality control. The water no longer belonged to the village to take from the moor. It became necessary to pay an annual licence fee to the Yorkshire Water Authority for the abstraction of the water and the Committee was also required to make a return of the estimated annual consumption. When the water authorities were privatised the Environment Agency took over the licensing for water abstraction and furthermore, so far as purity was concerned, the water became subject to six-monthly tests by the Environmental Health Department of Richmondshire District Council for which payment was eventually required. While these new administrative and financial controls presented the Committee with extra work and extra costs, they accepted them as necessary for the health and benefit of the village water consumers. The increased costs, together with the need to build up funds to cater for future improvements and emergencies, were easily obtained by increasing the amount that individual households contributed towards these costs.

However, those problems that presented themselves after the installation of the 10,000 gallon holding tank which were not so easy to solve, were, firstly, the ones connected with a renewed shortage of supply and, secondly, those of contamination. In 1976 and 1977 and then in the early 1980s there were several very dry summers and by early August 1981 the springs were producing very little water. Consequently, by September of that year the 10,000 gallon tank was nearly empty and there was evidence that leaks in the system were a large contributory factor, most of the leaks being from field troughs and the polythene pipes leading to them. Therefore garden hoses were banned and the stop-cock on the moor holding tank was turned off overnight to allow the tank to refill itself; in due course renewed rain restored the springs. In the meantime most of the leaks had been repaired. Four additional springs further along the moor were also tapped and the water from these new springs was brought down to the holding tank through a new but temporary pipe.

With regard to water purity, some of the early test results were poor and indicated high coliform bacillus contamination and specifically an unacceptably high E-coli level. It was therefore decided at the 1981 Water Committee meeting that owners of holiday cottages and those providing bed-and-breakfast accommodation should be advised to boil their water, not that anybody did so, nor were there any reported cases of ill effects! During this period the staff at the District Council were very helpful and the Committee had a good working relationship with them. The Council realised and understood that the village was doing its very best to improve the water quality and indeed the results of later tests were much better, probably partly due to the purer water that was coming from the additional springs. It was also discovered that the joints in the old mains supply pipe from the original springs had perished with the consequence that contaminated surface water was entering the pipe and going straight into the tank. Unfortunately, the lengths of pipe between the joint varied and no-one knew exactly where the joints were. After several days of gruelling work by Tommy Handley, John Watson, Roger Baxter and Dick Hall's grandson, Nicky Grundy, they were all found, dug up and replaced. After that stupendous effort, the analysis of the water, while not completely clear, ceased to be a cause for serious concern.

There was an attempt in the early 1980s by the public auditor who has responsibility for parish accounts to bring the West Scrafton Water Committee's accounts within his remit, but after correspondence it was agreed that, because this committee is not a parish-elected body, but a body drawn from the local village community who are themselves the only consumers, it is not subject to public audit.

The early 1990s saw the spring heads rebuilt in concrete blocks with a PVC collecting tank to reduce ingress of surface water. During the 1990s it became obvious that the 1976 tank would always be suspect. The household contribution had now risen to just over £30 per annum and by 1995 a reserve sufficient to pay for a second tank had been built up. This new tank of 12,000 gallon capacity was duly installed, built by John Watson and Kevin Utley alongside the 1976 tank, so that if and when necessary, either one of the tanks could be taken out of use for cleaning and refurbishment. However, by the end of the millennium only the 1995 tank was in use, as the older one had still not been attended to. During this time the amount contributed by each household had been steadily increasing and by 1997 it reached £44 per annum per household.

Although the water had greatly improved in purity, as evidenced by the 1999 test revealing only one coliform compared to over 180 in the 1990 test, it was still considered essential to provide guaranteed purity from bacteria by the provision of a sterilisation plant. In fact, the European rules which had now come into being demanded that there should be no bacteria at all in the supply. The 1999 test also reaffirmed the fact that the water was soft with no major chemical contaminants and, in this respect at least, all seemed satisfactory.

In 1999, at the end of the millennium, a £9,300 millennium grant was obtained to help pay for the purchase of an electric ultra-violet filtration and anti-bacterial treatment facility, which John Watson installed (see next section), the effect of which was to ensure that the water taken from the tanks on the moor was free from bacteria. The amount that each domestic household contributed to the improvement and maintenance of the distribution system was increased in 1998 to £88 in order to augment the grant, as the cost of the disinfection plant was of the order of £20,000.

While the West Scrafton village water system may not be unique, it must be one of the very few small community enterprises still surviving at the end of the second millennium. Some of the pipes in the system were still those which were laid in 1898 and those along Poverty Street had not been replaced until the 1980s.

Nevertheless, at the end of the millennium there was still a lot to be done to improve the service. For example, the old 10,000 gallon tank needed to be thoroughly renovated and brought up to scratch and there was still a significant quantity of old pipework which required to be replaced in due course.

Long may the West Scrafton Water Committee continue to survive. Its history illustrates the determination of a very small community to remain masters of their own future!

The Installation of the Water Sterilisation Plant

Installation of the new sterilisation plant for the village water supply began at the end of April, when John Watson built a stone housing for the electricity meter on a wall just before the entrance to Moor Ghyll. This was only a few yards away from an overhead supply pole from which the connection to the mains would be made.

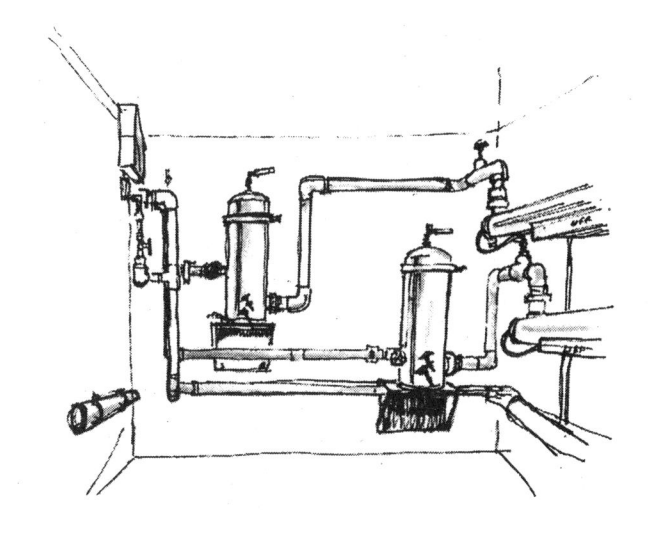

Not long after, John and Kevin Utley began digging in the electricity cable all the way from the meter box up to a site on Roova Moor to feed the ultra-violet treatment plant which was to be located in an underground chamber adjacent to the site of the old 620 gallon tank. Kevin dug the trench with his Ford digger machine and John followed up by feeding in the cable and filling in the trench with his Kramer. It seemed a very long way to go, and the process was leaving a great scar of mud across the fields, but it would soon disappear as the grass once again took over. The whole operation took about four days and during the exercise Liz took some photographs for posterity.

The purification equipment for the water treatment plant had been ordered by John in May and so the digging of the hole for the construction of the underground chamber could continue in earnest. John had made a temporary cable termination on a supply socket mounted on a post near to the chamber site in order to use his electric tools in the construction work, but unfortunately it transpired that it would be some time before the electricity company could come and connect the supply to the meter box. As it was only another few days before the hole was ready for the construction work on the chamber to commence, a portable generator had to be used to operate the electric cement mixer.

The morning of Wednesday June 23rd was misty, and John and Kevin completed digging the hole in which to build the underground equipment chamber. The concrete blocks for the walls had been ordered for delivery the next day, and Kevin had also arranged to collect the concrete for the base of the chamber on that day. John had finished the shuttering for the base and had laid the drainage pipes and they were hoping that the weather would stay dry so that the concrete when it was poured in would not get washed away down the drainage channel.

Luckily, Thursday was fine and dry and Kevin went to Masham to collect the concrete in the tipper-trailer. The blocks were duly delivered to East Farm; John had made a road-sign telling the driver where to deliver and off-load them.

A hole in the ground is always of interest to people and that morning saw a succession of villagers traipsing up the moor track to view the site. Sandra and Roger Baxter were taking their dog Meg for a walk up Roova, and Sandra returned home to make and drop off a couple of flasks of tea; she collected the "empties" on returning from their walk.

As it happened the day was so hot that the concrete started to dry out and set in the tipper-trailer before Kevin could get it back from Masham. It had been intended that it would be gently tipped from the rear of the trailer down some plywood sheets and into the base area where it would be shovelled along to form the floor of the chamber. However, the partly dried concrete did not start to flow until the tipper was raised to quite a steep angle and then it all came out in an uncontrolled rush, breaking the plywood sheets and splashing right to the far end of the hole; no shovelling along was necessary, but some of the concrete had to be taken out as a bit too much had fallen in (see fig 15). It proved to be too much to take out by hand and so the digger bucket had to be used.

The next day saw the start of the building of the walls and from now on a succession of viewers came to see the progress of the construction. There was a torrential thunderstorm that night and inspection of the site the next morning revealed that only one large landslip had occurred and this was on to the drainage pipe which was later found not to have been damaged. At least John's fears that the sides of the hole would slip in against the partly completed walls were not realised. On the Monday John progressed with the building work on the chamber, having first had a couple of electrical jobs to attend to elsewhere. As the forecast downpours did not occur, he worked on until 9pm to complete the construction of the concrete block walls. Several more villagers visited the site and Kevin had to bring up some more sand to allow John to continue without a break.

On the Wednesday the reinforcing bars were inserted, and the channels in the walling blocks were filled with concrete. A couple of days later John put up the props or wooden scaffolding for temporarily supporting the concrete roof of the chamber after he had collected the necessary timber from Leyburn. The next day temporary roof supports were erected and the shuttering for the roof was placed in position ready to pour in the concrete. There was a couple of visitors that day including Kevin Utley who came in the evening to make a check on progress and to see whether Monday would be the day for him to fetch the concrete from Masham.

It apparently was, so Kevin duly went to Masham on Monday morning to collect the concrete for the roof of the equipment chamber. There was apparently a problem with the concrete mixer at the suppliers so that the arrival of the concrete to the site was delayed for about an hour or so. Remembering the avalanche of concrete that had occurred when the floor was laid, and not wishing the same thing to happen again, this time the concrete was carefully shovelled out into the Kramer bucket from only a shallowly tipped trailer with John doing the shovelling standing in the concrete in the trailer. Kevin then repeatedly ferried the concrete in the Kramer and emptied it on to the roof. Again they had erred on the right side and obtained too much, but this time what was left was still in the trailer! Later on that day, luckily after the concrete had been tamped out to form a level roof top, the rain appeared and a plastic sheet was duly placed over the concrete to protect it not only from the rain, but also from the sun and wind to prevent it from drying out too quickly.

On the Wednesday the shuttering was knocked off the outside

edges of the roof and John measured up for the steelwork that consisted of the manhole cover, the entrance ladder, the ventilators and the shelving and fixings for the equipment. A few days later the heaps of soil which had come from digging out the hole were put back around the outer sides of the walls and most of what remained was then spread around.

A week or so after that, John came home one evening to find that all the galvanised metalwork needed for the water treatment plant housing had been left in his front garden. He made time to fit it all later that week. The next week, John ordered all the pipework needed for the connection of the water treatment plant to the main supply coming down from the water tanks on Roova Moor. The water would normally be diverted through the plant, leaving a short section of the original pipe shut off, but still able to be used in an emergency if the plant needed to be taken out of service for any reason. The next job was to install and wire up the electrical supply inside the chamber ready for the equipment, but it was another week before further work could continue as the water valves had not yet arrived.

At last John could now work on the treatment plant again, fixing the shelves on the wall on which the filters would stand and fitting the ulta-violet sterilisation units to an adjacent wall. He also managed to fit in some of the associated plumbing work. By now it was into September and John continued to work on the plumbing, this time concentrating on the joints in the plastic pipe-work. These were of the push-fit type which required solvent to "glue" them together to prevent the water pressure from pushing them apart and to make them watertight. A temporary fan was placed in the opening of the chamber to help extract all the fumes from the solvent; this proved to be a very necessary device as the fumes were rather overpowering. Geoff and Julie Forrest ventured up to see what was happening and went down in to the chamber; Julie gave lots of encouragement and they appeared quite impressed by the work done so far.

On Monday, John decided to take the bit between his teeth and name the day for the changeover, so he delivered the notices to inform all the householders that the water would be turned off between 10am and noon on Wednesday 15th. Several villagers went up to the plant on that Monday to see it before it would

Laying the Power Cable

Delivering too much Concrete!

Dealing with the Excess

Filling the Reinforcing Holes

The Equipment Installation

Fig 15   The Installation of the Water Sterilisation Plant

become out of bounds. Ed Hullah went up to make some sketches and Tony endeavoured to take a couple of photographs, but it was difficult to get far enough away in the rather confined space to get all the equipment in.

Wednesday dawned and the water was duly turned off at the tank at 10am and John cut the main feeder pipe where it passed the treatment plant. Both he and Tony, who was up there with him, were surprised that it took nearly twenty minutes for the water to empty out of the three hundred yards of pipe coming down from the tank. The two cut ends of the pipe were connected to the new system and the water was turned back on again by 10.40am, although not yet going via the plant. A few last minute checks and the plant valves were turned on in stages before the "straight-through" valve was turned off and the water for the village was fed via the ultra-violet plant. A Red Letter Day indeed!

The next two days were spent in finishing off and cleaning up the site. This not only entailed levelling off all the soil around, but also building a small chamber around the external stop-cocks. John had a small "trademark" which he left in the cement on his jobs consisting of two small footprints ingeniously made with his hand, and he duly put this mark on to the edge of the small chamber. There is also one on the main equipment chamber if you know where to look!

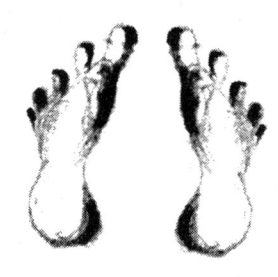

A few weeks later samples of water were taken from a few points at the extremities of the system and not a single bacterium was found in any of these samples when they were analysed. The great thing that all villagers were agreed upon was that there was no change to the fresh taste of the water as no chemicals of any kind were used to achieve this absolute sterility.

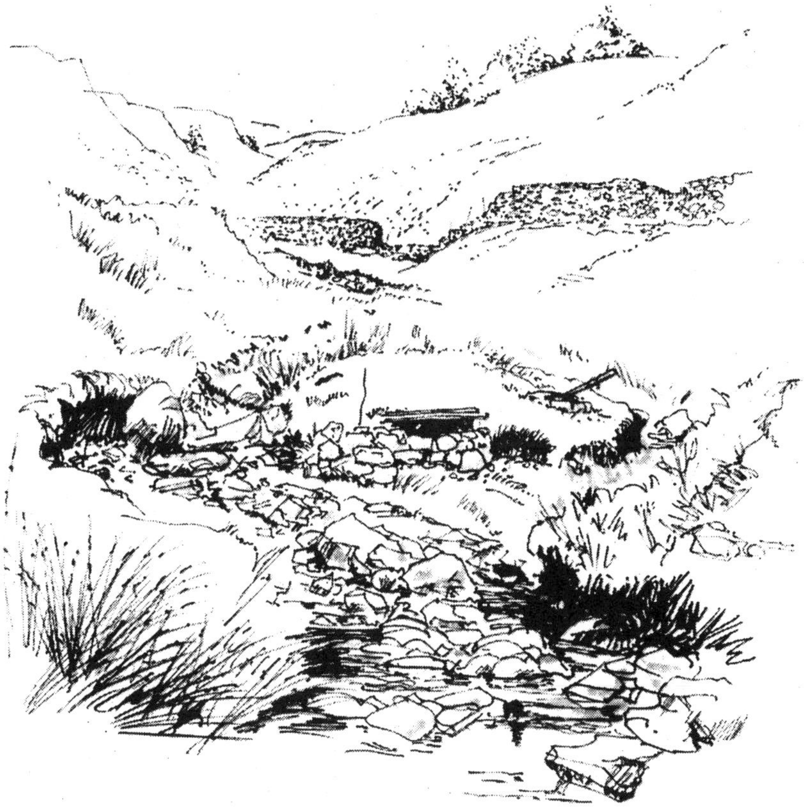

Postal Services

In this modern day and age many people order at least some of the goods they need by telephone, by mail order or over the internet, thus making postal and delivery services a much more vital part of village life than ever before, especially in isolated communities like West Scrafton. Hence it is an increasingly common sight to see the vans of the many different carrier companies careering along the country lanes in the dale, delivering the various items that have been ordered by village folk.

Postman Doug Gillam

One of these carriers is Parcel Post and some of their smaller items are delivered by the postman, who is, in spite of the more recent proliferation of electronic mail, still the mainstay of written communications. The days are long since gone when the postman had to travel for miles on a bicycle, but even nowadays postal services in the country areas are naturally much less frequent than in the towns. In Coverdale there is just one delivery a day, which usually arrives in West Scrafton somewhere between 11.00 and 11.30am. The service is operated from the local postal town of Leyburn and this particular postal round covers 270 addresses from Gale Bank Farm to Coverhead and then returning to take in West Scrafton, Swineside, East Scrafton and Caldbergh. The complete round is 41 miles long and is probably one of the longest in England to cover only 270 addresses.

In addition to delivering people's mail, the postman also has the duty of collecting mail from the various post-boxes which he passes on his way to Middleham. There is also a collection only service in the late afternoon which is operated by a larger van and covering a more extensive area. In the days when there was a post office in Carlton, the postman used to deliver newspapers around the dale, although this was an unofficial service.

Between 1983 and 1995 the duty was operated on a four-week rota system by five postmen. Many local people will remember Bob Strickland, Steve Wright, "Chalky" Mills, Paul Westwood and Steve Hemsley as the five stalwarts on the Coverdale round.

In 1995, a single fixed duty was introduced for this round and it has been operated ever since by our good friend Doug Gillam, who is shown in the picture. Over the years there have been times when he has had to struggle in his van in atrocious weather conditions and he can remember some particularly hairy trips between West Scrafton and Swineside. Over the last five years or so, however, there has been an increasingly rare number of times when the roads have been bad, but there have been other hazards to encounter in West Scrafton. For example, in the period between November 1996 and Easter 1997 he suffered from the proverbial dog problem, receiving no less than seven dog bites in that short space of time! He is, in fact, a dog lover himself and Sam, his faithful King Charles spaniel, often used to do the round with him in his van. Sadly Sam has now passed away. In spite of the dog bites, he has expressed the sentiment that the people living in West Scrafton are always very kind and helpful whenever he has needed it. We can return that compliment and continue to look forward to the daily visits of that cheerful face delivering our mail.

However, Doug is expecting to retire around July 2002 and we shall all miss him.

A Brief Look at Road Transport

Nowadays we are so used to cars that it is difficult to realise that for nearly the first nine-tenths of the millennium there was no such thing as mechanical road transport and all wheeled vehicles were pulled by some form of animal, mainly horses. Travellers had to go on horseback or, in the latter part of the period, in carriages drawn by horses. The roads in this area were not much more than rough tracks, but as time went on some were overlaid with loose chipped stones, a practice that had spread to all the main roads in the country during the first part of the 19th century. and until quite recent times all of the seven roads into the dale which were of good enough quality to be called roads were gated.

Around that time many of the main roads were also reconstructed and provided with a camber in order to drain off the surface water and help preserve the small powdery gravel that was used to bind the larger stones together. However, the country lanes and bye-roads, such as those serving the locality around West Scrafton, mostly remained as well worn tracks until well into the second half of the 19th century. Up to then each parish had been responsible for the upkeep of all the roads running through its area, but in the middle of the 19th century John McAdam, the surveyor-general of roads, managed to get parliament to agree that the administration of public highways and bye-ways should come within the authority of the government; in turn the government quickly devolved this function, for all but the main "trunk" roads, to local county councils. From that time on, the money needed for the provision and upkeep of roads was allocated from public taxes rather than from the collection of tolls, the system of funding which had been used for centuries before that.

As has been mentioned elsewhere, in the old days there was a much used "trade" route from London to Richmond which ran through Coverdale. In fact the first road atlas, which was produced in 1675 by John Ogilby, showed a main road running through the dale. The trade routes were formed originally by the repeated trampling of herdsman driving livestock to market towns. By the 17th century commercial necessity had developed what were called "road trains" which passed along these routes. A road train consisted of a team of perhaps 30 or 40 pack horses carrying all kinds of wares. Pack horses were chosen from breeds which produced strong persistent plodders that did not tire easily. The best types came from the south of Scotland and were known as Galloways. There were many of these road trains and some of the routes included passing places or divergent lanes to enable trains going in opposite directions to pass each other. The route through Coverdale went from Skipton via Kettlewell, up over Park Rash and then followed the river Cover. When these routes were later used by wheeled vehicles it must have been an extremely uncomfortable ride for those taking journeys in horse-drawn carts or carriages (and not very pleasant for the horses either!).

Towards the end of the 19th century a few steam vehicles came into being, known colloquially as traction engines. These were used for pulling heavy trailers such as cartloads of hay and farm animals; but they were slow, cumbersome, expensive and required frequent maintenance. The horse remained the mainstay of private and public local transport until well into the 20th century when petrol driven vehicles gradually took over.

There was, however, an extensive network of public horse-drawn vehicles running to regular time-tables organised by local operators. Although not very frequent by modern standards, they served the purposes of most people who, in those times, had little need to travel outside their own vicinity. For example, there was a service from Leyburn to Richmond twice a week and a weekly run to Bedale. Another went to Stockton on Mondays and Thursdays, returning on Wednesdays and Saturdays. There were a number of long distance routes running from Richmond to other large centres like Durham, Edinburgh, Leeds, Liverpool, London, Manchester and Newcastle. From remote places like West Scrafton, of course, one first had to get to the main towns in order to board one of these long distance carriers in much the same way as one has to get to a main line railway station today.

The general introduction of the bicycle during the latter part of the 19th century provided individuals with a new method of getting about. Although the old "bone-shakers" had solid tyres and were not very conducive to travelling on rural lanes, cycling did become a hobby, as the existence of a cyclist's map of 1881 (fig 16) shows. "Safety" bicycles were invented in the mid-1880s and rapidly became popular as they were the first bicycles to have two equal sized wheels and were geared by means of a chain connecting two different sized cog-wheels to make pedalling easier. It was well into the 20th century before rural cycling became comfortable, thanks both to the improvement in road surfaces and to the increasing use of so called "balloon" tyres. Lighting was also introduced by means of either acetylene or carbide lamps. No doubt the first people to really use such transport in these parts were the children, especially as children's tricycles were available at the turn of the century (for those that could afford them).

When highways were under the authority of the local parish, each village had to look after its own roads. The Parish Meeting would appoint a "Surveyor of Highways" and he would be responsible for overseeing the upkeep of all the highways within the parish, hardly a full-time job in West Scrafton. Each person in the parish was obliged to give 3 or 4 days "statutory labour" and pay a parish rate towards the maintenance of the roads. When the function of road maintenance passed to the county councils, it was they who appointed what were known as "length-men", each of whom was responsible for a length of road by keeping it free of dirt, repairing pot-holes, cutting back the verges, trees and side-growth and generally ensuring that the roads were clear for vehicles to travel safely. Length-men were in operation during the first half of the 20th century until such times as mechanical means of road maintenance were widely introduced and could be operated from a central depot. There was a length-man responsible for the road through West Scrafton stretching from beyond Nathwaite to the East Scrafton boundary (see page 45 for a note about James Utley, the last lengthman).

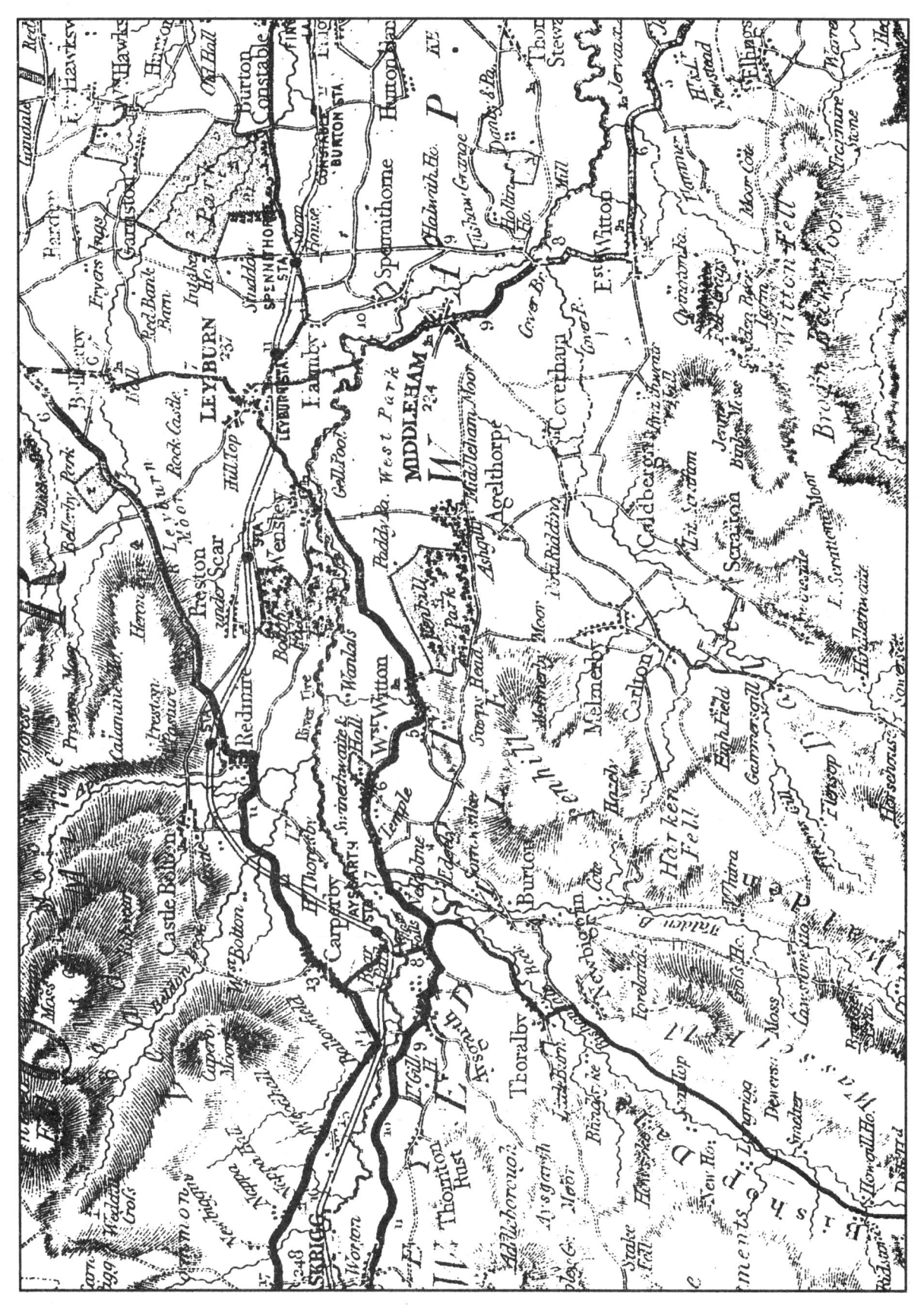

Fig 16   Cyclist's Map of 1881

The road through the village was tarmacadamed, or "metalled" as it used to be called, in the early part of the century and has since provided a very much more comfortable ride for people in cars and on bicycles.

However, central responsibility for road maintenance has its drawbacks in that we now have to await our turn and the necessary central funding for the upkeep and any repairs and changes needed on our local "bye-ways".

The Yorkshire Dales Railway Proposals

There have been several attempts to utilise the ancient trade route from Wharfedale through Coverdale to the North East as a line for a railway. Each attempt was promoted by interests that were remote from Coverdale, emanating mainly from Lancashire but also, to a lesser extent, from North East businessmen. Each proposal would have been primarily a route through Coverdale rather than into or out of it. Nevertheless, the effect on the dale and all the communities within it, including West Scrafton, would have been profound.

The story begins around 1845 when a proposal was made to construct a line from a point on the existing system near Skipton, going north through Kettlewell and then on through Coverdale to Middleham and ultimately joining the Richmond branch at Scorton. This line was titled The Lancashire and North Yorkshire Railway, but funds were not forthcoming and things lay quiet until, in the early 1860s, a Skipton, Wharfedale and Leyburn Junction Railway was proposed which would have followed the same route from Skipton but was to terminate at Spennithorne where it would have connected with the (then) Leyburn branch from Northallerton. This line would have provided a fairly direct route between North Lancashire and the North East but, as it is believed to have been planned to cross Coverhead on the surface, the gradients on both sides would have been fearsome. Under some pressure, and probably through inability to raise the necessary capital, the promoters in the end decided to limit their line to a branch ending at Grassington and not to attempt the Pennine crossing.

The same proposal was raised again in 1882 resulting from interests in the South continuing to harbour thoughts of infiltrating North Eastern Railway territory. Another attempt was made in 1895 and this time the company proposed was called the Yorkshire Dales Railway. At this time also it was proposed to continue the line directly to Darlington, Stockton and Middlesbrough.

Plans exist showing the proposed route of this railway through the dale (see figs 19 and 20). Most significantly, this time it was the intention to tunnel under Coverhead, thus reducing the gradients involved to something much more manageable than had been the case in the earlier proposals. An average gradient of about 1 in 100 from the crossing of the River Ure near Middleham bridge to the summit at Coverhead was now envisaged (see fig 18 for details).

However, the passing of the Light Railways Act in 1896 led to a series of schemes that were in effect revivals of the Yorkshire Dales Railway proposal but with the railway being built on a cheap and cheerful "light railway" basis. These proposals were put forward in 1903 and again as late as 1912. That none of these later projects came to fruition was due, in part at least, to objections from landowners along the route.

The plans for the Yorkshire Dales Railway referred to above show that the proposed line of the railway would not have entered the West Scrafton parish but would have held to the north-west side of the River Cover crossing the Nathwaite bridge road somewhat above the hairpin bend. It would then have run along the hillside below Carlton village crossing Goodmans Ghyll just at the top of the steep bank rising up from Caygill footbridge.

No indication is given in the plans of the proposed location of stations or other facilities on the line. It is likely, however, that had it been built, a station would have been located somewhere near to Carlton, this being the largest settlement in the Upper Dale. The crossing on the road up from Nathwaite would have formed an

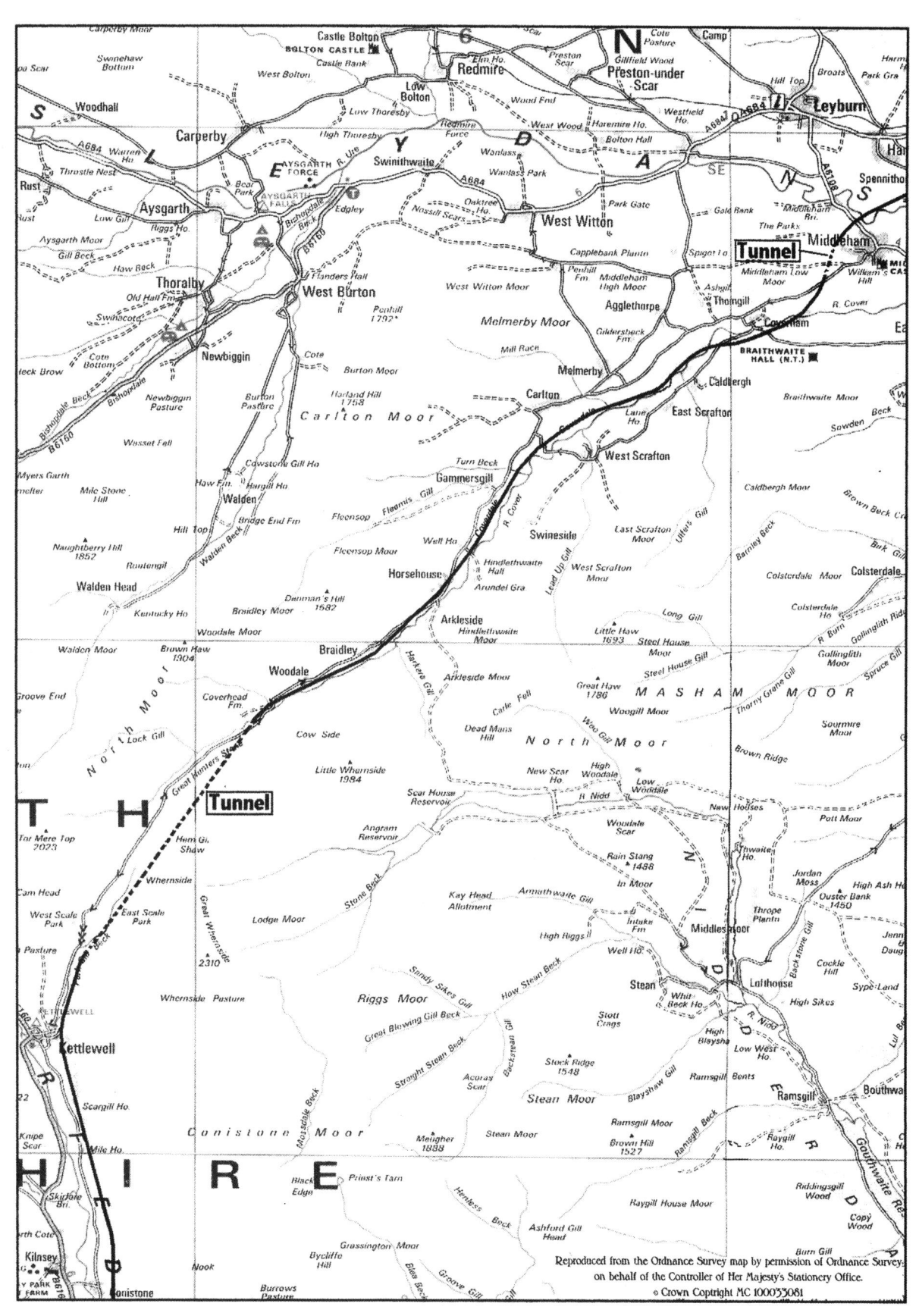

Fig 17   Route of the proposed Yorkshire Dales Railway

ideal place so that the station would have served West Scrafton equally well.

It is interesting to speculate about how the dale, and West Scrafton in particular, would have been affected if the railway had materialised. It would have greatly eased the movement of heavy goods in and out of the dale. We have heard that for many years coal and flagstones produced locally were exported to Lancashire over Coverhead and down via Park Rash! We have also heard that the reason for the mine at West Scrafton being re-opened at the end of the 19th century was that there was an understanding that the railway was coming! What might have happened if the railway had come? The mining operations may have lasted longer and may have been more intensely developed; who knows? West Scrafton might have become a mining village with rows of terraced cottages, etc! There were, of course, several other mines in the dale that could also have benefited, such as Fleensop. How much good roofing stone is still underground that might have been sought if good transport had been just a few hundred yards away? The dale and the village could have been very different places.

What is most likely is that, as has happened to so many others, the line would have been closed in the late 1950s or 1960s. It would by now have been a haven for wildlife and probably a quiet, easy and level(ish) walk through this beautiful place.

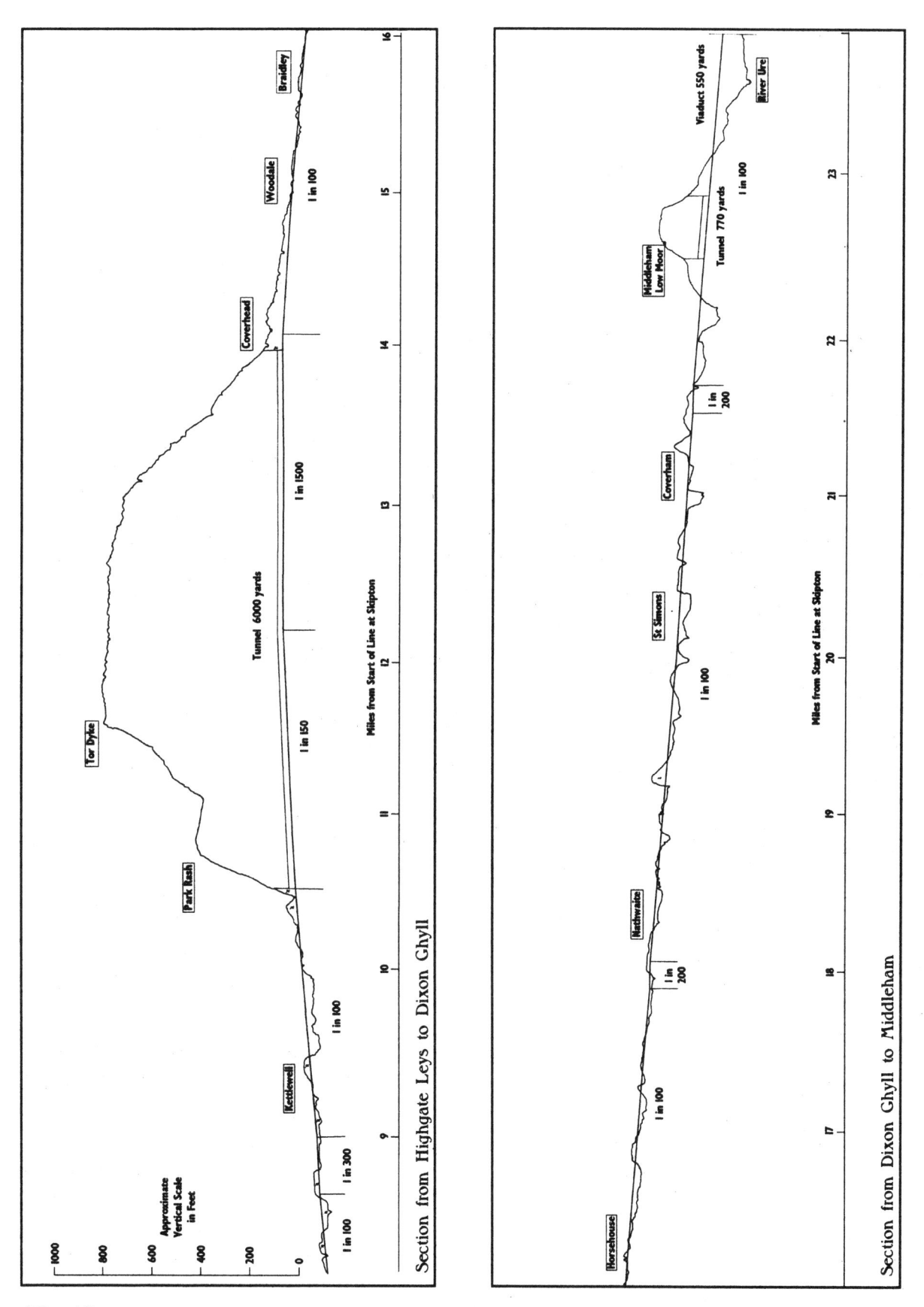

Fig 18 The Yorkshire Dales Railway Proposal - Gradients

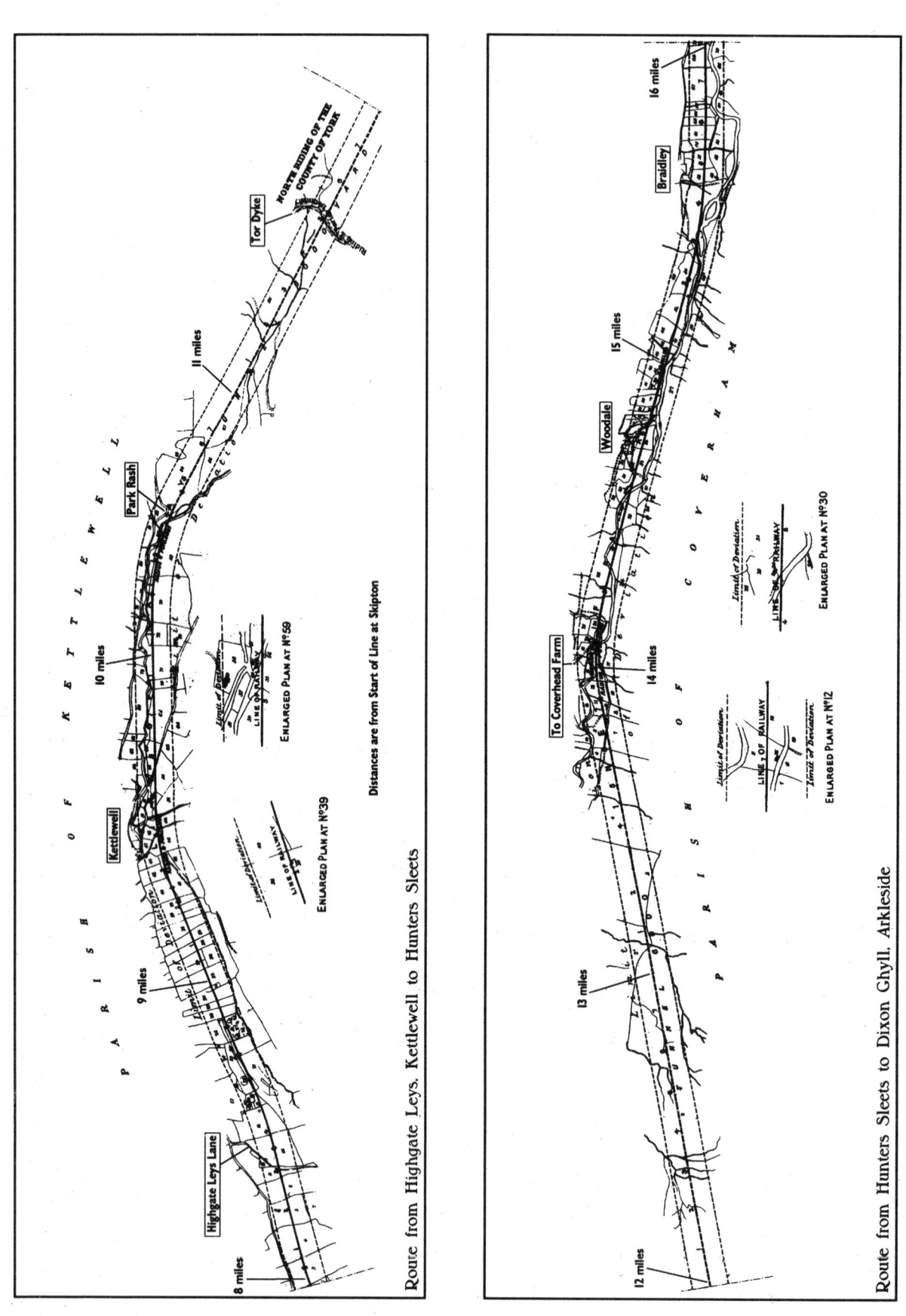

Fig 19   The Yorkshire Dales Railway Proposal - South

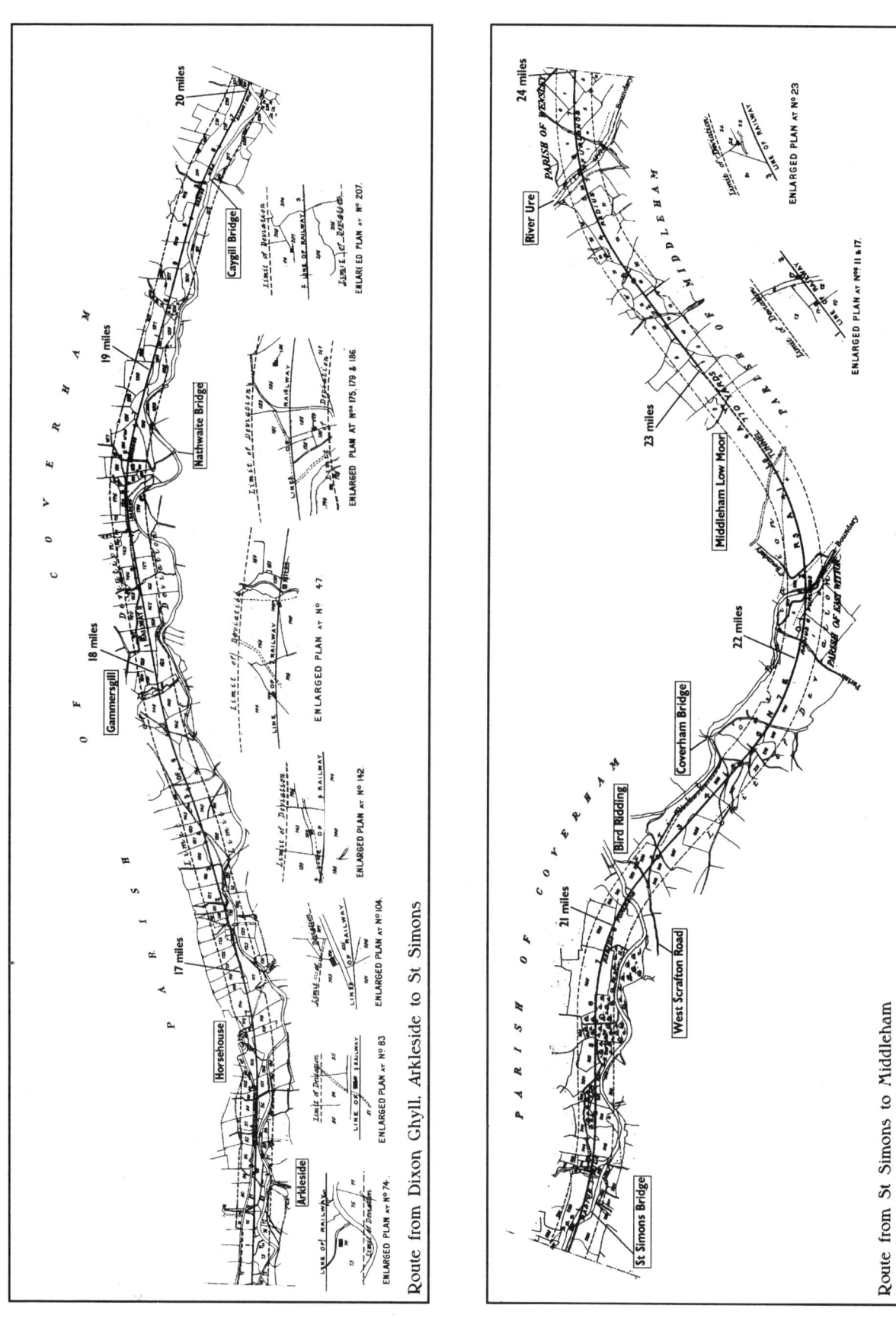

Fig 20   The Yorkshire Dales Railway Proposal - North

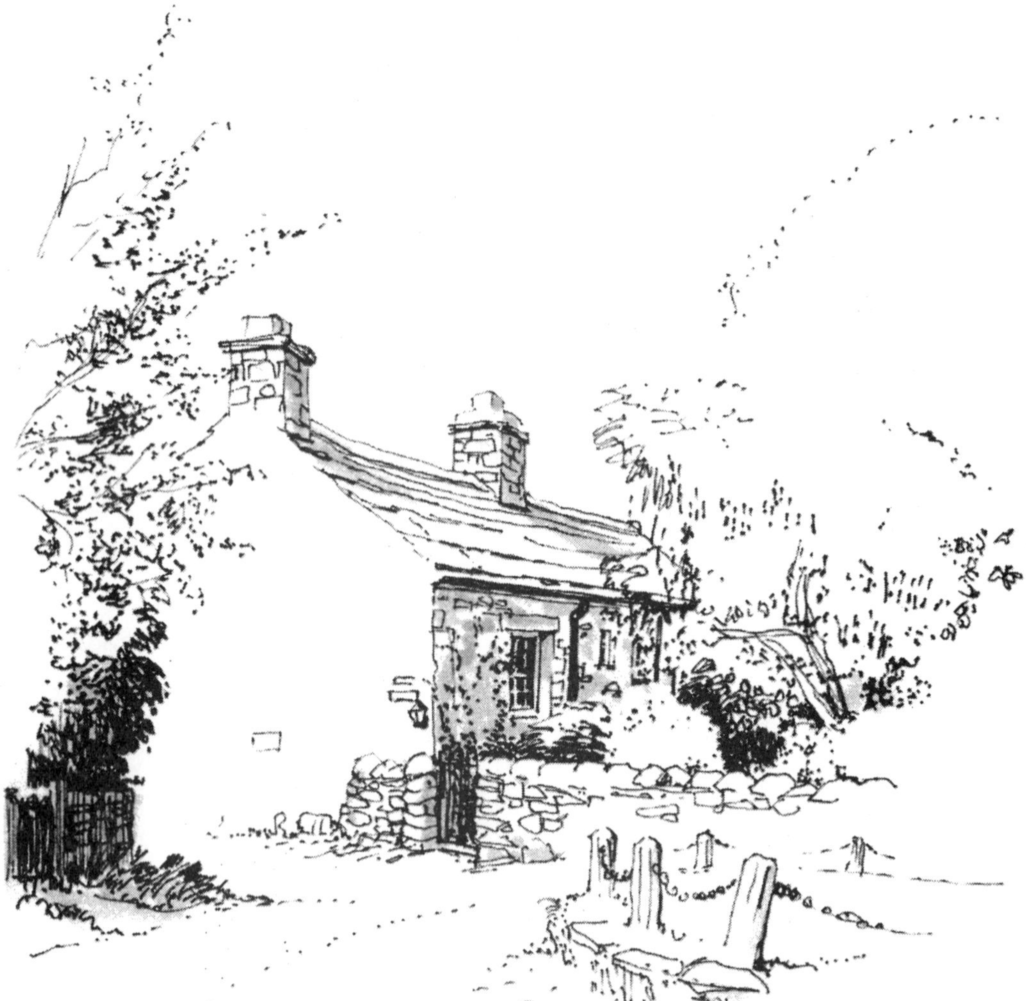

LOCAL ITEMS OF INTEREST

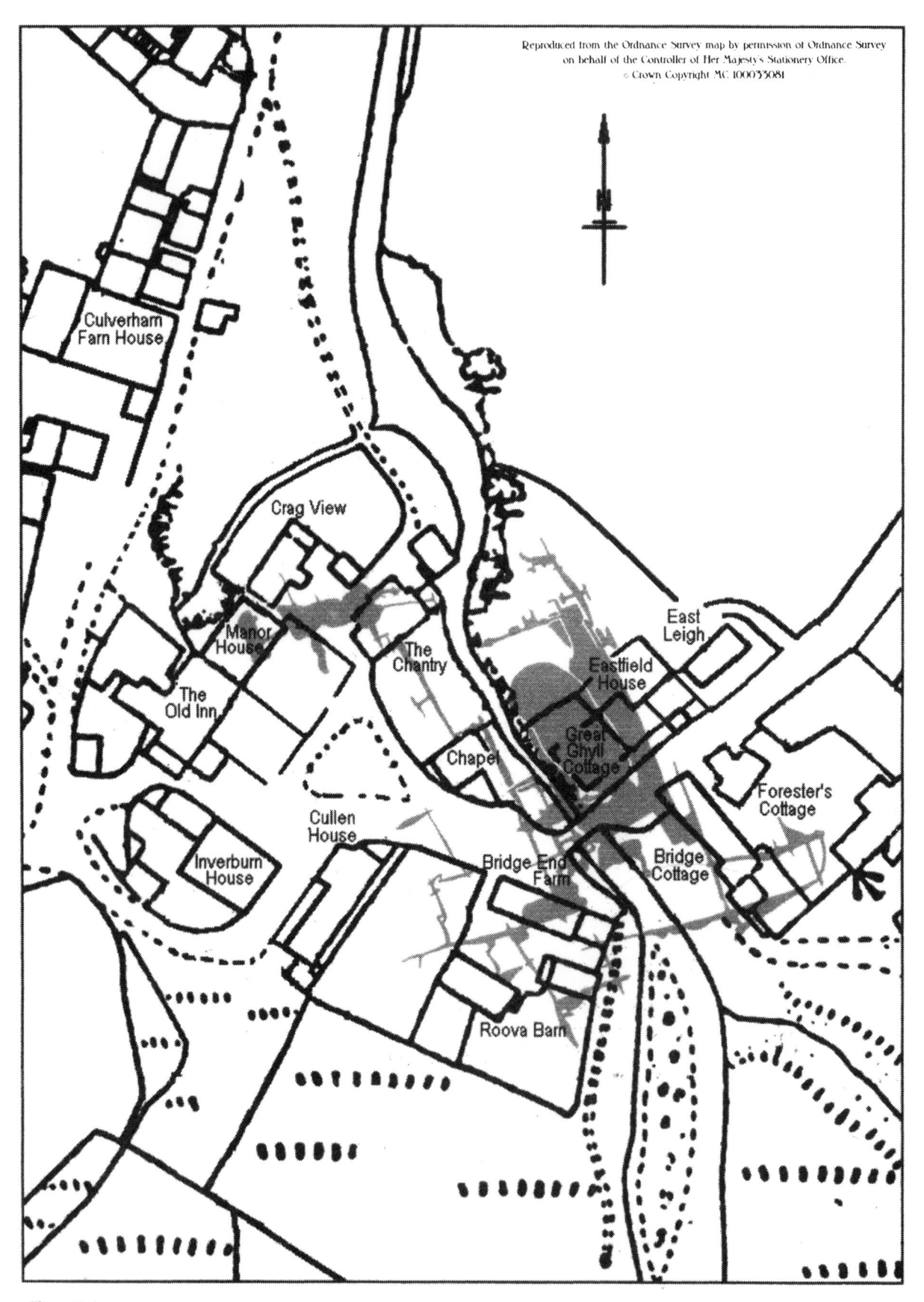

Fig 21   Map of Village showing approximate position of Scrafton Pot

The Pot-holes

There are several pot-holes in the vicinity of West Scrafton, one large one and a number of small ones, the large one being in the centre of the village and having a main cavern right underneath some of the cottages. The others are to be found in the gorge which carries Great Ghyll from the village past Caygill and down to the River Cover a few hundred yards to the north. According to the dictionary a "pot-hole" is a vertical hole, while a horizontal tunnel is known as a "cave", although the term "pot-hole" is popularly used to refer to any underground opening. Brief descriptions of the pot-holes are given here both for the sake of interest and to help make this book as complete a story of the village as possible. It must be stressed that this is not an invitation to non-pot-holing members of the public to explore, but if an interest has been kindled, then the reader must contact the pot-holing fraternity both for the sake of their own safety and for the preservation of the environment.

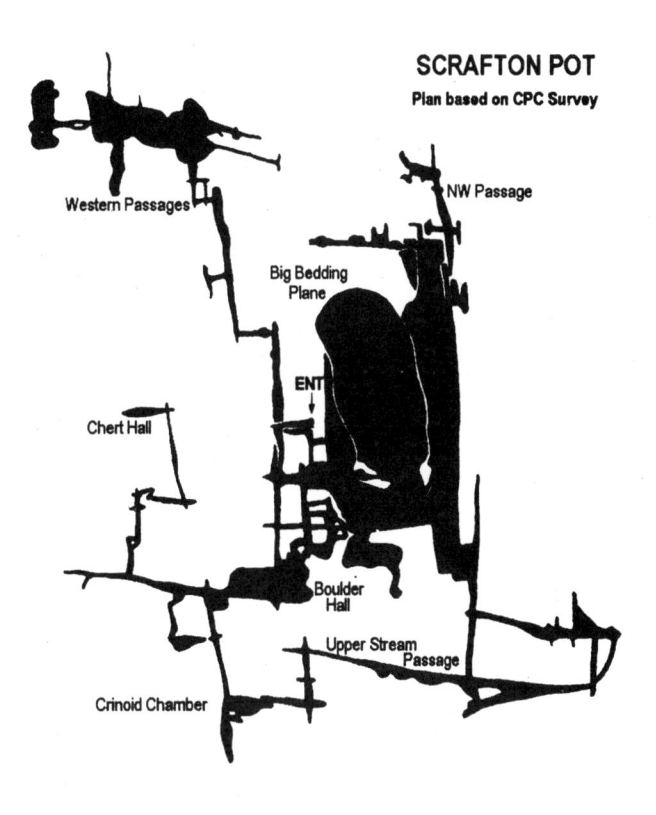

The rock around this area from which all the pot-holes are formed is known as middle limestone. The main pot-hole is known as the Scrafton Pot and the entrance to this is near the bridge by Great Ghyll Cottage. It was first explored by pot-holers in the mid-1960s who estimated its depth as nearly 150 feet. In wet weather Great Ghyll becomes rather full and there is an extensive flow of water down holes in the bed and through the pot. This drains down to the River Cover by way of Otter's Cave. By the bridge there is a fissure in the side of the ghyll from which there is a drop down on to a massive boulder. This gives access via a climb down to Big Bedding Plane, which is a large chamber, some 40ft wide by 85ft long, but quite low and eventually becoming too low to explore. Near the boulder there is a raised opening leading to a small chamber called Boulder Hall. From there a succession of passages lead to Stream Corner, where there are several high water inlets. Eventually Chert Hall may be reached, which is a choked sumped rift.

From the initial main drop a fissure leads past a maze of passages on the right connecting with Boulder Hall and emerges in a widening chamber near the start of which is a climb of around 20ft to Western Passages. Above Western Passages a high rift chamber may be reached by way of a further climb. A steep slope leads back up to Big Bedding Plane.

There are a number of other routes and fissures, a couple of which extend to the spacious Upper Stream Passage.

Frank Johnstone is the only resident in the village who has been down the pot-hole and about ten years ago he mentioned to a pot-holing colleague that he would like to have a go. Later he was told that a trip had been arranged down Scrafton Pot. In Frank's words "we met up one Saturday about lunchtime. The expedition was led by a man called Chris and his friends from the Swaledale fell rescue team. There was myself and five other people including a character who was wearing a boiler suit over a wet suit and who was called the "water baby" by the others. At the entrance, after crawling in for a few feet, we dropped down metal rope-ladders and set about climbing down the initial pitch. Unfortunately one of the party got cold feet and could not climb down the ladder and so was left to wait some six hours for us on the surface. After the initial big first drop of about 60ft I seem to remember that we went down one more short rope-ladder and that for the rest of the journey we did not need ladders. We had been issued with lamps for our helmets but I was last in the queue and instead of an electric light was given calcium carbide crystals on to which I had to pour water to get the gas required for a flame to light. I was at the back and frequently had to ask for someone to shine an electric light for me to see the way or to be able to see some feature more clearly. We travelled some distance, although this was difficult to judge. The "water baby" kept trying any small crevice or offshoot to see if it would lead to anything more. He would scrabble in the cold wet mud probing and searching like a mole. We saw some spectacular sights and I can remember coming across a huge cavern which I always recall seemed to be big enough to hold a cathedral. It was a wonderful sight and I was amazed to discover that all of this existed beneath our feet. I was very well looked after in spite of my dim lamp and by the time we returned to the surface I felt slightly relieved to have returned safely but also felt that my curiosity had been satisfied and that we had had a most interesting experience".

This pot-hole is right in the centre of the village and several of the old cottages are over the main chamber as can be seen from the map which shows the underground caverns in grey (fig 21). When the weather is very wet and the ghyll fills up, especially when large holes appear in the bed allowing the main flow to pour underground, there are perhaps exaggerated worries about the possibility of the ground opening up and swallowing up some of the properties.

Further down the ghyll is Shatter Cave, which is a small fissure on the right-hand bank. There is a low crawl ahead which leads to a 20ft wide chamber with water sinking through the floor. A 10ft climb to a shelf gives access to a short choked crawl.

The next pot-hole down the gorge is known as Lead Up Ghyll Pot, about half-way between the village and Caygill Scar. The opening is on the west side of the ghyll, about 5ft above the stream. There is a 12ft climb down through loose boulders and a squeeze into a steeply descending passage ending in a blank wall. The total distance is about 40 yards.

Tom Hunter's Parlour is a cave with a large entrance at the top of Caygill Scar. The long narrow climb goes up for about 30 feet and eventually opens up into a roomy rift passage ending in a choked inlet. There are two other small parallel passages with connecting fissures.

The last ones down towards the River Cover are the Caygill Scar Caves which are short dry caves with obvious entrances. The longest is about 30ft long.

Finally we come to Otter's Cave, which is a few hundred yards further down the River Cover, just before Thorow Ghyll. This is a tunnel about 500 yards long wending its way back towards the village. There is initially an easy walk back to the first sump which is in a large chamber. The passage continues through three more sumps, one of which is a long one of around 300 feet, to end in a boulder choke. There is a complicated way through this to two further chambers. The name is believed to be a corruption of "Otto's" Cave, Otto being the name of a man who is reputed to have lived in it. The photograph below shows the far end of Otter's Hole (as it is known locally) and the plan on the next page shows the extent of the underground passage.

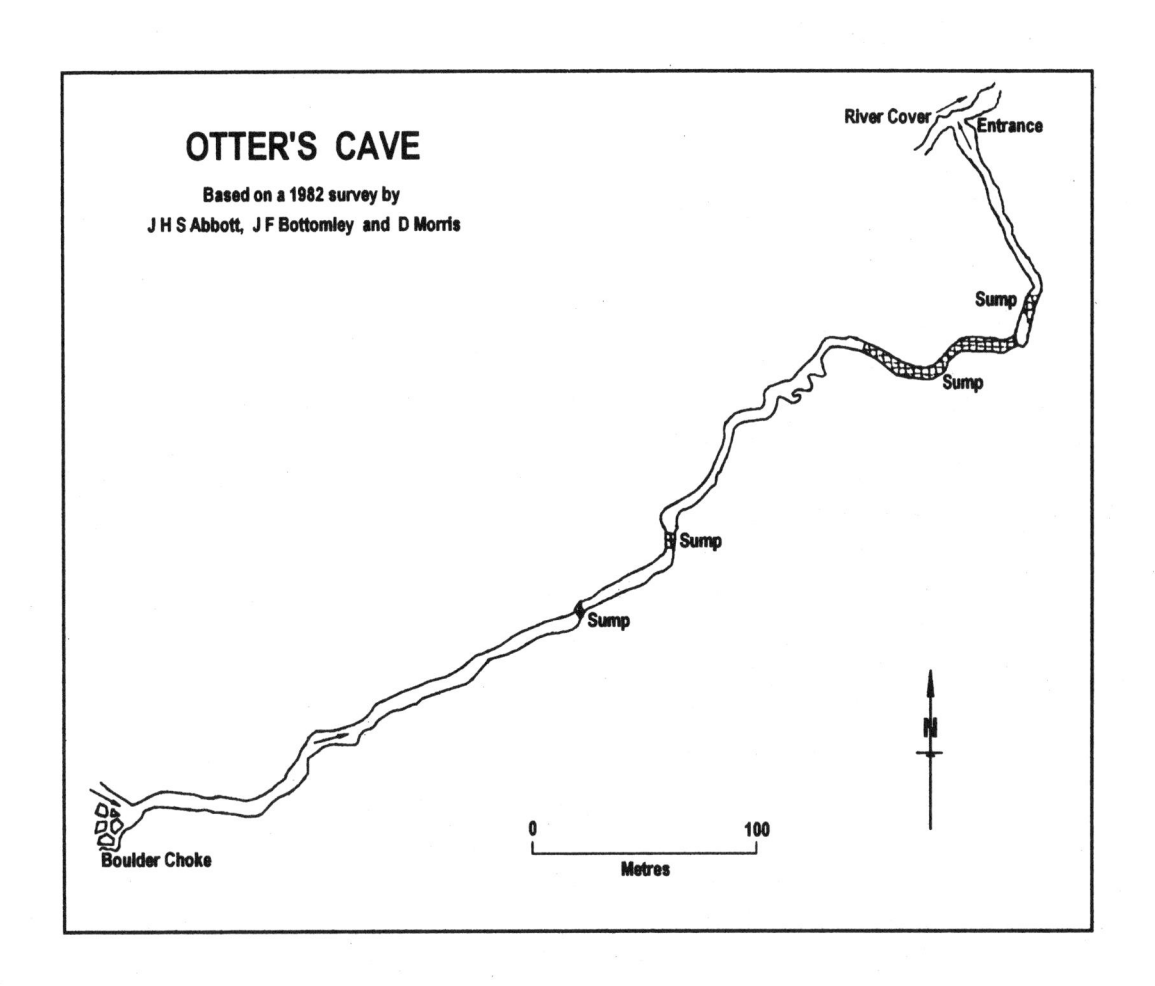

The Coal Mine

Over the last millennium there have been a number of coal mines in Coverdale. These were to be found at West Scrafton, Fleensop, Woodale and Coverhead but they have all have been closed down for a great many years. In 1738 the one at Fleensop had been acquired by the Pennyman family from Ormsby who also owned some nearby lead mines. Records show that this mine was extensively worked during the seventeenth century and that four yeomen lived there at the time.

Roova Crag stands over the village of West Scrafton above the moor where there are some disused coal mines. As has been mentioned previously, this particular site dates way back to beyond the 14th century when it was worked by the monks of Jervaulx Abbey. They went so far as to lay down a permanent road between the mine and their abbey to ease the transportation of the coal. Coal from these mines was once used to fuel the nearby lime kilns (see fig 24) after the ancient woodland had been burnt. Quick-lime was used to spread over the farmland to help pasturage to grow where bracken and heather had previously flourished.

The most obvious remains of the main colliery are probably the oldest part of the workings. The coal seam becomes an outcrop at about the 1400ft level on the moor to the south of the village and the series of spoil heaps along the moor mark the sites of incursions made into the seam to get at the coal nearest to the surface. Immediately above each heap lies a man-made gully and buried at the head of each lies a level. Most of these are undoubtedly collapsed but at least one of them was provided with a stone arch and has survived, although it is buried and is full of water.

On the top of the moor, enclosed by a ring of fencing, lies the site of the shaft that was last worked in 1912. Now buried under a large mound of spoil, the shaft was once some 360ft deep (see fig 22 for a plan of this last worked colliery). A few hundred yards to the east, a large spoil heap marks the site of another pit, presumably with a shaft of similar depth if coal was ever procured from it. Old large scale maps mark another disused pit a bit further to the east, but very little evidence of this is now apparent. Nearer to the village there is yet another pit, 145 feet deep and running for half-a-mile up Lead-up Ghyll.

In the mid-1700s a long airway and drainage system was constructed connecting the lower moor level with the coal workings at the shaft bottom level. This tunnel, shown on the plan and its position roughly indicated on the map in fig 23, clearly still exists to some extent and is still carrying out its drainage function, bringing heavily mineral-tainted water into the ghylls draining from the moor.

Tommy Handley's daughter, Linda, as a schoolgirl in the 1970s, carried out some research into this last worked colliery on West Scrafton moor for a school project. She started by enquiring of various people in the dale whether any of them could remember the time when the mine was last open. She eventually came across a Mr J Spence, who was then eighty-seven years old and living in Leyburn, although he had spent his youth as a resident of West Scrafton. He apparently had some memories both of his own youth and from the stories that his father had told him, the first of which was rather gruesome. In the 19th century, after the pit had been closed for the first time, some human remains were found there and an inquest was subsequently held at Carlton. An inquest held locally was apparently a bit of a novelty, and the story goes that from the evidence given the conclusion was reached that the remains were of two young lads who had unfortunately been caught in a snow storm and had sought shelter in the mine but for some reason had been unable to get out again.

In the late 1800s the mine was re-opened by a Mr Tennant of Middleham who went into partnership with a Dr Smeddle.

Mr Tennant also had interests in a pit on the outskirts of Shildon near to the station on the Stockton to Darlington Railway. Dr Smeddle lived in Shildon where he worked as a local doctor (see photograph). The two men were undoubtedly induced into the West Scrafton venture by the plans for a railway through Coverdale, the route of which would have run through the dale with the possibility of there being a station at Nathwaite; this could have been a convenient loading point for the coal and for its transportation to Lancashire or to the North East. They managed to drag the engine for the mine up over Roova Crag with the aid of seven horses that had been hired from Brown's of Leyburn. Mr Spence remembered that there was a very old cart track which went right up to the mine, probably the remains of the old monks' road.

He went on to describe one particular occasion when he went down the mine for coal; it was on a Monday morning and apparently he and three other men went down in the lift. He related how one had to be quick to avoid getting soaked as there was a lot of water in the mine tunnels. It was about a hundred yards down, the mine was not reinforced in any way and coal "shudders" were common. There was one such shudder when Mr Spence and his colleagues went in, but they managed to move it with sticks and stones. (A "shudder", as Mr Spence called it, referred to a minor collapse of the tunnel wall or roof). The tunnel was narrow for the most part, but its width varied in places. That morning he went forward with his pick to the coal face; in this particular tunnel there was room for about three men to work at the face. The coal seam varied in thickness and they got their coal back to the lift by means of a wagon running along a track.

Dr Smeddle

Mr Spence went on to say that the mine was about a mile long running in a southerly direction and that the face at which he was working was under Little Haw. There were very few ventilating shafts. At the top of the hill up from the village, near the mine entrance, there was an old stable built of stone in which miners' horses could be left while they were at work. The whole village relied upon coal from the mine for fuel and also upon peat from the moor which they collected for themselves.

Sam and John Neesham, their father William and a William Stubbs were four of the men employed by Mr Tennant to work in the mine digging out the coal. One day when they were coming up in the lift, something went wrong and the lift got stuck in the shaft. Luckily no-one was hurt and the four of them managed to get back down to the tunnels where they were forced to go back and crawl for half-a-mile along what Mr Spence described as a water drain. They eventually managed to escape to the outside world. After this incident the mine was temporarily out of use while Mr Tennant raised the funds necessary to pay for the repairs to the winding mechanism.

During the first part of the 20th century the mine continued to have a very chequered history. One day in 1912 there was a very bad storm and the mine was engulfed by a flood. As it happened, there was a local "feast" that day and the miners had been allowed to take the day off in order to attend. Two miners, however, decided to work, no doubt to earn a bit more cash, but they were caught in the flooding tunnels and were unfortunately drowned for their pains. They were buried in Coverham churchyard. The mine was then closed yet again.

In 1915 there was an attempt to re-open it, prompted by the renewed proposal for a Yorkshire Dales Railway to run through Coverdale. A steam pump was brought to the village in an endeavour to pump out the mine, but the attempt failed. Mr Tennant and Dr Smeddle could no longer afford the costs and the mine could not be not used while they waited for funds for repairs and further development. According to a contemporary surveyor's report (see page 285) it was "temporarily" closed down, but as it did not re-open it can be assumed that the funds were not forthcoming.

The entrance was fenced off as a protection for any roaming animals. However, there had been some "small" (pieces of coal up to about one inch across) thrown out when the mine was closed off and during the strike of 1926 a number of people used to go up Roova to collect it, although it was yellowish in colour and of very poor quality. In fact, the whole output from the mine was undoubtedly of low quality, as it used to be said that one could light a fire and put the kettle on, go away on holiday for a week and on returning find that there would be a nice fire going and the kettle boiling!

When the mine was in operation it is interesting to note that the present kitchen of Forester's Cottage was the "clog shop" for the miners. The mine manager's office was situated in the top end of what is now Bridge Cottage, while the lower part of the house was where the pit ponies were kept.

Shown below is a note containing some comments from the surveyor followed by the 1915 Report on the Abandoned Mine.

Report on Plan of Abandoned Mine

Under the _____ C O A L _____ Mines Act.

Registry Number: 30Cn306

Number of Plan: 6n82
(To be filled in at Home Office.)

County	Yorks, N.R.
No. of Division	2.
Name of Mine	West Scrafton.
Where Situated: Parish	Coverham.
Post Town	Middleham.
Name of Owner, and Address	The West Scrafton Colliery Coy., c/o Dr. Smeddle, New Soildon, Co. Durham.
Minerals worked, and in case of Coal, the name of Seam or Seams	Millstone Grit Coal Seam.
Date of Abandonment	November, 1914. (Temporary).
Cause of Abandonment	Standing for want of capital to develope.
Is the accuracy of the plan certified as required by the Coal Mines Act, 1911	Yes.
Name of the Surveyor certifying	F. J. Raine.
How Qualified	Surveyor's Service Certificate.
Does the scale on which the plan is drawn fulfil the requirements of the Act?	Yes.
Does the plan show everything required to be shown by Section 31 of the Coal Mines Act, 1911, or by Section 14 of the Metalliferous Mines Regulation Act, 1872?	Yes.
Is the meridian marked on the plan the true or the magnetic meridian?	Magnetic.
If the latter, is its date stated?	Yes.
Does the accuracy of the Survey depend upon the indications of the magnetic needle?	Yes.
If so, have proper allowances been made from time to time for the changes in the magnetic declination?	Yes.

REMARKS
(Under this head should be mentioned any points not included under the previous heads in which the plan appears to the Inspector to be irregular or unsatisfactory.)

This mine is situated upon the moors 2½ miles to the South of West Scrafton village. There are no roads or buildings within the vicinity to act as land marks.

The mine is expected to be re-opened at an indefinite date when capital for the purpose is available.

There is no regular section of the seam; it varies rapidly in thickness between 9 and 18 inches.

Signed J. R. R. Robson
H.M. Inspector of Mines of the Division.

Date November 26th, 1915.

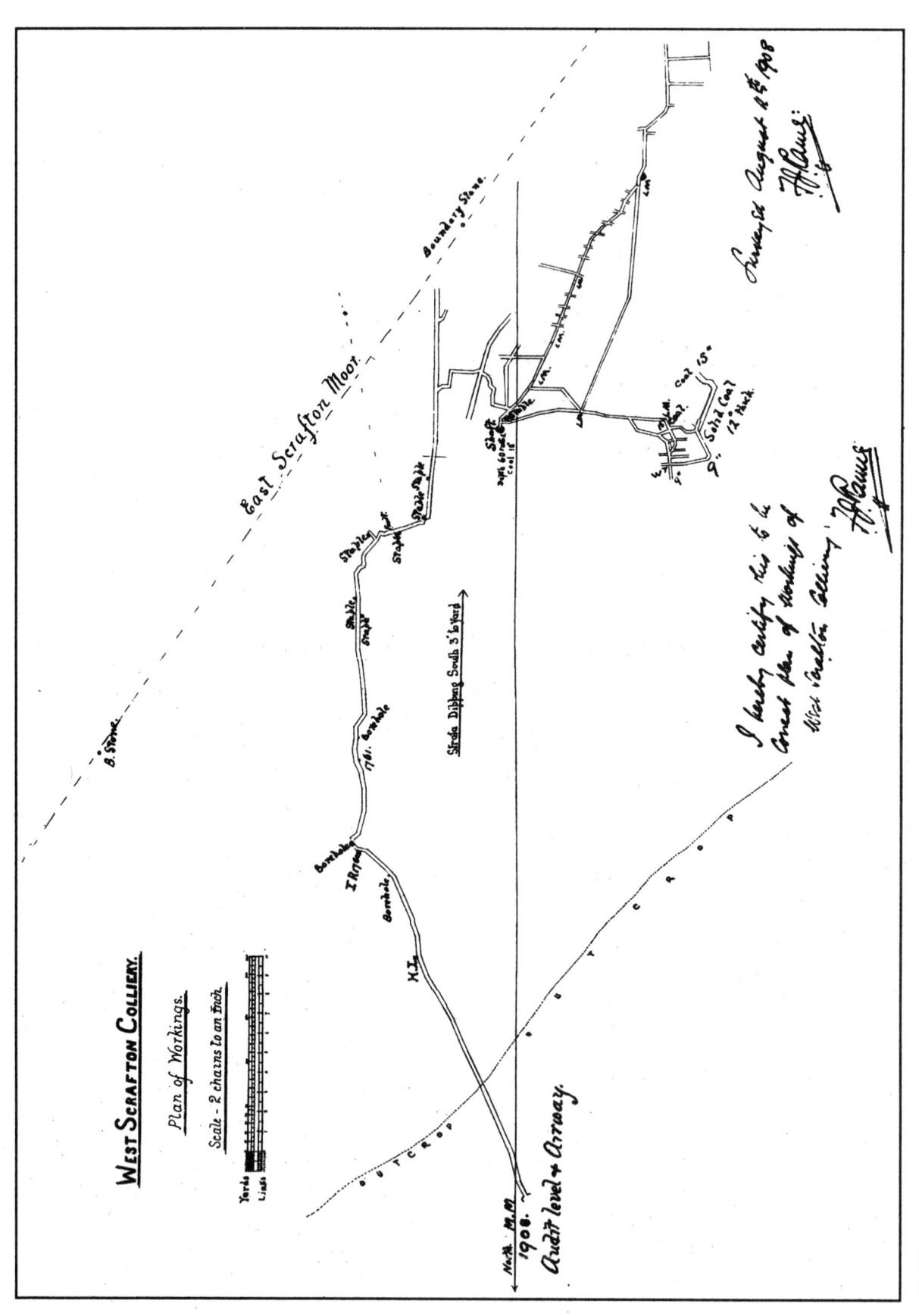

Fig 22   West Scrafton Colliery as surveyed in 1908

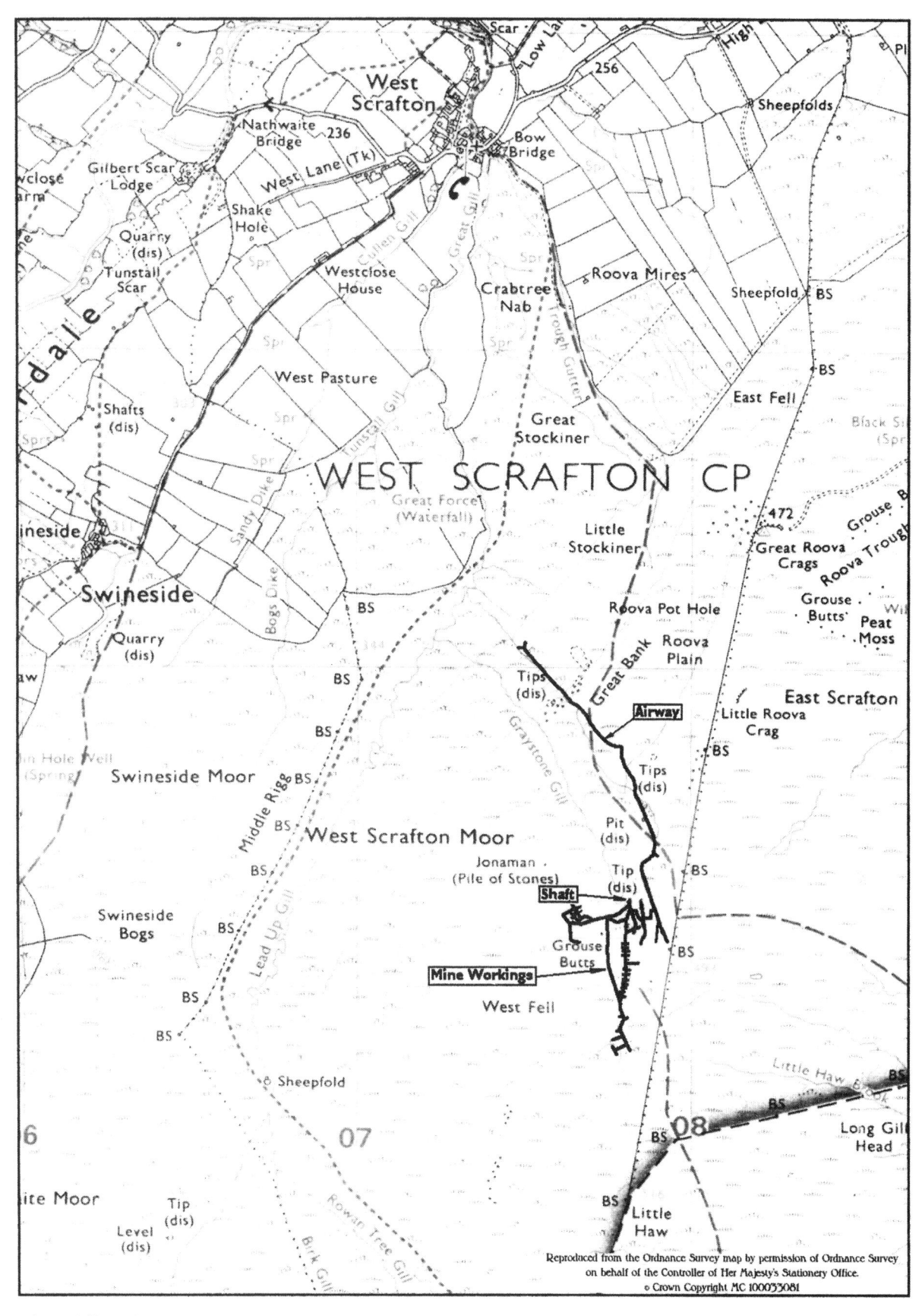

Fig 23   Map showing approximate position of Last Working Colliery

The Quarries

The local stone quarries have over the centuries been the source of much of the roofing material for the various buildings in the village. They should perhaps be called stone "mines" as the word "quarry" really refers to an open cast excavation whereas these are underground workings. At the end of the second millennium they are still very much in existence and are in extremely good condition (see picture on page 326). They are to be found close to the River Cover a little upstream from Nathwaite Bridge. The type of stone is naturally of the wafered sand-coloured variety known nationally as "Yorkstone". Many of the houses in the dale have roofs made of stone which have undoubtedly come from these quarries at Nathwaite.

There are four entrances to the quarries, each of which can be readily located and easily entered. Inside, in several cases the passages incline downwards away from the entrance and are therefore subject to increasingly deep water. Nevertheless, examination of some of the workings is possible. The high quality of much of the walling and arching is quite remarkable.

A great deal of the space that was opened up underground through extraction of the stone has been filled in with waste from workings further in. This was a regular practice in mining but it does unfortunately make seeing the extent of the excavations somewhat difficult. As in coal mining, the stones often used to be carried out by rail trucks and in one of the quarries some of the old railway lines are still in position. In one of the others, there are clear marks of wear indicating that in that particular mine the stones were brought out by the use of some form of sledge.

It is not known when the quarries were last worked, but they were probably abandoned during the first decades of the 20th century. In the West Scrafton census records, the last mention of a quarryman was that of J Butterfield who in 1890 was also a farmer.

As in the case of the collieries, had the proposals for a local railway come to fruition, the quarry workings might have continued for a bit longer, as a railway station would most likely have been only a couple of hundred yards away and could have provided a means of easy export to other parts of the country.

One of the quarry entrances

Wild Flowers

There is a considerable number of different wild flowers to be seen in and around West Scrafton if you know where to look. There are, of course, many common ones such as the snowdrop which usually appears in large groups around the river and ghylls and also on the grassy banks by the side of the road, especially if the preferred damp and sheltered conditions are provided by over-shadowing trees. A brief selection of these wild flowers is compiled below with a brief description of their main characteristics.

Coltsfoot (*tussilagu farfara*) plants are classed as perennial herbs with long stout white scaly stolens with furrowed stalks above. There are black toothed lobes which are heart-shaped at the base. The heads are between 15 and 35 centimetres in diameter and are usually on purplish woolly stems. There are a number of hairy bracts and the flowers are quite a bright yellow. These plants can be seen in a number of the hedgerows in and around the village, and sometimes grow in open fields, but usually there are too many perils there for them to survive.

Herb Robert (*geranium robertianum*) is another quite common plant to be found around the area. It is mostly pink in colour but sometimes has a tinge of red. The stems often lie along the ground and rise at the ends showing extremely dense hairs on the underside. They are branched at the base and are quite brittle.

The leaves grow in pairs on either side of the stem, have deeply cut lobes and are strong smelling. The plant flowers between May and September and is to be seen not only in woods but also on rocks where the sun turns the leaves to a brilliant crimson colour.

Red Campion *(silene dioica)* has deep pink flowers with jagged teeth-like petals. It has five styles and a fairly stout stem with quite hairy leaves. It is a fairly common plant in these parts and is to be found mainly in the hedgerows in June and July, but there do not seem to be many specimens in wooded areas. The White Campion *(silene alba)* can also to be found, but there are not so many of these around.

There are a few woodland areas in which Bluebells *(hyacinthoides non-scripta)* grow in profusion in May and June, but these are mainly further downstream towards Coverham. The flowers are so well known that description is hardly necessary; they are bright blue in colour, cylindrical in shape and with outward curving tips to the petals. The anthers are yellow and the flowers hang downwards from bent-over stems.

A similar plant to this is the "Bluebell of Scotland", or Harebell *(campanula rotundifolia)* as it is known south of the border. The flowers of this plant are a light blue and do not hang over to such an extent as those of the bluebell as the stem is thicker and stiffer. They are to be found in dry grassy places, such as on the banks beside the road and they flower later than the bluebell, between July and September.

Primroses *(primula vulgaris)* are another type of plant that is so common throughout the country that description is really superfluous. However, these plants have long pedicels with lemon coloured flowers and the throat of the corolla is quite narrow. The leaves are long and narrow below. Primroses can be found in abundance in Coverdale from February to May, mainly in hedgerows, on grassy banks and in wooded places as well as in some gardens.

The leaves of the Oxslip *(primula elatior)* are narrowed sharply below the flowers which are yellowish in colour and all turn to face one way. This is not a very common plant around the vicinity of West Scrafton, but it may be found by searching in local woods between April and May.

Cowslips (*primula veers*) are very much more common and can also be found in the woods and other shady places in April and May. Its flowers are of a lemon yellow and quite small and its leaves, like those of the oxlip, narrow abruptly below. Primroses, cowslips and oxlips are usually to be found growing in the same areas.

The Celandine comes in two types, known as the Greater (*chelidonium majus*) and the Lesser (*ranunculus ficaria*). They have slightly bluish flowers, those of the Greater type being rather brittle, with almost pinnate leaves and between five and seven leaflets. The terminal leaflets are often three lobed, the lateral ones having a stipule-like lobe on the lower side and all the leaves are crenate toothed. Its sepals are greenish yellow and the petals are bright yellow with the filaments thickened above. The Lesser variety is a perennial plant and is very common in the local hedgerows.

Wood Anemones (*anemone memorosa*) have stems that are about six inches long bearing flowers which are normally white, although sometimes pale lilac or pale blue ones can be found. They are extremely common plants in this locality and can be seen growing in woods and in fields near to water courses during the months of April and May.

The Sweet Violet (*viola odorata*) has bluish purple flowers and the petioles have deflexed hairs. The plant itself has stolons and is to be found between April and June in the hedgerows and woods around the area.

Wild or Wood Garlic (*allium oleracium*) has an abundance of broad fleshy leaves and small white flowers. They are quite common plants, growing in moist shady areas around the village and they give off a strong garlic-like smell when crushed under foot. There is also a related variety known colloquially as the Ramsons (*allium ursinum*) distinguished by the three-lobed fruit sheath instead of the two lobes of the garlic.

The common Forget-me-not (*myosotis sylvatica*) has stems and leaves which are covered with spreading hairs. It has a short style and a calyx with many hooked hairs. The flowers are mainly blue, but get paler and fade towards white in older specimens. This is another plant that is very common in Coverdale and grows in many of the woods and hedgerows.

* * * * *

To give the reader a much better idea of the extent and range of wild flowers to be seen at this altitude of nearly 1000ft, listed below is a range of wild flowers seen in the lanes and fields around West Scrafton. The list was compiled between March and August some years ago by Norman Oddy's late wife, Irene, and it is surprising how many varieties there were. She used the common names and the latin names have been added for interest where these are known.

March
Celandine *(chelidonium majus)*
Sweet violets *(viola odorata)*
Wood anemone *(anemone nemorosa)*

April
Primroses *(primula vulgaris)*
Woodruff *(galium odoratum)*
Dandelion *(taraxacum officinale)*
Creeping speedwell *(veronica persica)*
Cowslip *(primula veris)*
Barren strawberry *(potentilla sterilis)*
White deadnettle *(lamium album)*
Forget-me-nots *(myosotis sylvatica)*
Ground Ivy *(glechoma hederacea)*
Lesser stitchwort *(stellaria graminea)*
False Oxslip

May
Wood sorrel *(oxalis acetosella)*
Water avens *(geum urbanum)*
Dog's mercury *(mercurialis perennis)*
Rock cinquefoil
Greater stitchwort *(stellaria holostea)*
Eyebright *(euphrasia nemorosa)*
Welsh poppies *(meconopsis cambrica)*
Pignut *(conopodium majus)*
Bush vetch *(vicia sepium)*
Buttercup *(ranunculus acris)*
Cow parsley *(anthriscus sylvestris)*
Sorrel *(rumex acetosa)*
Wavy bittercress *(cardamine flexuosa)*
Bastard toadflax
Lady's smock *(cardamine pratensis)*
Marsh marigolds *(caltha palustris)*
Sweet Cicely
Lady's mantle *(alchemilla)*
Butterbur *(petasites hybridus)*
Herb robert *(geranium robertanium)*
Red campion *(silene dioica)*
Black medick *(medicago lupulina)*
Bluebell *(hyacintoides non-scripta)*
Ramsons *(allium ursinium)*
Common speedwell *(veronica officinalis)*
Daisies *(bellis perennis)*
Townhall clock

June

Birdsfoot trefoil *(ornithopus perpusillus)*
Sandwort
Tormentil *(potentilla erecta)*
Common mouse ear *(hieraceum pilosella)*
Burnet rose *(rosa pimpinellifolia)*
Hardheads
Heath bedstraw *(galium saxatile)*
Shepherd's purse *(capsella bursa-pastoris)*
Valerian *(valeriana officinalis)*
Red clover *(trifolium pratense)*
Rose bay willow herb *(chamerion angustifolium)*
Broad leaved willow herb *(epilobium montanum)*

Bugle *(ajugo reptans)*
Silverweed *(potentilla anserina)*
Yarrow *(achillea millifoleum)*
Hedge parsley *(torilis japonica)*
Dog rose *(rosa canina)*
Meadow cranesbill *(geranium pratense)*
Foxgloves *(digitalis purpurea)*
Hedge woundwort *(stachys sylvatica)*
Meadow sweet *(filipendura ulmaria)*
White clover *(trifolium repens)*

July

Hemlock *(conium maculatum)*
Nipplewort *(lapsana communis)*
Honeysuckle *(lonicera pericyclenem)*
Teasel *(dipsacus fullonum)*
Bell flowers *(campanula trachelium)*
Ox eye daisy *(leucanthemum vulgare)*
Wild marjoram *(origanum vulgare)*
Policeman's helmet
Meadow vetchling *(lathyrus pratensis)*
Square-stemmed St John's wort *(hypericum tetrapterum)*

Harebell *(campanula rotundifolia)*
Self heal *(prunella vulgaris)*
Black horehound *(ballota nigra)*
Lady's bedstraw *(galium verum)*
Marsh orchid *(epipactis helleborine)*
Hoary plantain *(plantago media)*
Common agrimony *(agrimonia eupatoria)*
Tufted vetch *(vicia cracca)*

August

Marsh bedstraw *(galium palustre)*
Great burnet *(sanguisorba officinalis)*
Welted thistle
Hogweed *(heracleum sphondylium)*
Autumn hawkbit *(leontodon autumnalis)*
Greater burnet saxifrage *(pimpinella major)*

Narrow-leaved bittercress
Pineapple weed *(matricaria matricarioides)*
Thyme-leaved speedwell
Common hawkbit *(leontodon officinalis)*

Birds

Around the West Scrafton area we are very lucky to have a wide variety of birds of all shapes and sizes ranging from the small wren right up to the large buzzard. Although the latter are more likely to be seen over the moorland areas, a pair has been spotted in the vicinity of the village.

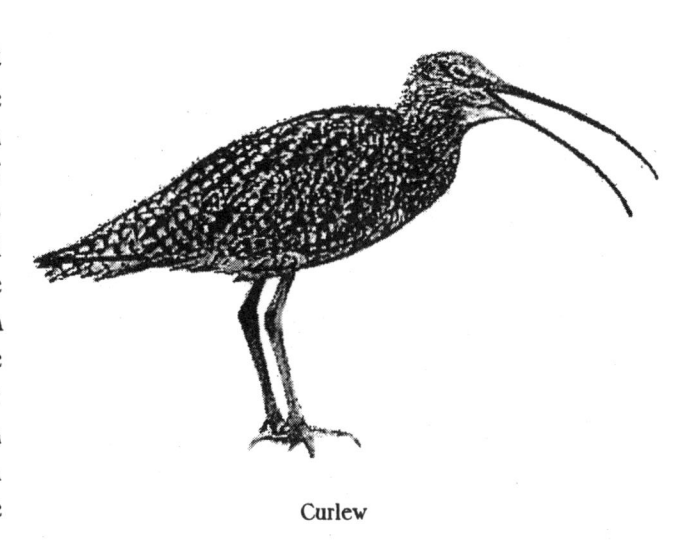

Curlew

A list of the more common varieties of birds which are to be seen in abundance in the area is shown below, but it is very far from being complete and certainly none of the birds in the list is in any way unique to this part of the world.

Chaffinch	Brambling	Bluetits
Great tit	Greenfinch	Goldfinch
Starling	Jackdaw	Blackbird
Thrush	Dunnock	Sparrow
Wren	Grey wagtail	Pied wagtail
Spotted woodpecker	Pigeon	Snipe
Cuckoo	Curlew	Oystercatcher
Little owl	Barn owl	Short-eared owl
Spotted flycatcher	Tree creeper	Kestrel

Many people in the village have bird tables or some other kind of bird feeder. David Thomas reported that spotted flycatchers nested in one of their hanging baskets recently. They moved the basket not realising that there were babies in the nest. Apparently the flycatchers didn't seem to mind and eventually the family duly took off. The Thomases have a barn attached to their house and every year from April onwards they leave the barn door open to allow swallows to shelter inside. Each year one arrives apparently on a reconnaissance mission and then disappears, but about a week later the rest arrive, about ten in number, chattering endlessly. Jackdaws can be a nuisance and they can monopolise the bird tables in the early morning. David woke one morning hearing a loud tapping on the window; he saw that the noise was caused by a jackdaw that was obviously incensed because he hadn't restocked the bird table!

* * * * *

In addition to the types of birds which are mentioned above, every so often the RSPB carries out a survey of waders in the area and for this an accurate count is made of the wader population in a well defined square kilometre. The area used for the Coverdale survey is grid reference SE 0683 which has Nathwaite bridge at its approximate centre. Three visits were made by the RSPB personnel in 1998 and the results of their count are shown in the following table.

Date	Oystercatcher pairs	Little ringed plover singles	Drummers Snipes	Curlew pairs	Curlew singles	Redshank singles	Other bird species
6 May	1	6	0	4	5	0	2 brown hare 9 stock dove
22 May	1	12	0	4	6	0	6 brown hare 1 Pr. grey partridge
9 June	1	4	0	4	5	0	2 brown hare 1 Pr. Linnet male redstart
Prs. Total 1998	1	6	0	4		0	

This next table compares the survey results for 1993 and 1998.

Year	Oystercatcher pairs	Little ringed plover pairs	Snipe pairs	Curlew pairs	Redshank pairs	Total pairs target waders	Other species maximum counts
1993	0	2	0	1	0	3	--
1998	1	6	0	4	0	11	6 brown hare 9 stock dove 1 Pr. grey partridge 1 Pr. Linnet male redstart

The Brothertons made a record for the British Trust for Ornithology of the birds seen in the garden of Moor Ghyll during 1999. This record is shown in the following tables.

Resident Species

Species	Jan to Mar	Apr to Jun	Jul to Sep	Oct to Dec
Blue tit	6	4	4	4
Great tit	2	3	3	1
Coal tit	2	1	0	2
Chaffinch	22	14	11	20
Green finch	8	9	10	7
Gold finch	3	4	5	2
Blackbird	4	3	3	2
Song thrush	1	1	1	0
Mistle thrush	1	1	1	1
Robin	2	1	2	1
Wren	1	3	1	1
Dunnock	4	3	2	2
House sparrow	4	11	21	9
Pied wagtail	1	2	2	5
Starling	4	6	>100	2
Wood pigeon	0	1	1	1
Jackdaw	10	8	3	16
Rook	0	3	0	3
Magpie	0	0	0	1
Pheasant	0	0	0	3
Tawny Owl	1	2	1	0
Srarrowhawk	0	1	0	1
Kestrel	0	0	0	1

Summer Visitors

Willow warbler	0	1	1	0
Chiff chaff	0	1	0	0
Spotted flycatcher	1	1	0	0
Grey wagtail	0	2	1	0
Wheatear	0	0	1	0

Winter Visitors

Brambling	1	0	0	2
Fieldfare	>50	>10	0	0

A Local Lime Kiln

Great Ghyll Dam built by the Children

One of the old Village Standpipes

The Bee-boles at Culverham House

Joy French's Weather Station

The Shoe Concealed in Fell View

Fig 24   A few local Items of Interest

Some Walks around the Area

We are blessed with plenty of good walks around here, and all the ones that are included in the next few pages are properly signposted, pass through glorious countryside and incidentally the going is invariably firm. If those of the "right to roam" persuasion wish to end up in a bog, that is their lookout, because if one does stray off the beaten track by chance one can be in pretty muddy trouble.

The walks that mentioned here are all shown on the Ordnance Survey Outdoor Leisure map 30, Yorkshire Dales Northern & Central areas which are on a 1/25,000 (2½" to 1 mile) scale. Footpaths are indicated on this map by green dotted lines.

Walk 1   To Carlton village via Caygill bridge.

There are two ways to commence this walk. The first is to leave West Scrafton on the road to East Scrafton and then in about a hundred yards to turn down the track on the left of The Batt called Low Lane; this is the old drovers' road. Carry on over the stile and across the field to Caygill House. Leaving the house on your left, go over another stile and continue down the field to Caygill bridge. Alternatively, you can go through the village and down the "no through road" on the right. Then take the signposted track to "Carlton" about a hundred yards down on the left between Lane End Cottage and Chapman's Cottage. Following the signposts, go along the side of a field, through a "kissing gate", and then down the hill to Caygill bridge as before. Go over the bridge and then diagonally up the hill until you reach Carlton. You can return to West Scrafton via the road by walking up the hill through the village, bearing left with the road at the top, and then, in about a further three hundred yards, taking a turning to the left signposted "West Scrafton". The walk is about 2 miles.

Walk 2   To Horsehouse.

Go through West Scrafton village and take the uphill turning signposted "Swineside" on the left of a grass triangle. Continue up this road for about three-quarters of a mile, then cross a cattle grid and bear right and through the hamlet of Swineside. Carry on, on the footpath across the fields, for about another mile when you will reach Horsehouse. Again, you can come back on the road by turning right at Horsehouse and continuing up the road for about 1½ miles, through the village of Gammersgill, until you come to the turning on your right signposted "West Scrafton". This walk is around 5 miles.

Walk 3   To Swineside and Nathwaite.

As in the previous walk, go up to Swineside, but then, instead of passing through the hamlet, go through the old Coverdale Hotel car park, which is on your right as you enter the hamlet, and then take the right-hand footpath down the hill to Nathwaite bridge; you can then return to West Scrafton either by turning right and up the hill, or halfway up the hill you can take a signposted footpath by a gate and continue back to West Scrafton across the fields. This round is roughly 2½ miles.

Walk 4   To Gammersgill.

There are two ways to extend the above walk. The first is to turn left after reaching Nathwaite bridge, and continue along the road up the hill until you see a signpost pointing to the left across the fields to Gammersgill. Follow this footpath, and when the road is reached just before Gammersgill village, turn right on to the road and return to West Scrafton by taking the next road turning on your right via Nathwaite bridge. The second way is to take the left-hand footpath after leaving the Coverdale Hotel car park, which will lead you down to Gammersgill, where again you can turn right on to the road and back to West Scrafton via the Nathwaite Bridge road as above. This walk is between 3 and 3½ miles depending on which way you go.

Walk 5   Up and Over Roova Crags.

For this walk you need to go through the small gate on the north-east side of Bow Bridge, pass in front of Bridge Cottage and continue up the track, reaching the old mine workings below Roova Crags in just over a mile. If you are feeling energetic, go straight on up the hill to Roova Crags. If you are so minded and are feeling even more energetic, you can carry on past the disused mine works and over Street House Moor, arriving after about a further three miles in Nidderdale. Another mile-and-a-half to the right will take you to Scar House Reservoir, or if you take the path to the left you will eventually finish up in the village of Lofthouse. To the reservoir and back is around 11 miles but a return trip as far as Lofthouse is nearer 18 miles.

Walk 6   To Scar House Reservoir.

Once again you need to start by going up the Swineside road, but this time carry straight on after crossing the cattle grid instead of turning down to the hamlet. This bridle path will take you over Hindlethwaite and Arkleside Moors and on the way you may find yourself surrounded by 3 ft high ponies that belong to Barbara Johnson who used to live in East Leigh where Jane and Peter Gower now live (she used to keep these ponies in my barn!). After that slight diversion you can carry on and, after passing Dead Man's Hill on your left, reach Scar House reservoir. It is about three miles from Swineside making the complete return walk about 9 miles.

Walk 7   To St Simon's Chapel

This is a much shorter walk and from the village you go along to The Batt again and down the old drovers' road, Low Lane. Follow it round and across the fields and you come back on to the West Scrafton to Coverham road. Turn left and continue down the road to the East Scrafton turning on your right. Opposite this is a signposted footpath on the left. Go over the stile and follow the footpath across the field and down the hill to St Simon's Chapel which is on the banks of the River Cover. You can then continue over the bridge, taking one of two paths up the hill and soon reach the Carlton road; turn left, reaching Carlton in under a mile and you can then take the footpath on your left from the village back to West Scrafton via Caygill bridge. The whole walk is of the order of 4 miles.

Walk 8   To Pinker's Pond

There is a route across the fields to Middleham if you are so minded. Proceed as above to the East Scrafton turning and then take this turning towards East Scrafton. In about a hundred yards, before Corner's House, turn left on to a signposted footpath and follow the track to Caldbergh. Beyond Caldbergh there are two alternative tracks, both coming out on to Hanghow Lane. Turn right up the lane and take the path on the left just before Braithwaite Hall. This will take you over Hullo bridge and up to Pinker's Pond. It is roughly 4 miles to Pinker's Pond.

There are numerous variations to these walks. The Ordnance Survey map mentioned above indicates the routes clearly as green dotted lines. The green dashed lines represent public bridleways. Although these are public rights of way and are usually clearly signposted, it helps considerably to get the 1/25,000 scale map.

A MONTHLY DIARY

Compiled by a few Residents

This, alas, is not a diary which reflects the activities of the whole village, as it has been woven around narratives provided by only a few who were able, or perhaps rash enough, to make such personal records as a diary requires. The result may be a little egocentric; it is certainly not comprehensive, but for all its warts, it is still a small slice of life in West Scrafton.

January

It was New Year's Eve and a warm, dry but humid night which was perhaps a little unusual for the beginning of a new year. The Hullahs greeted the occasion at midnight by going outside and listening to the total silence; there was apparently no noise at all apart from the trickle of water in Great Ghyll. After popping open some champagne, they shouted "Happy New Year West Scrafton" into the night but got no response. Perhaps this was because everyone had two-foot thick walls and sounds of revelry could not penetrate either way. There must have been some revelry, however, because the Brothertons were having supper at the Thomas's together with Graham and Ruth Burgess and they did not emerge until two o'clock in the morning. Everyone at that party had contributed a course for the meal and the roast beef had made a very welcome change from turkey and trimmings. When the party finally broke up, the New Year was seen to have begun with a clear, starry night.

New Year literally came in with rather a bang for Mabel and Tommy Handley. They had spent the New Year celebrations, together with the Utleys, at friends in Masham, but on arriving home early in the morning, they discovered that they must have left their house keys back in Masham. The only way to get in to the house was by breaking in and one of Mabel's shoes presented itself as being the time honoured and only readily available weapon in the circumstances; the heel certainly brought the pane of glass in the door to shatters!

On New Year's Day, Ed and Joan Hullah invited a number of the villagers to lunchtime drinks and food. It was at this gathering that the first ideas and proposals for this village book were mooted and discussed. Although most of the people that were there were what one might call newcomers, having come to the village within the last six or seven years, the idea took root and was followed up with growing and spreading enthusiasm by a number of villagers two or three days later.

Philip and Kate Hudson were such newcomers, having arrived in the village only the previous year and they were deriving pleasure from their new garden as they were not at all sure what was in it and were constantly being surprised by the gradual appearance of various plants.

The following week tended to be rather wet and gloomy with a strong gusty wind, which proved to be a precursor for the type of weather that was to come. Nevertheless, the local wildlife was being its usual hive of industry. Bluetits were making serious inspections of the various nesting boxes that many of the inhabitants of the village had provided. Moles were pushing up their unsightly mounds of earth all over the place and that night Ed noticed a badger crossing the road at Coverham as he was coming home in his car at about 10pm. Perhaps it was the bad weather that had encouraged all this activity, especially as it was quite mild for the time of year.

Tony Harrison, whose wife had died three months earlier and had left him with two Afghan hounds to look after, walked them on the moors every afternoon, whatever the weather. So far this year they had hardly had dry feet and much time was spent "bucketing" them to get the mud off their very hairy legs. They were not the only dogs whose feet got bucketed after they had been out; Meg, the Baxters' Rough Collie, also had to undergo such treatment. Unfortunately, the two Afghans did not like each other and fought whenever they met, so they not only had to be kept apart in the house, but they had to be taken to the moors and walked separately, one by one. When the ground was dry, they were taken for walks on the roads to help keep their claws in trim, but there was much more freedom on the moors and less likelihood of meeting farm animals. Of all the previous Afghans that the Harrisons had had, these were the only two that had been at daggers drawn with each other, although they had individually been perfectly friendly towards the others. They were therefore quite lonely now that they had to be kept apart.

The first week of the year saw the first snow of the winter as there had been none before Christmas, but it was not very much more than a light covering and was gone from the village in no time, although signs remained on the surrounding hills for a few days. It was icy on the track up to the moor behind Moor Ghyll and as the Brothertons made their way up for a morning walk, Meg, their Border Collie, disturbed a snipe from an unfrozen patch of ground by the track about a hundred yards or so above the bridge. They continued up Roova and for a change there was a beautiful clear blue sky with all-round views from on high; they regretted, not for the first time, having left their camera at home.

On the 11th there was a fire at the White Swan Inn at Middleham in the late evening. Durrant's, the shop next door to the White Swan from which the villagers of West Scrafton obtained their papers, was luckily still operating and so the paper round continued undisturbed. A weekly rota system was operated whereby those West Scrafton villagers who had papers took it in turns to collect them from Durrant's and deliver them around the village, having a natter in the process.

There was a little more snow the next day and young Joseph and Thomas Forrest were to be seen trying to sledge down the slopes on plastic sheets, but, disappointingly for them, there was hardly enough snow to cover the rocks. As it was not very pleasant outside, Brenda Thiede spent some time that day choosing colours for decorating the rooms at Great Ghyll Cottage. Her house had been undergoing reconstruction work for some time and this had virtually been completed; the "kitchen" man was now hovering. When the Hudsons had moved into their house last year they had inherited planning permission from the previous owner for a "sunroom" to be built on the eastern end of the house. They had decided to continue with this plan and they hoped that work might be started quite soon, although the weather would be a deciding factor in this matter. The Gowers, who were soon to be spending a period in Australia, were also having building work done; they were having the buildings behind East Leigh enlarged and renovated and this work was gradually coming to an end. When it was all totted up, there seemed to be rather a lot of renovating and building work going on in West Scrafton at that moment.

There continued to be gales and rain for a number of days, with small pockets of snow still clinging to the upper reaches of Roova and Penhill. Sheep were huddled in the gulleys on the moor and lined in single row in the lea of the walls on the west side of Nathwaite Bridge. Great Ghyll and the River Cover were both roaring in flood. The road was flooded by the Batt, as the drainpipe, which was supposed to take the water flowing off the fields under the road, was apparently blocked. One got to know those sections of the road that became flooded when it rained heavily and this wasn't normally one of them. Liz Watson was lucky in getting her vehicle through, although it spluttered for a time afterwards, but Matthew Gower was less fortunate as his car came to a halt.

The 21st proved to be a fine bright morning but the ground was very soggy after all the rain. The gate to one of the fields on the track up to Roova and Crabtree Nab had been left open; this was unusual and Ed, who discovered it, told Charles Utley. At about half past two that morning Roger and Sandra Baxter had seen lights on the moor and had been wondering what action to take as it took courage to ring your neighbours at that time in the morning, especially as it became evident that the "lampers" (poachers) had chosen a wet and windy night for their operations. As it happened, several of the farmers, returning home from a "farmer's dinner", had also seen the lights. It transpired later that, with the aid of Mick Southgate, the gamekeeper from Lane House, the lampers' car had been located and its registration number noted. Stories were going around that the car tyres had been let down, but nevertheless the lampers had apparently managed to get away undetected. Contact with the police the next day revealed that they had known the car involved from the registration number and had apparently said that it was "not local".

The rough weather had caused the sheep to move down from the moor and there were now about 150 ewes and two tups huddled together behind Moor Ghyll, seeking shelter and looking longingly in at the kitchen window. This presented a colourful sight to Ian and Jenny Brotherton as the Utleys' sheep had blue and red markings and the Hoggs' had black shoulder stripes; there were also many displaying psychedelic bums, some red, some yellow, some blue and some green, these various colours indicating the time of lambing. In addition, a number of multi-coloured ones were to be seen vying for the limited amount of shelter.

Tony went to Darlington on the 29th to pick up 1½ hundredweight of frozen raw tripe, which was enough to last his *Afghans* for about ten to twelve weeks. Tony's late wife, Doreen, used to show the dogs and they had both won their way through to Cruft's. Ruth Burgess had Keeshonds and she also exhibited these at dog shows. They, too, had qualified for Cruft's and in fact both mother and daughter (seen below) were champions. It seemed quite remarkable that, in such a small isolated village as West Scrafton, there were two families both with dogs that were qualified for and exhibited at Cruft's.

February

Winter was very much with us for most of the month and, although there was not much snow, we continued to have extremes of wet and wind, which seemed to have become the norm for the moment. However, the weather had apparently been kind to this part of the country at the beginning of the month, defying, thank goodness, the dreadful forecasts. The snowdrops were out in masses and were just at their best; it must have been the bursts of mild weather that had brought them out a little earlier than usual. The Hudsons noticed the spotted woodpeckers that frequented the trees by the ghyll which ran straight down from their garden and one of them came to their bird feeder to try out the nuts. These birds had been around for at least four or five years and they sometimes came to the bird feeders in the back garden of Curlew Cottage, although they had not been seen there for quite some time. The Handleys had also had them at the back of Culverham House, even though their rear wall was quite close to the house.

On returning home from work at about 6.30pm one Monday evening, Liz Watson pulled in to her "garage" to find a robin sitting on the aluminium trunking in one corner, with not a peep coming out of it. It was just keeping its beady eye on things in the dark. The word "garage" has been put in inverted commas because it was, at the moment, only a shell. John was in the process of erecting a building that comprised both the garage and a workshop, the latter being large enough to house his Kramer mechanical digger and shovel. The inside shell of breeze blocks was complete and the roof with its waterproof lining was in place, although this lining was still bare. The main double doors for the Kramer and the side door to the workshop had been installed the year before and about half the outer stonework had been completed. The part that was used for Liz's garage had no doors as yet and therefore performed only a temporary "garage" function and allowed access for the local birds. John hoped to complete the building when time (and the weather) permitted.

The first Sunday in the month dawned clear, sunny and cold with a very thin covering of dry snow over everything. Ed walked up the track to the moor and met Charles Utley coming down with Joe Forrest riding in the trailer behind the Landrover. Charles had been putting out feed for the sheep who

John Watson's workshop

had herded together to feast on it single-mindedly. By the wall between the moor and the pasture to the west, Ed came across a dead new-born lamb, frozen. It was presumably premature but looked full-term to him. The umbilicus was still fresh so he assumed that it had been dropped that night. When he came down, he reported this finding to Kevin Utley and Curly Harrison who happened to be talking to each other by Hilltop Farm. They asked if he had seen the mother but he had seen no solo ewes at all, so he guessed that it must have been with the others tackling the fresh hay.

The next morning was clear with not a breath of wind in the morning, but there was a crisp temperature of -1°C, making it was an ideal day for a walk up the fell. It seemed amazing to Ed how warm freezing conditions can feel when there is no wind; and that was before the sun had risen above Rooval He reflected that it was good to walk on ground that was frozen hard instead of the wet soggy surface that had presented itself for some time past. Tony, walking an *Afghan*, shared the same thoughts, especially as he would not have to spend time washing the dog's feet when he got back home. The still air made the water in the ghylls sound even clearer than usual. The sheep were continuing to enjoy yesterday's delivery of hay and the aborted lamb was as yet untouched by predators or scavengers.

Some time last summer five dead moles were hung from the gate in the wall below the waterfall on the way up to Roova and Ed noticed that they were still there, although their skeletons were beginning to show through their dried pelts. He thought that he must try to find out who had put them there. It continued to be a fair day, although there was a thin flurry of snowflakes in the late afternoon. The flurry must have been very local as Tony, on Middleham High Moor with the other Afghan, missed it but noticed the slight whiteness on the edges of the flagstones in the drive when he got back home.

A young rabbit was grazing on the Poverty Street green in front of the Watson's house on Saturday morning. John wasn't around as otherwise its days would have been numbered. He kept an air rifle and often took shots from his upstairs window to help keep the rabbit population under control. The rabbits seemed to have started coming out rather earlier this year, which did not augur well for the garden plants. For the first two years that the Harrisons were in Curlew Cottage, no rabbit was seen there and no plant damage was suffered. The Hendersons, who were the previous occupants, had apparently had no trouble with them either, but last year, notwithstanding the Afghans, quite a few came in towards the end of March and a number of plants were totally destroyed. Tony had therefore put wire-netting all round the boundaries. This seemed to prevent them getting in from around May onwards as by this time they had apparently grown too large to force their way through the 2-inch mesh. Unfortunately, this year one or two had already been seen in the mornings playing on the grass within a few feet of the house windows through which the barking dogs did not seem to present any deterrent.

Towards the end of the month, the Baxters' daughter and son-in-law from Colchester came to visit them for a week, bringing with them four grandchildren. At eight years old, Thomas was showing signs of becoming a hill-walker. He was keen to walk anywhere with Roger, Sandra and their dog, Meg, especially up to the top of Roova Moor. Alexander, who was six, was not so keen on walking but enjoyed playing hide-and-seek on the moor. He was still small enough to be able to hide among the reeds and didn't seem to notice the mud! Hannah was three and seemed to like walking but couldn't quite manage long distances as yet; however, she did make it to the water tanks and back, which was quite a feat for a three-year-old. While their visitors were here, Roger and Sandra took them to Harrogate to see the latest Disney film, "A Bug's Life". They were not prepared, however, for the "bugs" which they had somehow collected during the week and which laid both Sandra and Roger low, luckily for only a day.

By now, building work was progressing really well on the Hudson's new extension. Most of the stonework was up to roof height; the roof had been felted and some slates were being fixed by the Thursday of that week. The construction should have been reasonably weatherproof by then and therefore they were not expecting any undue hold-ups because of bad weather. The stonework looked really good as they were using old stone that had come from the "lean-to" that used to be at the east end of the house which helped it to blend in with the rest of the building. Their garden was suffering somewhat, like most people's, due to the soggy ground and the high winds. However, the weather had been remarkably kind to them so far as, apart from one day of freezing temperatures, their builders had been able to work for a full day every day.

The last Sunday in the month was a bad day for Tony when the washing machine turned nasty. He was halfway through doing some washing when water started dribbling out of the front of the washing machine; and then the door fell off! Luckily, it was in a part of a washing programme that only took in a little water so that there was not too much of a mess. Investigation found that the very weak and thin plastic moulding, into which the door hinge was screwed, had snapped. How this design had lasted for eight years or so will never be known. A new door would no doubt be unnecessarily expensive, as well as incurring the inconvenience of having to traipse to Darlington in the hope of finding one in stock. A little thought suggested that small bolts right through the plastic door would be a much quicker, cheaper and stronger solution. Luckily, he managed to find some suitable ones and was soon back in business and able to finish the washing. In fact, for the first time for ages, the door shut with a gentle click instead of having to be banged; it must have been out of alignment for some considerable time. It was a good job that he was at home when it happened and he vowed not to leave any of the self-destructing machines on when he went out in future (if he could avoid it).

There were definite signs of spring at the end of the month, with daffodils suddenly showing buds and flowering currant showing green. Some varieties of aubretia were also beginning to show signs of colour. A wildlife visitor to the village at this time was a kestrel that came to the garden of Appletree House. Further arrivals later that same week were the lapwings, the Baxters having noticed them for the first time. Surely spring could not be far away now, could it? Judging by Friday's weather, though, it was still winter, with snow blowing in the very cold wind. Notwithstanding the weather, numerous birds continued to come and feed on the nuts hanging in the gardens; blue-tits, coal-tits, chaffinches, green finches, robins, wrens and sparrows, plus, of course, the larger birds like thrushes and blackbirds that perched on the overhead wires or strutted over the grass looking for worms.

March

March is usually the month in which the weather changes to more pleasant spring conditions. This year was no exception and the month saw a lot of spring-like weather right the way through, although interspersed with a few very wet interludes. When he was walking on the moor during the first week of the month, Roger noticed that some of the pools had begun to show signs of frog spawn. That must surely have been an indication that spring was on its way. In addition, the sound of the curlew was heard that week while the Hudsons were out walking up near Swineside, even though it seemed to them to be only at "half bubble" as they put it. Owl hootings had also increased both in the evenings and later at night. A few daffodils were already in flower in the village and here and there were just the very first signs of green on the hawthorn hedges.

The second week, though still mild, was prone to outbreaks of heavy and prolonged showers accompanied by gusty winds. On the Monday, although the weather was not too bad in West Scrafton, the electricity went off for about three-quarters of an hour. Whether this was due to wind or some other weather condition was not known. Interruption to services is one of the hazards of living in a rural community. Overhead distribution of essential services such as electricity and telephone makes them vulnerable to adverse weather conditions and, with the growth of cottage industries, working from home and the recent explosion in the use of electronic mail, rural communities are increasingly dependent upon their reliability.

West Scrafton, it seemed, had been very fortunate with the weather, as some parts of Yorkshire had been subjected to serious flooding. The areas around Malton and Norton were particularly badly affected, as the River Derwent was causing major flood damage due to the excessive amount of water coming off the North York Moors.

The weather was very much better again the following week and over the weekend the roads were quite busy with many cars carrying the first day trippers through the Dales; a number of these were open-topped, driven by people braving the slightly milder atmosphere than of late. This good spell persisted right through until the following Thursday when it turned a bit cooler again. The Hudsons even sat outside after lunch to have their coffee, although they admitted that they had had to wear their coats. In addition to the usual birds gobbling nuts as fast as Kate could put them out, one of the spotted woodpeckers had made several visits to their nut-hanger. The rooks were beginning to destroy their old nests, producing a mess of twigs and debris beneath their favourite trees.

The first few lambs appeared in the fields behind Curlew Cottage, an event which, each year, aroused the interest of the Afghans. They stood up on their hind legs and looked over the wall with fascination and curiosity at the gambolling, only barking with excitement if one started to run fast. More rabbits were appearing on the common ground beside Poverty Street. So far the Hullahs had not seen any of them venture in to Culverham Farm House garden and they were banking on the several new notches that John had marked on the barrel of his air rifle, which they thought could probably be counted as deceased rabbits. They knew that John had a mission to keep their numbers down and this would in turn help to keep their garden looking up. Last year, the rabbits had gnawed through the netting defences on the gates in order to ravage the early growth inside and they were grateful for John's accurate aim.

For the greater part of the month a "flu bug" had attacked a number of people in the village and, although it was not serious, it was very long-lasting, leaving those affected with a nasty cough that persisted for a number of weeks. The bug was part of a nation-wide epidemic according to reports from friends and relatives in various parts of the country. It was rather a pity, as it was somewhat spoiling the enjoyment of the much improved weather for those unfortunate people who were afflicted.

Building work was still progressing well on the Hudson's extension, although this was less visible now that the main construction of the walls and roof were more or less finished. The builders had now cut a doorway through from the sun-room into the existing sitting-room; this was something of a messy job in spite of their best efforts to keep the dust and debris to a minimum. In addition, the floor had been laid and the window frames were in position. The following week had the electric wiring and plaster-boarding in place and the finishing touches were carried out on the ceiling; even the glass had been fitted in the windows and it was at last beginning to look like a room! The outside had been tidied up, concrete laid round the back and the retaining wall for the garden completed. The flagstones were expected the following week and they did actually arrive! They were laid outside the new extension, vastly improving its appearance. The joiner came on the Thursday to install the windowsill boards which in turn enabled the plasterer to complete his part of the work. They were hoping that the plaster would dry out quickly enough for them to paint at least those parts of the walls that would be behind the two radiators, as this would make life easier later on. They were also hoping to get the beams stained before they were put in place; these were to make the room conform more to the style of the rest of the house. Unfortunately, the following week, the building work stalled, as there was very little activity while they waited for the French doors to arrive and for the remaining electrics and plumbing to go in.

There were no street lights in West Scrafton and, in 1998, the council had offered to pay for a few to be mounted on existing structures if the villagers so desired. At a village meeting that had been held in the previous October, it had been agreed by a substantial majority that street lighting would tend to "suburbanise" the village and this was not a characteristic that people wanted. In any case, a number of houses had external lights which helped to illuminate a good proportion of the roads and therefore the council's offer had been rejected. Tony had always intended to place some form of lamp on the end of the front wall of Curlew Cottage and he had purchased one last autumn waiting for some better weather to mount it in position. He took the opportunity to carry out the work one weekend as he had missed the good weather of a couple of weeks before due to having had the flu bug. The lamp had looked quite large in the shop but now that it was on the wall he thought that it was rather too small; anyway, it would have to do for the moment. The light it gave was quite good enough and served, not only to light the drive, but also to provide illumination for a good portion of the otherwise unlit part of the road leading past Curlew Cottage and on to Burnside and Caygill House

Two village meetings were held this month. The first was the annual meeting of the Water Committee which was convened at Culverham House. Two environmental health officials from Richmondshire District Council attended to give advice regarding the water sterilisation process that was planned to be brought into operation later in the year. It was decided that there would be no further increase for the coming year in the contribution that villagers provided for the distribution of the water; this had already been doubled for the current year to help pay for the new filtration plant and last year it had been indicated at the annual civil parish meeting that this increase would last for a couple of years. The water sample taken from the Watsons' kitchen tap the previous month had apparently only contained one E-coli, which was an improvement on some previous samples.

The second meeting was the annual civil parish meeting with tea and biscuits to follow, this year held in the home of Charles and June Utley. One of the main concerns of the evening's discussion was the 17-tonne weight limit that had been temporarily applied to Bow Bridge. There was some likelihood that this could become a permanent feature as apparently the Council could not find the necessary money to strengthen it sufficiently to take the weight of fully laden tankers. The other major topic was a situation report on the village water supply. Discussion centred on

Bow Bridge

whether or not to take out some form of temporary insurance against the possibility of the water causing illness before the time when the proposed ultra-violet treatment plant was brought into use.

The final Saturday in the month saw the Watsons going to the cinema to see "Lock, Stock and Two Smoking Barrels" at the Elite cinema in Leyburn. John had been busy building a stone pillar in which he planned to house the boxes for the electricity meters for the UV water treatment system. Liz said that he was so engrossed in this work that she had had to threaten him with two smoking guns himself before she could drag him away to ensure that they got to the cinema in time! On the Sunday, John's enthusiasm for this work again prevailed and he spent the day building some dry stone walling to hide the meter pillar that he had now completed. Planning permission for the UV treatment system had been requested some time before but had still not arrived.

In the last week of March, Jonathan Watkins cut his section of the grass on the village greens for the first time in the year. This first grass cutting round was much later than it had been the previous year but at least it hopefully heralded the beginning of summertime activities.

April

Perhaps the best way to describe this month is "very variable". We had a complete mixture of weather, changing literally on a daily basis from quite warm and spring-like to bitterly cold with heavy snow showers. Halfway through the month there was a return to real winter with an inch or so of snow lying on the ground after an exceptionally heavy breakfast-time shower lasting for about an hour and a half. Ed and Joan had made a quick family visit to Holland earlier in the week in an attempt to get all their travelling done before the peak holiday cottage season set in and on their return they awoke early to a surprisingly mellow light which emanated from a layer of snow, with more still descending. Liz wondered why it was that, once all the daffodils were in flower, it snows and flattens them all, but Kate took the opposite view and thought that it was spectacularly pretty, as it was the wet stuff that clung to everything. Although it had stopped by about 10 o'clock and had melted soon afterwards, it snowed again in the afternoon, but only lightly this time.

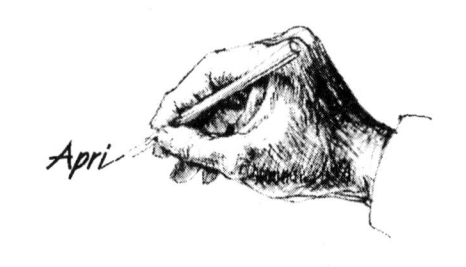

But the following day, Ed was cutting his lawn in very bland weather and admiring the progress that John Watson had made on the stone cladding to his workshop; another couple of courses had been added and on the roadside wall he was in some danger of reaching the eaves. However, the next day there was a very heavy frost, apparently heavy enough to warrant the gritting lorry coming through. Breakfast time saw a repeat of the weather of a couple of day's before, this time even more ferocious, with about two to three inches of snow falling within about an hour. Some of the snowflakes were extremely large. However, although most of the snow had disappeared by the afternoon, the mower of lawns was able to congratulate himself on his exquisite timing and muse on the total absence of boredom as a feature of the local weather pattern.

Good Friday was not a bad day, considering that it was the start of the holiday weekend. It was dry, warm for the time of year, and reasonably bright and the first bees of the season were now hovering over the few flowers and blossoms that were beginning to appear in the gardens. It was apparently the warmest Easter holiday day for a considerable number of years, which probably accounted for the fact that the first butterflies were about. When Tony took the dogs on to the moor in the afternoon, after having spent the morning tidying up the garden, he noticed for the first time this year that the skylarks were skimming over the surface of the grass and then ascending to the heavens, warbling their spring songs. New leaves on the trees were beginning to be noticeable now and the primroses were plentiful and beautiful. At long last there were all sorts of signs of spring. The holiday season had really started in earnest and, as well as a family staying in Laneside, The Old Chapel had paying visitors, which was its first let of the year.

The holiday Saturday was not quite so pleasant and John spent a couple of hours with his Kramer mechanical digger spreading gravel over the private roadway leading past Curlew Cottage to Burnside. Every so often this job needed doing as pot-holes quite readily kept appearing in the mud and gravel surface. In the afternoon he cut the rest of the Poverty Street grass, finishing off the work which Jonathan had started a week or so beforehand. He was pleased that his mower started at the first attempt after its winter break, but, needless to say, it ran out of petrol before the job was finished. The early morning sunshine on Easter Sunday spurred him on to do a little more construction work on his new workshop-cum-garage. He had felt a little guilty, as the date stone proclaimed that the building had been erected in 1997 and there were at the moment only two and a half courses of stone facing above that, so he had thought that he had better spend some time that day adding a few more. Liz remarked that, if he kept this up, it might be completed by the millennium.

About half way through the month, the weather men had been forecasting that there would be a complete reversion to winter conditions, with wind, bitter temperatures and snow, perhaps up to two inches in places. About two weeks beforehand, Northern

Electric had sent a notice to everyone in quite a large area of the dale saying that the power would be cut off for a whole day from 8.30am to 4.30pm to allow them to carry out some replacement work on the high voltage overhead feeder lines. Unfortunately, the weather men were right for a change; the temperature dropped to a daytime low of 4°C and there was quite a fall of snow, especially in the afternoon, although it did not last long on the ground. With no power, it got very cold indoors for those whose heating systems depended upon electricity for their control. Still, it was only going to be off until 4.30pm and a number of residents went out for at least part of the day. As it turned out, the power was not switched back on until nearly eight o'clock that evening, causing some people to have rather late meals. No doubt the electricity company put the blame on to the weather.

Early on in the month there were more rabbits in Curlew Cottage garden than usual and on one morning one of the Afghans caught one when he was let out. He chased it under a shrub and then managed to reach for it and kill it before tossing it up in the air and playing with it. Tony managed to catch the dog and take him indoors before too much fur had been eaten. He thought that it might be a good idea to leave the dead rabbit on the lawn for a day to send a message to the others and to act as a deterrent against future invasion. He guessed that it would be a bit of a forlorn hope, though. However, after a week had gone by, Tony had not seen another rabbit in the garden, so perhaps the ploy of the rabbit being left on the grass had worked after all; or perhaps it had been the short squeal that it had given as it had been caught that had sent the message to other would-be intruders. Each time the dogs went out now they were on the lookout, carefully sniffing under every bush.

Building work on the Hudson's house extension had picked up again. Various final stages of finishing off outside were now completed and the electrical installation had at last been completed with the visible bits, like switches and sockets, installed; but there were still no French doors! There were, luckily, some good drying days and the plaster was drying well. As he had hoped, Philip managed to get some emulsion paint on the crucial bits of the walls, such as those parts which would soon be obscured by radiators. Their outside retaining wall was soon finished and the plumber at last came to fix the radiators, but, typically, one of those he brought with him was the wrong size, so a return trip would be needed. The actual building work was now complete and all the rubbish cleared away. The project was to all intents and purposes finished but the French doors were still nowhere to be seen; instead there was a gaping hole covered by boards which were wedged in place with planks.

One Wednesday morning, when Liz went to her garage on her way to work, she noticed a song-thrush sitting on the roof of her car. It looked most disgruntled at being disturbed and it only flew off after she had told it that it would have to move! About this time in the month, Joan saw the first swallows of the season as she and Ed were inbound to West Scrafton just west of Coverham. This was a cause for pleasure as the sighting was a herald of summer and anyway they are supposed to bring good luck. It also caused a *frisson* of anxiety in their minds, because soon work would start on converting the old milk-house at Culverham Farm House into their garage and that particular building had been a nesting place for swallows for years, maybe for the half a century since it had been built by Tommy Handley using stone from the old lime kiln above Cullen House. The door of the fuel store was locked open in the hope that the swallows would use that as an acceptable alternative to the milk-house. The plans for the conversion to the new garage included a "swallows gate" in the eastern gable as a further encouragement to get them to stay. They would have been very sad to lose them as tenants; swallows were part of summer and were happily forgiven for their bombing of the car and garden furniture.

It was also time to remove the bird nesting box from the north side of the milk-house before the building operations began. Blue-tits had started lining it with moss and feathers, so rather than disrupt a growing brood, the box was transferred to the centre of the cottage wall where it was surrounded by honeysuckle and looked very enticing. Alas, when the blue-tits returned to the old site with beaks full of nest-building material they were very puzzled when they found that their box had gone. So far they did not seem able to recognise it in the new location on the barn wall; but on the other hand, these particular birds may have been the ones which had occupied yet another box on the garden side of the fuel store. Meanwhile, not to be outdone at the building game by a pair of tits, John had added yet another couple of stone courses to his workshop!

While Jonathan was working in the garden of the Old Inn for Mrs Neale, Norman Oddy went to have a word with him. Norman and Dick Hall usually cut the grass in and around the small central village green as it was near to their properties, but Norman pointed out that Dick was away a lot and he was finding it difficult to spare the time to do it all himself. Jonathan agreed to include it in his round of cutting on the condition that he could cut off the lower branches of the two crab-apple trees on the green if other nearby residents did not object. In the event they agreed and so Jonathan duly cut off the offending branches on the Monday morning. From then on his new extended mowing duty would be less hazardous.

Tony's son and daughter-in-law came to stay over the last weekend in the month and, as the Saturday was a nice sunny day, they decided to have a day out at Malham Cove. When they got back, Tony took one of the dogs on to the moor, but on returning to the car, he found that the jinx that had affected his washing machine had transferred its attentions as the "bleeper" would not open the car door and the key had to be used to get in. He then found that the engine would not start as the immobiliser was still in operation. After leaving the dog in the car and hitching a lift back home, his son Paul took him back to the car and they then had to call the emergency breakdown service. The man who came at least managed to get the car started but said that it would have to go to the dealer for examination to discover what had gone wrong. On the Monday the car was taken to the garage where it was kept for the whole week as the problem was eventually traced to a main cableform which somehow had some totally corroded wires in it. As the car was only eight weeks out of guarantee, the manufacturers agreed to replace the cableform without charge. Not only that, but the garage kindly steam-cleaned the remnants of some rough cow-muck off the car which had persistently remained there ever since February, despite the many subsequent pressure cleanings.

May

During the first week in the month, many people in the village heard the first cuckoos of the year. They seemed to be arriving a little later over the last several years. In the old days, they could be heard from around the 23rd of April and not much more than a day or so either way. In recent years, it seemed that their sound was not heard until the beginning of May. Philip heard it for the first time while he was out running above East Scrafton to Caldbergh. Could this gradual later arrival be something to do with global warming?

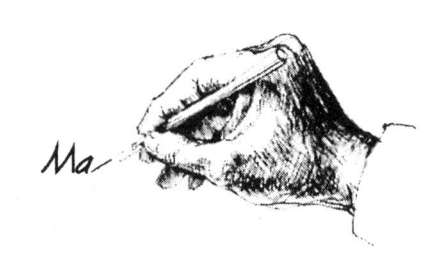

This warmish weather, although still with an unwelcome amount of rain, had also had its effect upon the local vegetation. A good many trees were now in full leaf and the marsh marigolds and "milkmaids" were now appearing in the wetter hedge-bottoms and fields. The grass was growing at an unconscionable rate and needed quite frequent mowing, a task made more difficult by the fact that it hardly ever dried out.

John and Roger went to Nenthead one Sunday afternoon to explore the "Small Clough" lead mine. They both thought that this had been a very interesting experience and it had whetted their appetite for more of this type of exploration, perhaps in the local mines. Therefore, a bit later, John and Roger, this time with Sandra as well, took themselves up to Roova moor to investigate what was left of the West Scrafton coal mine. They took a couple of spades with them so that they could have a dig if necessary! The digging proved fruitful, as it led them to discover what they took to be the entrances to two of the levels of the mine. Roger managed to retrieve a piece of the mine "timbers". Later that week John, Roger and Sandra had another "expedition", this time down to Nathwaite. With Sandra staying outside acting as safety warden, they went exploring the slate mines and managed to get in to three of the entrances for a cursory inspection with a view to returning later in order to penetrate further in. This next time they would make sure that they were armed with a powerful torch and a camera. The following Sunday, the three of them went up to the coal mine again to continue their investigations of the remains of various entrances, if this was in fact what their diggings had begun to reveal. They were now really getting bitten by the exploration bug! They continued on up to the "red pool", coloured by the presence of various minerals in the ground through which the water filtered; this is the cause of Great Ghyll often having a reddish hue and sometimes being known as "Red Ghyll".

Inside Nathwaite Slate Quarry

Ruth Burgess and Ed had been chatting outside Bridge Cottage very early one Monday morning and she had mentioned the fact that the pot-hole below the bridge was now taking all the water from Great Ghyll, leaving the lower section of the ghyll quite dry. By a strange coincidence, only a few hours later, a new hole had opened up in the bed of the ghyll above the bridge and half the stream was disappearing down it. It was not a gaping hole but it was clearly taking a substantial amount of water and causing an equal amount of comment. Later in the day, Will Utley manoeuvred his mechanical shovel into the ghyll and shifted enough rock and earth to stem the flow. There was a high degree of uncertainty about the layout of the pot-holes beneath the ghyll and surrounding area and this gave rise to an instinctive unease whenever there was a marked change to the normal flow of water over or into one of those holes. The pot-hole runs underneath two or three of the cottages (see fig 21) and, although they have been there for centuries, there could easily come a time when nature took its toll!

One day John came to repair Tony's roof. This had been leaking earlier in the year during some rainy weather when the wind had been blowing very strongly from the north-west John had been waiting some time for some dry and reasonably windless weather before venturing up on to the roof to carry out this task and at last such an opportunity had presented itself. Tony would now have to repaint the bedroom ceiling which had been stained by the leaks; this was a difficult task as the ceiling was a tall pointed one and the ladder would have to be carefully manoeuvred between the roof trusses.

He had been complaining about the poor quality of reception of television pictures ever since they had arrived in the village and had been thinking of changing the aerial system, especially since a recent gale had blown off one of the arms. John had agreed to put a new one up for him when they were talking about this while the roof was being done. He returned to do this one Saturday and managed to get as reasonable a picture on all five channels as was possible, considering that West Scrafton was a known "black spot" for television reception, as it was shielded from the main transmitter at Bilsdale by Flamstone Pin. As a consequence, not only did it have a low signal strength, but it was also subject to "multiple ghosting" caused by the many strong reflections from the surrounding hills. Digital terrestrial television was now transmitted from Bilsdale, but, as the power was so low, West Scrafton was on the "no go" list as far as the cheap or free set-top box providers were concerned.

After John had renewed Tony's aerial, he and Liz thought that they would go and see the much proclaimed film "Shakespeare in Love" at the Elite cinema but unfortunately all the seats were sold. Although this was, of course, a nuisance, they conceded that it was good that such a small local cinema has new highly rated films in its offerings and could manage to sell out.

The weather had continued to improve, producing some quite warm days without that almost incessant wind. The farms were beginning to have their first cut in several of the fields across the other side of the dale; they were working flat out in the fields down from Carlton one night and in one area they were on the go until almost midnight, working with the bright floodlights mounted on the top of the tractors.

Philip and Kate's elderly cat had taken to having long naps in warm "nests" in their garden, which was taken by them to be a sign of increasingly summery weather; it also started on a lengthy circuit of the field and footpath immediately below their house, an activity which it hadn't done since they had moved in. Decorating the new sun-room was proceeding slowly at Burnside. There were lots of fiddly bits and an odd error of judgement on Kate's part resulted in her having to strip and rub down the door into the sitting room and start again in order to get a better finish on it. When it had been re-stained it certainly had a much improved appearance. Curtains had already been ordered from what the Hudsons described as an amazing curtain material emporium in Harrogate, the discovery of which was one result of a "shop-till-I-drop" policy on Kate's part. The day was rather marred, however, by torrential showers. The next thing would be the carpet choosing and this was becoming imminent. By the end of the month their second radiator was fitted and the decorating in the new sunroom was almost complete.

The month saw district council election day and a number of people diverted their respective journeys to go via Carlton where the local polling station was sited in the Coverdale Memorial Hall. Sandra and Roger walked Meg that way, Tony stopped off with an Afghan on his way back from the moor and Liz and John voted on their way to see the film "Life is Beautiful" at the Elite. This time they had managed to get in!

For once, the early May bank holiday weekend was favoured with reasonably good weather and, not only did this unusual phenomenon make for a goodly supply of walkers traipsing the public footpaths in and around the area, but also allowed John to get on with the stonework on his workshop, a job which he diligently continued to carry out from the Sunday right through to the following Tuesday. At the end of these three days of work the front of the building was almost completed up to the eaves. He would now have to think about doing some more work on the back and sides. The idea was to get the visitors that he and Liz were expecting for the Spring bank holiday to help clear up the rubbish from behind the workshop and to start moving some stone ready for the next onslaught.

Spring bank holiday weekend came and the weather was not too bad. On Saturday, John and Liz went to the Elite yet again, this time to see "Waking Ned". They had some more visitors on Sunday and John took them down to the Nathwaite slate mine equipped with torches, waterproofs and wellingtons. On their return they were a little damp and muddy but quite impressed with their exploration of the mine. The next day, bank holiday Monday, they had their first barbecue of the year, but it was not really warm enough to sit outside to eat it, so it was a case of kebabs in the kitchen.

June

Perhaps the rabbit population will gradually diminish, hoped Tony, as John managed to achieve some success with his rifle early in the month, reducing their numbers by two. They were everywhere this year, on the Poverty Street green, in the Watson's field and now back again in Curlew Cottage garden. Tony actually saw one climb over the wire netting and another take a running jump at it! So far they had not been in the Watson's garden but they had visited Joan and Ed's.

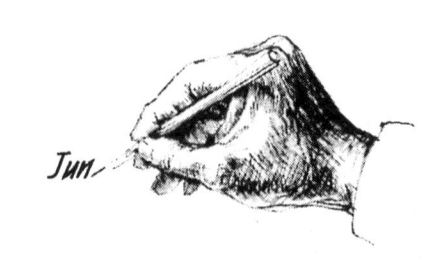

Tony's son and daughter-in-law came for another weekend visit and on the Saturday, as it was a fine, dry day, they went to Fountains Abbey which none of them had ever visited before. It was a very pleasant day out and they came back via Gouthwaite and Lofthouse. They noticed that the holiday traffic was beginning to build up, although as yet there had not been many occasions on which they had needed to pass other vehicles on the narrow single track roads. The next day was wet and the three of them walked up to Roova Moor to see the remains of what had been the local coal mining industry. On the way back they passed other drenched walkers who stopped and said "what on earth are we doing out walking in this dreadful weather when its too murky to see anything. We must be mad". There seemed to be no accounting for the odd way in which human beings appear to get their kicks!

On the following Friday, itchy eyes and runny noses were in evidence; this was because silaging had begun, with cutters and spinners working overtime in many of the fields around the village. The next day John received a phone call from Charles Utley at round 9.15 in the morning. It was to ask if John could assist in throwing the old car tyres over the sheets of plastic covering the silage clamp in order to hold it firmly in place in the wind. That Saturday was also the Forester's day in Carlton and John was again summoned to the rescue, this time to unblock the drains in the Memorial Hall. With all this extra work for John's services, Liz thought that it was strange that 18 years ago a village meeting voted against their planning application for a house to be built in a part of what was then Tommy and Mabel's garden, the reason being that they probably wouldn't be able to find sufficient employment to sustain their remaining in the village!

One afternoon a few days later, Liz attacked the jungle at the base of their house and cleared away the weeds that had died as a result of the weedkiller which she had applied some weeks before. The tough docks needed another dose but according to the weather forecast it was due to rain in about six hours from then, so she thought that there was no point in applying it; it was a bit tricky getting the timing right given the vagaries of the current weather. The warmish humid weather had brought the midges out in their swarms and this year they seemed to be more vicious than ever; Liz was covered in bites. It was later given out on the radio that Scottish midges were migrating southwards and North Yorkshire was mentioned as being one of the areas for their colonisation!

One Monday in the month, Richard and Bruce Tunstall, the third generation of builders in Harmby, arrived at Lane End Cottage together with Barry Fawcett with his JCB. Jonathan Watkins had arranged for them to come and do some work for him. At the back of the cottage there was a three-foot wide concrete strip and a dry stone retaining wall with half a dozen slippery uneven steps leading up from the back door to the ground level. Jonathan wanted the wall moved back to where an existing curved wall ended, giving him more space outside his back door. The final plan was to erect a covered porch that would be a place in which to dry his dogs before they went into the house and also it would act as an air lock to help keep the heat in and the draughts out. However, the builders did not think that it was safe to dig out so much soil as it was rather close to a two-storey outbuilding wall that had, over the years, badly "bellied out". It was ultimately decided to take that section of the outbuilding wall down first, then dig out and build the new retaining wall before rebuilding the outbuilding wall again. Before they did that, a large 7½ft × 3ft flagstone, which had formed part of a walkway in front of the outbuilding, was moved to the front garden where it could be used as a path between the steps and the front door. The next day the outbuilding wall was taken down, the digging began and Kevin Utley took away many tons of subsoil and rocks with his mechanical shovel.

Before Jonathan had signed the contract to purchase Lane End Cottage, he and John Watson had collected a pair of stone gateposts from one of Jonathan's customers in East Witton. The elderly lady had just bought a new car which was slightly wider than her old one, and she had told Jonathan that she would like the posts removed to make the access to her drive easier. He had then thought that they would look better than the concrete ones at the back entrance to Lane End Cottage, so he and John took them out on the understanding that, if his house purchase fell through, John would have them. As it turned out, the old concrete posts were removed and used as lintels above an internal door in the outbuilding which was being renovated. The first of the stone gateposts was put in at the rear entrance but the second one would have to wait until all the work was done and there was no longer any need for large equipment to be taken in to the back garden.

The following Saturday ended with a thunderstorm and the electricity went off for a few seconds three times at around two o'clock in the morning. There was one intense thunder clap which started the Afghans barking and the lightning caused the earth trip in Curlew Cottage to operate. Tony wandered around in the dark with a torch calming the dogs down and it was some minutes before he realised what had happened and that the supply to his house had in fact been interrupted only momentarily. The lightning had also started his phone ringing so he unplugged it to prevent this from happening again but when he reconnected it on the Sunday morning he discovered that the pre-programmed numbers had all been wiped out!

The last morning of the month dawned with a heavy mist, which was not very good for the Baxters as they had a 3am start to travel to Ardnamurchan on the west coast of Scotland for a caravan holiday. They were certainly travelling into midge territory! In West Scrafton the sun eventually did come out and it was warm, if a little breezy. Liz walked up to the moor with ready-made iced orange squash, as John was busy building the walls of the chamber that was to become the underground housing for the water treatment equipment; laying concrete blocks in a hole on what was by then a good sunny day was rather warm work. She met Tony on his way down; he had been up to take photographs of progress. Ruth and Graham Burgess had also been over to inspect the hole while they were out walking their dogs. Pete Hullah also arrived and offered his assistance by passing some blocks down to John in the hole ready for future laying. John got home early in the evening and was having a bath after his hard day's work, when Charles came round to see if he could assist in collecting bales of silage from Highfield. After bathing and having his tea, John went off to unload a trailer of completed bales, but he also got roped in to assist in wrapping large bales of silage that had been collected the day before. Life is anything but boring in rural England!

Sheep being herded in Poverty Street

A Dry Stone Wall under construction in Back Lane

Fig 25   A couple of Rural Activities

July

The pheasants and partridges were now about in considerable numbers. This year in particular, they seemed to like settling in the roadside verges, much to the interest and sudden surprise of the *Afghans* as they sensed their presence and caused them to take to the air with much squawking and flapping of wings. A couple of partridges scurried across the road by the entrance to East Farm and into the gateway as Liz was driving to work one day. This seemed to be a very good year for wildlife in general. Several villagers who frequented the road to Coverham had seen deer on more occasions than in recent years. One or two sightings of badgers had also been reported nearer to Coverham and there were also instances of unusual types of creatures such as the two (at least) white pheasants which were around. In addition, both Tony and Liz had noticed black rabbits in the West Scrafton area; perhaps they were descendants of some tame pet rabbit that had escaped. In recent weeks the Watsons had noticed a dunnock flying in and out of the honeysuckle in their garden and on Saturday they decided to have an inspection. This revealed four fledglings with gaping yellow mouths. They also spied a shrew diving out from underneath the "Lady's Mantle". Further inspection of the honeysuckle on Sunday revealed five gaping beaks!

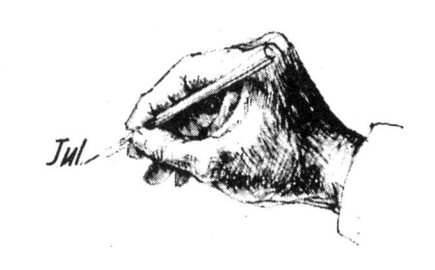

There was a "Seventies" concert at Middleham School on the 5th, in which two West Scrafton children, Hannah Utley and Joe Forrest, took part. It was deemed to have been a splendid occasion, with *Abba* and other songs of the period being thoroughly enjoyed by family and friends alike. That week Hannah's younger sister, Elizabeth, had a trial afternoon at Middleham School as she would be starting there in September. As with all children at that age, this change would be a big milestone in her life and having a foretaste of what the school was like was a great help in reducing "tummy butterflies".

A friend of Kevin and Clare Utley, who was also a godparent of their offspring, came to stay with them for a short while. Their grandmother, June, who lives in Cullen House, looked after the children in order to allow the grown-ups to go on a shopping trip to Harrogate to look for a birthday present for young George who would be three on the 9th of the month. The Watsons went to his party, but decided not to venture on the bouncy castle that Clare had hired for the occasion! The party went with a swing, and luckily the weather was fine and hot, allowing both tea and games to be held outside. The eleven children had a great time while their mothers took the opportunity to sit and relax. Clare had made a birthday cake in the shape of a crocodile, as this was George's favourite animal!

The Hullah's grandson Colin arrived from Vancouver, an excited and exhausted 12-year-old making his first long trip alone. Within a few days, Thomas Forrest agreed to act as local guide on an exploration of the gully and the Highwayman's cave which included some pretty rough going, but it wasn't the climbing up and down that inhibited their conversation; after talking less and less frequently for an hour it became apparent that a strong Canadian accent was as much a foreign language as a strong Yorkshire accent and they were mutually almost incomprehensible.

Every day there was something new to be done but when there wasn't, a quick game of cricket (not baseball) on the front lawn soon got rid of any surplus energy any one might still have. But the one great expedition was to discover the "source of the Nile". Inspired no doubt by Burton and Speke, Colin recruited his grandfather and David Thomas as guides and potential bearers, stocked up on Mars Bars and set out for the head waters of what looked remarkably like Great Ghyll. But the discovery of a fascinating ants' nest delayed progress for a while, and then almost stepping on a hare crouched on its form created another diversion. Meanwhile there had been too much laughing and joking with the frankly rather aged guides, who seemed to have consumed most of the rations anyway, so eventually the expedition was abandoned, considerably short of its objective, but just in time for tea..

In the last few days of his visit, Colin's grandmother treated him and his grandfather to a balloon flight. A perfect, cloudless, calm evening saw ten people and a pilot lay out the vast envelope, climb into the wicker basket and, with burners roaring, lift off from a site near Skipton and drift east a couple of thousand feet above the river Aire in great tranquility and total isolation from the real world. However, the approach to landing was less serene, the wind increased to close to maximum landing speed at ground level and touch down was violent, but what more could a twelve-year-old wish for? Moreover, in the dark drive home to West Scrafton, the live rabbit count in the headlights was just over 300 in the five miles between Kettlewell and Coverhead, which gave rise to lengthy speculation about how many there must be on the hundreds of acres of moor either side of the road.

Hannah Utley had her tenth birthday later in the month and, as luck would have it, it coincided with the first day of the school holidays. They all went to the cinema at Teeside Park to see the "Rugrat" film and afterwards lunch was organised at Pizzaland. Brenda Thiede's daughter Alex, Clare's sister, arrived with her offspring to spend a few days with her family. They loved the village, and the children spent hours together on the ghylls, building dams and having reed boat races. The eldest boy liked to help Kevin on the farm. When they were on their own again, Kevin and Clare took a trip to the Great Yorkshire Show with some friends. It was hot and crowded but they had a very enjoyable day. They tried out various new cars that were on show on some of the sales stands and enjoyed sampling the tasty morsels which were on offer at many of the stalls in the food section.

On the 10th, Ian and Jenny Brotherton's daughter, Vanessa, married Richard Adams at Coverham church. Luckily, the weather was gloriously sunny with not a cloud in the sky. People came from all over the country and, indeed, from all over the world, with Vanessa's brother Simon, his wife Liz and their children Sam and Jack, flying in from New Zealand and some of Richard's relatives arriving from Australia and America. Coverham used to be the parish church for most of Coverdale, but is now owned by the

Churches Conservation Trust. The ceremony was performed by Reverend David Eyles who also looks after Middleham, East Witton and Thornton Stewart parishes. The reception was held in the Blue Lion at East Witton and took the form of a meal and dance in a marquee behind the hotel. The next day the party moved to West Scrafton where there was open house at Moor Ghyll for wedding guests and local friends.

John and Liz had evolved an improvement plan for their back garden and Liz decided that, as the weather was being kind at the moment, she would attack the unwanted greenery. She finally removed all the dead weeds, moss and muck from the area and levelled it off. Their plan was to cover the terrace with decking, make a flagstone path, and build several sets of steps to make it more easily accessible. In the evening, when the sun came round more to the west, it made the place a real hot spot and they thought that it would be very pleasant out there when the plan was finished. A day or two later the Watsons retrieved some old carpet that was stored in John's workshop and placed it on the soil outside the back door as a weed mat held down with the garden chairs; not everyone has fitted carpet in their garden! When Liz returned home from work one evening a few days after that, she found John using the pick to break up the now weed-free soil on the back terrace in preparation for the timber supports on which the decking would be placed.

Towards the end of the month there was yet another electricity failure, this time at around a quarter past eight in the morning. Several people noticed that, although nothing was working, some domestic equipment was still humming slightly and that their electricity meters were still going round! Some people's lights were just about glowing. Tony thought that with some types of switches, such as pull-cord and push-on/push-off types, there was no way of knowing whether the appliance was on or off; therefore he had to guess before he went out shopping. On his return about an hour later, the power had been restored and he found the waste-disposal unit merrily going round with no water to lubricate its bearings. It had apparently been going for about half-an-hour but luckily it seemed that no damage had been done.

John was still waiting for the electricity company to come and connect the meter that he had installed near Moor Ghyll ready to serve the water treatment plant and he had laid the cable from there to the site that he was preparing for the installation of the equipment. The main supply was available from a pole which was just a few yards away from the meter box. At last a team came to do the job, but it only laid the cable between the electricity supply pole and the new meter box; this team apparently was not supposed to connect it up to the meter. Later a second team arrived to connect the cable to the overhead supply line but found that the first team had already connected it! Unfortunately, no-one came to connect the other end of the cable to the meter! However, some days, later a third team arrived and did make the necessary connections. This state of affairs seemed to be reminiscent of the days when the electricity authority was a public body; who would have thought that a supposedly efficient private company would have acted in this seemingly manpower wasting and petrol consuming way?

August

August began with good, hot, sunny weather and some Coverdale residents had organised a car boot sale at Leyburn on a site just off the Harmby Road that was quite often used by various organisations for such events. Liz Watson set off with a wallpapering table and a car that was packed with a load of "junk" that they had decided to get rid of. It turned out to be quite a profitable day for her as she returned home with £50 in her pocket. While she was away, John finished putting gravel on the weed mat outside the rear terrace, and in her absence he had ended up having Sunday lunch at Clare and Kevin Utley's.

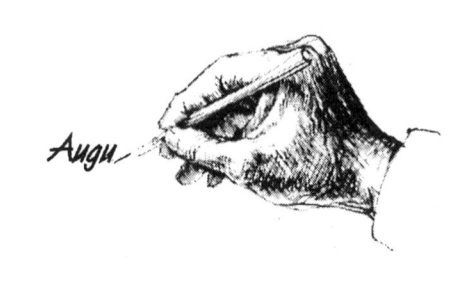

On Liz's arrival home one evening she discovered that a gent's urinal had been mounted high up on the rear garden wall. In it was a lupin growing in a plant pot! As yet she and John had been unable to resolve the problem of what to put on the rear wall and so John had taken this unusual step in the hope that it might encourage a decision. Shortly after that, they made a trip to the builder's merchant in Northallerton to have a look at what flagstones were available to lay outside on their rear path. Having made a note of the various sizes, they returned home to work out how many they might need. On their way home, they bought a dwarf *Juniperous squamato* conifer that was to go in a glazed pot that Liz had bought earlier. Her idea was that it should detract from the urinal which was still adorning their rear wall.

Life this month was quieter for the Hullahs without a twelve-year-old around. Breakfast could be taken leisurely outside on the paved *stoep* and frequently warranted a sun umbrella. Several meals had been quite lengthy, starting at a civilised 8.0am, but being extended as visitors passing by on Poverty Street stopped for a chat and yet another cup of tea. On a couple of occasions, it was 11.0am before the table was finally cleared; a refreshing change of pace from July.

The much heralded eclipse of the sun came early in the month, on the 11th to be precise. The morning was duly overcast although, luckily, most of the cloud was rather thin and the sun could be seen through it. West Scrafton was due to experience only an 80% eclipse and therefore it was not expected that it would get particularly dark. In the event, as there was a variable amount of cloud around, if you had not known that the eclipse was happening, you would simply have thought that a darkish cloud had come over. However, Clare and her children, as did Ed, Joan and the Watsons, watched the whole thing through welding masks and the children were terribly impressed. In 1929, when the last total eclipse visible in this country had occurred, West Scrafton had been right in the centre of the line of totality.

Early in the month John Watson arrived home one evening to discover that all the galvanised metalwork needed for the water treatment plant housing had been left in the front garden. He now had to find the time to take it up to the site and fit it all. This he managed to do a couple of days later. The next week, he ordered all the pipework required to connect the plant to the main supply coming down from the water tanks on Roova Moor. There was another occasion, a bit later in the month, when John came home to find that a further delivery had taken place; this time it was the flagstones for the back terrace of their house, so the plan for the rear improvement scheme was another step nearer completion. This, together with the remarkably sunny weather, gave Liz the incentive to make an attack on their front garden by weeding the path and cutting back three sackfulls of rubbish. Ed was also busy gardening and he leaned over the wall to invite her and John over for a barbecue that evening. John, who had laid the flagstones as soon as he had arrived home, just managed to finish pointing them in time to make this supper date.

The Hullahs had been invited to judge the childrens' fancy dress competition at West Witton "Fun Day", because they lived far enough away to be free of any accusation of nepotism (and, it was hinted, safe from retribution for unpopular decisions). It was a beautiful day with a happy crowd at West Witton, but the Hullahs found the judging difficult, of course. The expected Pony Girl, Bo Peep and Cowboys solemnly circled the judges along with identical twins in a box labelled "twin-tub" and an alarming Batman. All had real merit but the prizes inevitably went to the ones who had tried hard or looked the most innocent. Sophistication is right out at a Fun Day in West Witton.

Another of the activities held in a number of dales villages during the summer months is fund-raising by what is known as a "scarecrow" trail. The idea is that a number of "scarecrows", each representing a different theme, personality, television programme, etc are scattered around the village and have to be identified by a set of usually rhyming clues on an entry form for which there is a charge of £1. These "scarecrows" are made by the villagers and the proceeds from the sale of the entry forms are donated to local charities. John and Liz went to the one held in East Witton towards the end of the month and they thought that the "Ground Force" one in Lowthorpe was very good as was the one called "Vets in Practice".

When Tony had installed his outside light earlier in the year, he had bought, almost a year beforehand, a daylight-sensitve switch (of a well-known national make) for it so that it would come on in hours of darkness automatically. This first one had failed after about five days by switching on in the middle of a bright sunny morning so he took it back to the shop which kindly exchanged it for him. The second one suffered the same fault after about eight weeks and a third one was installed. This failed after only two days so, by now fed up to the teeth with the whole thing, he sent it back to the manufacturer together with a letter explaining what had been happening. The manufacturer rang to apologise and sent a fourth replacement. Tony had little hope now, except that he thought that maybe this one would be of a new and different manufacturing batch and that therefore it might just last a little longer. However, his worst fears were realised as it also failed after a few days. This one was sent back with a letter saying that he had lost faith in the device. He suggested that perhaps the firm ought to do more rigorous life tests on their products and informed them that he would be obtaining a different make. He told John Watson about this and by chance John had one (of a different make) in his stock of electrical goods. This one was duly installed and the lamp switched on and off overnight perfectly from then on. A couple of weeks later Tony was surprised to receive a parcel containing a garden lighting set as a gift from the manufacturer of the faulty switches for the inconvenience that their products had caused. These later came in useful for illuminating the outside of the Thomas's barn where the village millennium party was to be held.

Some friends of Kevin and Clare arrived to stay with them for a week during August. They came two or three times a year and always had a wonderful time with the family. At the end of the month, the local play-group organised a trip to the theatre in Darlington for the children to see "Play Days". The Utley children and their friends went along and they all had a great time.

Another outing that was attended by three West Scraftonians (Joan, Ed and Tony) was organised by the local "Probus" branch. Probus is an organisation for retired PROfessional BUSinessmen and several of the villagers were members of the Leyburn branch. The outing in this case consisted of a visit to the Maritime Museum at Windermere, which houses some very interesting vessels and old boat engines going back to the Victorian era. Luckily the weather was just right, as after lunch the visit included a trip on the lake in one of the old steamers. It had been a very refreshing day out. This had been a first for the local Probus branch in order to test the enthusiasm of the members for such events.

The 20th dawned warm even before the sun rose over Roova Crag and by 7.0am, walking up the moor, it seemed to Ed positively hot in the still clear air. The silence was absolute and so disturbing several grouse was a heart-stopping shock as they clattered protesting away up the moor. Later, there was the sound of horses hooves on tarmac, but so unsullied was the air that they could have been in West Scrafton rather than where they were, just visible, up wind, six hundred feet lower and a mile and a half away beyond Melmerby.

September

Luckily, the month got off to a good start weather-wise as there were celebrations all round on the 4th. It was Liz and John Watson's 23rd wedding anniversary, Clare and Kevin Utley's 6th wedding anniversary and also Thomas Forrest's 13th birthday, all on the same day; and to crown these events they were favoured with a gloriously sunny day. Liz and John ventured to Harrogate for lunch and then on to do some shopping. This was followed by a visit to the Craft Fair at nearby Newby Hall, which was very well attended, although it got very hot in the marquees with the sun blazing down on the canvas. Liz bought a stoneware gecko which she hoped would eventually go outside on the wood-clad wall in their back garden.

Later in the month, she and John went to Darlington to see "The Importance of Being Ernest" at the Civic Theatre. Dora Bryan, now 76 years old, played Miss Prism. It was very foggy on the way back, both on the A1 and over the "tank" road from Richmond. The next day was clear here, but foggy by the time you got to Middleham. It gradually cleared as Liz approached Tees-side on her way to work. John spent the morning sorting out a problem with Ed and Joan's electricity supply which had failed at around 9am. The fault was cleared, at least for the time being, well before lunch.

A flurry of activity started when the Schofields decided that they would like to buy the cottage which had once been called Swallows Nest only to be renamed Lane Side by the Hullahs and finally labelled Gillside Cottage by the new owners to be. Distant solicitors in the south had difficulty grasping the eccentricities of land and property in the dales and initiated lengthy debate. Long forgotten drainage lines beneath the yard had to be established and dividing walls between the two cottage patios and the rest of the property had to be arranged.

A "Red Letter Day" for the village this month was the final installation and turning on of the new water treatment plant, details of which are included in the chapter on "The Installation of the Water Sterilisation Plant". John Watson, helped by Kevin Utley, was the main architect and provider of this new addition to village amenities, and he took his faithful Kramer up to the site on Roova Moor in order to do much of the hard work. It was very unfortunate (or perhaps fortunate) that almost at the end of the final clearing up and levelling off process, one of the rear wheel axles of the Kramer sheared off, making it "finishing off" day in more ways than one! Kevin also had a mechanical digger that he used for farm work and he took it up to the moor to help John get his broken one down. The process took over an hour as the rear end had to be held up by Kevin's machine and the two had to proceed very carefully together down the steep and very rutted track from the moor to the road below and then on and into John's workshop without dropping or further damaging the broken Kramer. The next day, a temporary repair was made by cannibalising a part from another machine that the local agent had in stock until a replacement axle could be obtained from Germany.

For the last few weeks, Pinker's Pond had been bone dry, but there had been some heavy showers lately and Liz noticed on her way to work one morning that it at last had a little water in it, making a rather large puddle a more accurate description than a pond. On her way home, however, she noticed that it was now almost full and that the River Cover was flowing rather fast, too. The rain must have been quite heavy on the hills to have made this difference in such a short space of time. A swan returned to

Page 345

Pinker's Pond the next day, now that it was full again; was the swan the same one that had been there earlier in the year, Liz wondered? It was also there the day after but it had disappeared when Liz came home that evening. At the weekend there was still no swan, but instead a goose had appeared on the pond. While on the subject of wildlife, one day on her way home from an evening with some friends in Sowerby at about 11pm, Liz came across a deer apparently feeding on a rotten tree stump between Bird Ridding and Caldbergh; she was not sure who was more startled, the deer or her! It ran quite a distance to the first bend in the road towards Caldbergh before it leapt up the bankside on the left and over the fence. She then passed two owls, one on the grass verge by the footpath to St Simon's Chapel and the other sitting watching her pass from the fence a bit further along the road below Lane Farm House. There was also a dead rat on the road near Bird Ridding; ugh! Several people had noticed grey squirrels around recently; both Liz and Tony had seen one near Coverham. This would not normally have been worthy of mention, but they seemed to have almost disappeared from around this area over the last two or three years.

The end of the month saw Kevin and Clare Utley and their children off on their holiday which was to be their first family holiday abroad. Their destination was Majorca and they later reported that they had had a fabulous time and that no-one had wanted to come home. John and Liz also went off on their holiday to Cornwall with stops at Bridgewater and Dartmouth on the way, and Stratford-upon-Avon on the way back. Before they had departed they had sent their apologies for not being present at the meeting that had been arranged to take place while they were away, the purpose of which was to make tentative plans for the millennium party that was hopefully to be held in Felicity and David Thomas's barn on New Year's Eve.

By way of light relief, David Thomas and Ed Hullah decided to walk the six miles or so cross country to Middleham. An idyllic day enhanced the always beautiful view across Coverdale from above and beyond Caldbergh. The day grew hotter, and a bit of a struggle finding the best track up to Middleham Castle whetted the appetites even further for a quick refreshment at Durrant's Cafe. On a chilly day earlier in the year Ed had parked a half-bottle of cognac there just to sharpen up the occasional coffee taken on the way home from market. And so, as a result, reasonably fortified and showing more euphoria than common sense, they spurned the pre-arranged lift home and set off to walk back. The day got hotter, the dale grew steeper and West Scrafton seemed eternally beyond the horizon but eventually hove in sight. "Where are you walking to tomorrow, then?" got a non-committal reply and some mutterings about three-score-years-and-ten or so and not wanting to push one's luck.

October

The owls were beginning to make themselves heard in the evenings now that they were drawing in. There were so many calling to each other on one evening that Liz said that there was a positive opera of them, and wondered what the collective term for a number of owls was. The blackbirds were starting to swoop very low, flying fast for quite long distances over the grass as they seem to do at this time of year, perhaps on the lookout for worms as they went. The rabbits were still about, but fortunately there seemed to be less of them around now. Rooks were collecting on the tree tops and took off in great clouds whenever they were disturbed. These were all signs that winter was yet again on its way!

There was a concert in the Chapel at Harvest Festival. The greater part of West Scrafton, perhaps forty people, was there to listen to the Uredale Singers, a pianist and six ladies, singing in an atmosphere that epitomised the village. It was almost a family gathering, totally without ostentation and devoid of sectarianism; an opportunity to enjoy well made, simple music amongst friends. Perhaps as incomers it struck the Hullahs as being singular, whereas for others it had been a regular part of life for generations. Certainly there are few places left where such things can be enjoyed - and enjoy it they did.

Kevin and Clare went to see "The Thomas Crown Affair" at the Elite cinema in Leyburn and, although it was an old film, they thoroughly enjoyed it. To "crown" their day, when they got home they found that their four new pullet hens had laid their first eggs; the children were thrilled and were given their first baby "dippy" eggs for tea that day! During the month, Clare went to a tutorial workshop on flower arranging in Catterick Village; she thought that this was well worth while and came home with two new flower arrangements and some new ideas on how to improve and expand her capabilities.

One of the highlights of the month for Hannah was when she went on a school trip to Beamish Museum. At school they were learning about the Victorian era and this visit formed an interesting part of their education. It made her mother wonder what this present period will be known as; perhaps Elizabeth's (as opposed to Elizabethan) so as to distinguish it from the first Elizabethan period. Later that month, Hannah, together with Kevin and Clare, went to an open evening at Wensleydale School where she would be starting in the following September. They thought that it was a very interesting and informative visit and that the staff there were very friendly and helpful.

The 20th saw Beth's fifth birthday. A tea-party was, of course, the order of the day and this was complemented on the following Saturday with a trip to "Captain Coconut's" accompanied by a number of her friends. "Captain Coconut's" was rather like a large barn, specifically equipped for children and had many interesting and exciting activities available for them.

One of the facilities enjoyed by the village was a mobile fish and chip van which normally visited the dale villages on a weekly basis and was due in West Scrafton at around 6.30pm each Thursday. One Thursday evening Charles and June sat with Roger and Sandra hopefully waiting for him to arrive, but in vain. No mobile fish and chip van appeared, so they assumed that he must either have been on holiday or was temporarily indisposed.

Later in the month, from upper windows in the house, the Hullahs watched an early morning mist develop into fog as it moved slowly up the dale, filling the lower ground with dense swathes while the upper parts of trees and the moor stood sharp and clear. Further down the dale, towards Middleham all was totally immersed, but here it was like a sea shore with the grey tide of vapour moving slowly further up the land - a fascinating theatrical scene for half an hour before we too were enshrouded for the greater part of the day. This mist often seems to invade the dale from below when the weather forecast says that the mist will lift from the Vale of York during the morning. The dale is where it lifts to!

Each year, before Guy Fawkes night, there were collections around the village, both for money for some fireworks and for rubbish for the bonfire. This year was no exception and collection day was arranged for the 27th. John and Kevin both helped in transporting large items of combustible rubbish, heavy branches and old fence posts, etc to the site of the bonfire in their Kramer shovels. The bonfire usually reached about ten foot high and this year was no exception.

The month saw the Harvest Festival at the school; Hannah and Beth Utley both took part; together with Joe Forrest. A service was held together with songs and actions, followed by a silent auction of the harvest gifts. Half-term which followed always seemed to come round very quickly.

Hannah managed to accompany June to the opera at Leeds twice during the month, once to see "The Mikado" and the second time to see "Die Fledermaus". She apparently loved both of them. Clare and Kevin attended a local couple's wedding at the Middleham Key Centre on the 30th. Many local people were there and, to use a cliché, a good night was had by all! A chapel service was held on the last Sunday taken by the Reverend Lunn. The children were captivated by her stories.

It had been arranged that the Hallowe'en custom of "trick or treat" would be held early in the village this year, as many of the children were away over the weekend; therefore many children came round on the 29th instead of 31st. However, there were more "trick and treat" youngsters on the 31st as the Southgate children live outwith the village and had not heard about the change of date.

The mornings were now crisp, the virginia creeper was turning a coppery red and sadly it seemed as if the swallows, the essence of summer, had finally gone. On the other hand the Bomb Squad had arrived! A casual query to the police about the safety of a small calibre shell which had been electroplated and had stood in the family display cabinet since childhood, suddenly resulted in a large white van appearing outside

Culverham Farm House with Bomb Squad writ large. A policeman and three military disposal experts whipped the offending ordnance away. Rumour ran rife and the truth eventually seemed rather tame compared with some of the conjecture.

November

November saw the first of the frosts and there were also some very strong gales on a couple of occasions with gusts reportedly reaching 80 miles an hour. One morning, after a very gusty night, John awoke to find that part of the roof lining on his unfinished garage had been blown off. It was, of course, still bare to the weather and only held down by the wooden battening. Luckily no further damage had been done and the roof lining was put back in place quite quickly.

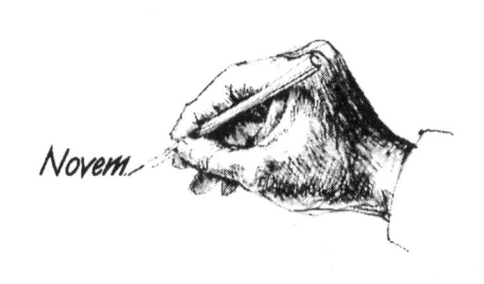

School re-opened after half-term and Beth Utley was apparently looking forward to seeing her friends again. Had it seemed that long a break? Later that month, Clare attended a workshop in Carlton that was all about the design of Christmas crackers and she had come home with four fabric crackers which she thought had looked rather pretty.

The Hullahs had decided to sell their second holiday cottage, Barn End, and within a day of the estate agent's notice, they had a firm offer from Rob and Kath Hannabuss. This signalled the end of their holiday cottage business. By April 2000 the venture would be over with no regrets, but with new friends and oft times neighbours for them.

Being November, it was, of course, firework night on the 5th and West Scrafton these days celebrated this historic event with a village bonfire on the island in the middle of Great Ghyll by Bow Bridge. Years ago the bonfire used to be on the Poverty Street green and had remained there even after Mabel had started to mow the grass in the days when she and Tommy used to live in Culverham Farmhouse. As far as memory could tell, it was in the mid-1980s that the event had moved to the island. £130 had been raised for the fireworks this year and Kevin, the pyrotechnician, had gone for quality rather than quantity. The bonfire grew even higher during the day as further rubbish was piled on to it. It was lit at about 7.15pm and the guy on the top very quickly disappeared. The evening's celebrations were supported by some refreshments and, as usual, a trestle table and floodlights were put out and the villagers brought food and drink, including sausage rolls and mulled wine; pop and crisps were provided for the youngsters. People always seemed to provide a greater variety of food when there was no organisation of who was to provide what and it was left to individual judgement! For once it was a dry evening and it was very lucky that it had been put off from the 5th to the 6th, as the 5th had been very wet and the occasion would have been a complete wash out.

The prefabricated sections of the porch that was to go at the rear of Jonathan's house were delivered and erected during the month. After all the laborious work of getting the site ready and the steps and handrails completed, the erection of the actual porch took only a few days; and it all appeared to fit! There was one slight readjustment of a length of guttering that was required and the job was done.

Once again, the electricity was turned off for a day from 8am until around 4.30pm, this time to allow the electricity company to carry out a programme of tree lopping in the dale! Some two or three weeks before, the village had been surveyed, along with others in Coverdale, to see which trees needed to be lopped to prevent their branches from touching the electricity distribution wires. By the allotted hour of 4.30pm no sign of tree loppers had been seen in West Scrafton as they were still only half way up the road in Carlton. However, it was getting dark and the power duly came back on. We were left wondering when the power would be turned off yet again to permit the job to be finished.

On the third Tuesday in the month the library bus made its three-weekly appearance, pipped its horn and waited alongside the green for the usual handful of people to stagger out under the piles of books they would be returning. Inside this book-lined mobile library there is only just enough room for browsers to pass one another and any queue to make the transactions with the two librarians/drivers is, of necessity, limited to two. But is a very comforting and cheerful service, where any known book that is still in print can be ordered and delivered, often on the following visit, if it can't be found on the shelves. Fifteen minutes later, it's gone on its way up the dale.

There did not seem to have been much activity to note about the wildlife in the area this month. Liz, coming home about 10pm on 13th, spotted a dark furry animal by the roadside either eating or playing with its supper. In the darkness, she thought that it could have been black and wondered whether it could have been a pine-martin. She also noticed that a swan had again returned to Pinker's Pond. They seemed to have made Pinker's Pond one of their regular haunts these days, when it had water in it, that is. There were also sightings of herons and Liz noticed that there was one standing sunning itself in the field of sugar beet by the bridge at Coverham, undisturbed by traffic.

At the end of the month, we saw the first heavy frost of the winter. It remained with us for several days and did not disappear during the daytime except for those places where the sun had managed to melt it. Tony was rather glad about it as it meant that the dogs' feet stayed dry and did not have to be washed after coming back from walking on the moor.

December

For once, December was not a particularly cold month and we actually had some quite reasonable weather for the time of year, although it was tempered with one or two periods of heavy rain. At the beginning of the month the Cover was in full flood and there were some falls of snow and hail on more than half the days leading up to Christmas. But certainly not all was grim. There was a motionless early morning when, again from the upper windows, the Hullahs watched the day emerge over West Scrafton, the moor and Roova Crag, all still covered by a thin layer of frost and snow. As the sun rose, it lit the mist from behind, giving it a mellow glow, while the leafless trees, branches and twigs were also suffused in the same light, making a remarkably delicate screen to the view beyond. It only lasted for half an hour before standard winter reasserted itself.

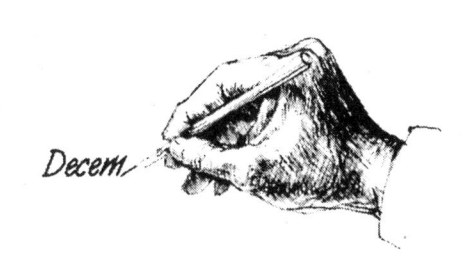

Earlier in the year, Tony had finished preparing a new rose bed that his late wife had started the year before and he had ordered some roses for it by mail order which he had expected would arrive some time in October or November. As they hadn't come by the beginning of December, he thought that it would be the spring before they arrived. Unfortunately for him, they were delivered unexpectedly at the end of the third week in December during a period of several days of heavy and incessant rain and flooding. Although the bed had been prepared, it was now just a soggy, squelchy mess and he had to dig "wells" in which to plant the roses. He hoped that this would suffice at least until such time as the weather allowed him to do the job properly. The next week was very frosty and the ground was frozen solid so he hoped that the roses would survive satisfactorily. He had bought some more wire-netting which he intended to put round each rose in the hope that this would protect them from the rabbits when they reappeared in quantity in the spring!

John saw a sparrow hawk sweep down in front of him as he was walking down Poverty Street the week before Christmas. It took off again from the Baxter's garden carrying a blue-tit that it had taken from their nest-feeders. Normally by now, the rabbit population was safely tucked up in its burrows and being a nuisance to no-one, but this year the mild weather had kept up their numbers and a few were still in evidence along Poverty Street. Unless we had some really freezing weather in January or February, we would undoubtedly have to contend with an even greater number of these pretty, but destructive, animals in the millennium year.

On the 19th a team of villagers spent the morning clearing out the Thomas's barn in readiness for the millennium party, putting up the Christmas tree and starting with the decorations. Several people had loaned sets of coloured lights, lengths of tinsel and other baubles and they made quite a show. The 10ft high tree had to be tied at the top to a beam to keep it upright and the base was wedged with large stones as it had proved to be rather too heavy for the tree stand that Tony had brought along. Room was made for some trestle tables, several sets of garden furniture and three heaters to make the barn more habitable for the evening's entertainment.

Christmas Eve, as always, was a double-barrelled affair. The carol service in the bitterly cold, evocative and candle-lit Coverham church, where mulled wine and mince pies by the font rounded off the service for the heavily muffled congregation, was followed by another carol service in the West Scrafton chapel, with just sufficient time to cover the three miles between them. The latter was always warm, lit by a vast number of candles and becoming hot when the eighty or so congregation packed inside had begun to give full voice to good old-fashioned hymns and a dozen or so residents had read lessons to the perspiring gathering. According to the Hullahs, the contrast in

Can't Wait for it to Start

Brenda bringing in the Food

Tommy Handley's Wig

Ruth, Tommy and Guest

Charles and Julie

Fig 26   The Millennium Party

temperature between the two services was similar to taking a midwinter mass in St Petersburg and ten minutes later singing your heart out at a midsummer service in Athens · not that they had done either. Still, Ed, with the help of a torch, did manage to read, somewhat imperfectly, a lesson in both places and so feel well set up for Christmas itself.

The Christmas holiday period was a long one, as it always is when Christmas falls at a weekend, but, as a change from previous years, at least the weather was dry. During the following week some final preparations were made for the millennium party, but when it came, the attendance was unfortunately depleted somewhat, as a number of villagers were struck down by a flu bug which was reportedly the worst for a number of years. Felicity Thomas, who had spent so much time and effort in getting everything ready, had to take to her bed just after the party had begun; it was the third recurrence of the flu that she had had since November. Some of the residents had had visitors staying with them and had brought them along to the party, confident that alcohol was adequate protection from infection. At midnight, after Auld Lang Syne had duly been sung, everybody trouped outside to watch the celebration rocket being let off. As might have been expected, there were several rockets to be seen and heard around the dales that night marking other distant celebrations, but the West Scrafton party eventually retired, content that theirs had been well worth the effort and not in the least surprised that they had contributed far more food than they could possibly cope with.

With all the celebrations and the past year behind us, we could now look forward to the first year of the next thousand!